EVIL'S ORIGIN

By Christian Laursen

EVIL'S ORIGIN

Christian Laursen

© 2023 Christian Laursen Inc.

All rights reserved. No part of this publication may be reproduced, stored in a retrieval system or transmited in any form or by any means, electronic, mechanical, photocopying, recording or otherwise without the prior permision of the publisher or in accordance with the provisions of the Copyright, Designs and Patents Act 1988 or under the terms of any licence permitting limited copying issued by the Copyright Licensing Angency.

ISBN-13: 979 8 98526 820 1

Published in Arizona, USA

Printed in South Korea

***Dedicated to all victims of evil...**な*

in this world, past, present and future.

Contents

CHAPTER 1: PROLOGUE 1

CHAPTER 2: ADAM AND EVE 5

CHAPTER 3: WHAT IS EVIL? 9

CHAPTER 4: DOES EVIL EXIST? 15

CHAPTER 5: EXAMINATION OF OURSELVES . . . 17

CHAPTER 6: EXAMINATION OF EVIL 25

CHAPTER 7: THE DIFFERENCE 41

CHAPTER 8: CONCLUSION 71

CHAPTER 9: THE DEFINITION 81

CHAPTER 10: DO MONSTERS LAUGH? 87

CHAPTER 11: KNOW THE MONSTER 103

CHAPTER 12: TRAPS & ILLUSIONS 109

CHAPTER 13: TO JUDGE... 141

CHAPTER 14: A MONSTER'S MASK 153

CHAPTER 15: SEE NO EVIL 159

CHAPTER 16: HEAR NO EVIL 185

CHAPTER 17: SPEAK NO EVIL. 197

CHAPTER 18: IAN BRADY 217

CHAPTER 19: THE MONSTER GENE 225

CHAPTER 20: THE HIDDEN MOUNTAIN. 233

CHAPTER 21: AMNESIA 247

CHAPTER 22: THE BIG DILEMMA 253

CHAPTER 23: TRIBES OF VENEZUELA 257

CHAPTER 24: TRIBES OF ALOR 263

CHAPTER 25: THE MISSING LINK 270

CHAPTER 26: THE PUZZLE PIECES 289

CHAPTER 27: DO WE HAVE A MATCH? 299

CHAPTER 28: THE WALL OF DISCOVERY 307

CHAPTER 29: THE FIRST YEAR 313

CHAPTER 30: THE SOURCE 321

CHAPTER 31: THE SECOND BIRTH 333

CHAPTER 32: THE NEED OF EVIL 339

CHAPTER 33: DOES GOODNESS EXIST? 343

CHAPTER 34: PREPARE 351

CHAPTER 35: KNOW ITS DEPTHS 363

CHAPTER 36: FIGHT EVIL 369

CHAPTER 37: IT CAN BE DONE... 375

Acknowledgements 381

References 385

CHAPTER I

PROLOGUE

WHY THIS BOOK?

My desire to write this book started almost twenty-five years ago when I began to question life. What is this world all about? I always wondered about evil and goodness. I saw both all around me. I didn't grow up during a war or in a violent environment. Still, I saw how some people treated my sick father, who had multiple sclerosis. For more than thirty years, he was bound to his body without being able to use it. At the end, he could only blink, swallow, and breathe. Yet he was the kindest man I have ever known. Even though he was very sick, he never took his disappointment or anger out on me, my sister, or my mother. He was funny, and his eyes would shine with love when I came to visit.

Yet... my father was looked down upon by certain people. We had caretakers daily who helped my parents, and most were kind. But some of the caretakers were cold, and in a subtle, yet real way, seemed to enjoy making my mother break down and cry. Thinking about it, was this the source of my drive towards wanting to understand evil? I don't know. But I know I was affected by it.

When my father passed away, I felt the deepest feelings of sadness of not being able to protect him or my mother against those who didn't treat them well. I could not fight back and stop them from hurting my parents.

Was it evil in a mild form? Or human nature?

Either way, I saw the effect it had on our little family.

When I got older and learned about the great evil in our world, seeing just how dark some of the world is, a strong fire lit from within me. I wanted to understand evil. I wanted to fight it. Not as a soldier but as an artist. This led me to two decades of studies, and now, finally sitting down and writing this book to hopefully shine a light on the darkness that surrounds us all.

Agenda

I have an agenda, and I want to share it with you as honestly as I can.

I see a world that is mostly blind and lost. A world growing ever so darker by the years, and it worries me.

Too many good people do nothing.

It is often too late when people finally wake up. Sure, we have been fortunate to turn it around in the past, but only after millions of people were tortured and murdered. Next time, The ramifications could mean worldwide darkness for decades or centuries. Where we are going? What are we doing?

Goodness cannot survive if it is not strong.

This book was born from my prayers and worries.

PROLOGUE

I believe in God. I am a Christian. Yet I want to emphasize this book will not go into the theology of evil or the various religious views on evil.

The book will also skip questions about the supernatural. Not because I do not think it could exist and have an influence in our world through thoughts and ideas. The devil and hell could be very real. The same with a spiritual world. Other realms could be as real as ours.

But all those questions are separate matters that I simply have no answers to.

That said, I believe the answers you will find in this book, behind the mystery of evil, could be enough direction for us-without needing to explain beyond this world.

If any questions in my book should offend some people, it is not my intention. I grew up in a home where questioning was encouraged. So if I say something that offends you, please know it's not personal, and I encourage you to challenge anything you find offensive.

Question everything you read.

Question my conclusions and use the book to inspire your own journey through the big questions on good and evil. I want good people to be strong and recognize evil, then find the courage to fight it-in whatever way that works for them and their own abilities and skills, through love and strength.

Why? Because there's too much fear, weakness, or ignorance among good people.

This must change. That's my agenda.

To invite you to take this journey together.

A journey to understand the dark and the light. I will lead you along the path I have found and show you what has been given to me by the wisdom of many great thinkers: authors, psychologists, and philosophers. Let's ask questions and, hopefully, by the end of the book you will have a slightly better understanding of evil and its nature. My hope is to help you navigate the world better and be able to recognize evil, big or small, and lead you on the path of strength. You must do the work. You must question everything with courage and honesty, including everything in this book.

Sounds like a journey worth taking? Then, let us begin...

CHAPTER 2

ADAM AND EVE

The Tree of Knowledge of Good and Evil

Close your eyes for a moment and imagine standing in the center of the garden of Eden. A thick old tree bearing fruit stands proud before you: The Tree of Knowledge of Good and Evil. Its crown and large branches are hanging low with ripe fruits. One particular branch is right above you and is low enough to reach.

Would you reach up and grab a fruit? Would you eat from the Tree of Knowledge of Good and Evil? Why would God *not* want Adam and Eve to eat from this tree?

This is the question that I asked myself one day while sick in a desert motel room after three days of working on a film and getting little to no sleep. I picked up the Bible next to me on the nightstand and began reading the first chapters of Genesis and thinking of Adam and Eve...and the tree.

Why would God not want Adam to eat from this tree? God told him, he would certainly die if he did.

My insomnia took me to thoughts that I could not get out of my head.

They may be related to the Bible's story or they may not be.

But I kept asking myself, "Would God not want me, and humankind, to know the Knowledge of Good and Evil?"

At the time, I didn't understand all the different viewpoints of the story. The different interpretations between the Hebrew Bible and Christian version of the Old Testament. I just asked God, like a child, "Why would you not want me to know the difference?"

I did not understand that it might not have been the devil. The serpent might have been a symbolism of temptation. Or maybe the translation of Hebrew to English was not about evil but about bad. The Knowledge of Good and Bad. Of Human Sin. The story of how humans got their nature of sin.

Still, these thoughts started my journey with this book.

I asked, "If the serpent was the devil and he temped Eve to get Adam and her to eat from the tree, how would the devil benefit?"

I began to follow this path of logic.

If one ate from this tree, what would happen? Maybe you would get the Knowledge of Good and Evil? The knowledge to know the difference. Perhaps you would know goodness and recognize it. And perhaps, more importantly, you would know evil and recognize it.

So I continued down the path and asked, "If we humans had this ability, who would be happy for us and welcome our knowledge, and who would fear our knowledge?"

ADAM AND EVE

Would God not want this?

Imagine you ate from the fruit, and then you saw God. What would you see? If God is love, which I deeply believe, you would see God as all good. You would be able to recognize and feel his goodness.

What about humans?

If a stranger came up to you and was a decent person, would they have a reason to fear you? A fear that you would see their goodness? Wouldn't it be a help to them, for you to know they were good?

But, what about the devil?

Would he have anything to fear?

He could come to you and lie. Put on a perfect "mask." Transform into the serpent and try to seduce you, lead you into trouble. What would you see? You would see the truth and recognize his lies. Same thing with a human who was a liar, or worse. You would know their lies and be able to tell their fake masks.

So if we saw the story from this angle, if we had the Knowledge of Good and Evil, who would be happy for us, and who would fear us?

I believe God would be happy for us. Decent people would be grateful to us. But evil, bad and indecent people who lie and deceive... would fear us.

Does that make sense? Even if this logic isn't the true purpose of the Adam and Eve story, it made me think...

What is evil?

Do people know evil and recognize it? Do we have this knowledge?

Dare to dive in? I only ask you to leave your ego, your fears, and all taboos aside...

CHAPTER 3

WHAT IS EVIL?

WIKIPEDIA'S ANSWER

What is evil?

It's an age-old question and one of the great mysteries.

Before we begin our path through the darkest corners of our world, it is important to know where we come from. What are our current beliefs at the moment as a culture on evil? How do we define it?

Let us look at the most influential encyclopedia right now: Wikipedia, an ever-evolving website that shows us our current understanding. It might be a bit convoluted, but bear with me. There's an important point.

One of the first sentences we read.

> *Definitions of evil vary, as does the analysis of its root motives and causes. However, elements that are commonly associated with evil involve unbalanced behavior involving expediency, selfishness, ignorance, and neglect."*

Take a moment and reflect on that and, if needed, read it again. Does this sentence give you a clear insight into what evil is?

Let us continue and read a bit more.

> *The philosophical question of whether morality is absolute, relative or illusory leads to questions about the nature of evil, with views falling into one of four camps: Moral absolutism, Amoralism, Moral relativism, and moral universalism."*

It then goes onto Western philosophy and mentions two people, Spinoza and Nietzsche.

Benedict De Spinoza states in his book *Ethics*:

> *We call it good or bad, and so knowledge of good and evil is nothing other than the idea of pleasure or pain which necessarily follows from the emotion of pleasure or pain."*

Let us reflect on that. The knowledge of good and evil is the idea of feeling pleasure and pain.

Is that true?

Good isn't pleasure. It's much more. If you try to save a child from drowning would that be painful? Would it be scary? Yes. Would it be pleasurable? No. But it would be good.

Evil isn't pain. Yes, it causes pain. But have you ever seen videos of people who have killed and how they grin when talking about their crimes during interviews?

WHAT IS EVIL?

In Spinoza's written work on "the improvement of the understanding," he holds good and evil to be relative concepts and claims nothing is intrinsically good or bad except relative to a particularity. Later in his final parts of *Ethics*, Spinoza insists on a completely ordered world where "necessity" reigns. Good and evil have no absolute meaning. The world as it exists looks imperfect only because of our limited perception.

I have no doubt Spinoza was a great thinker and influenced the world. But do his views of good and evil seem clear? If one were to follow his thinking, could one not easily come to the conclusion that evil doesn't exist and it is all relative?

Maybe Spinoza was right? Maybe evil has no meaning?

Let us go to the other philosopher Wikipedia chose for us, Friedrich Nietzsche rejected the Judeo-christian morality:

> "the natural functional non-good has been socially transformed into the religious concept of evil by the slave mentality of the weak and oppressed masses who resent their masters."

Poetic but hardly clear. We don't have Nietzsche here to clarify for us, but he might be saying that evil is made up for religious reasons out of spite against the "non-good" of the natural world. That evil is a concept to help the fearful rationalize the non-good. That when bad things happen, we call it evil. The thought could almost make evil seem good in a non-good way. That evil is the natural world. To be fair, maybe Nietzsch reflected on religion's use of the word more than the idea of evil itself.

See how things are getting convoluted? At least for me.

Wikipedia's definition of evil then goes on to psychology and renowned psychologists, Carl Jung and Philip Zimbardo.

Carl Jung, especially his book *Answer to Job,* he depicted evil as the dark side of God. Jung also implied that Jesus was an account of God facing his own shadow.

Besides an explanation of how he struggled with God and evil, which is very understandable, the thoughts and questions by Jung seem to be based more in theology than psychology. Because of this, let us skip these thoughts and continue to the psychologist Dr. Philip Zimbardo.

Zimbardo suggested that people act in evil ways as a result of a collective identity. His hypothesis was published in his book: *The Lucifer Effect. Understanding how good people turn evil.* which was based on his famous Stanford Prison Experiment.

Think about that. A collective identity can turn you evil.

Sounds scary. What does "collective identity" mean? Can groups turn you evil? Do we all have evil inside us? Does it only take one group to turn us into monsters? Zimbardo seems to want you to believe this.

Do you think he is right?

Wikipedia then goes into religion, which we will skip as the book's journey is about seeking the universal truth of evil. Something that should transfer across culture, time and belief systems.

Now, let us sum up what we have learned. There is no doubt the definition of evil is hotly debated and argued.

WHAT IS EVIL?

Some argue it's relative. Some argue it's absolute as moral, religious sins and supernatural. Others say evil is an idea that comes from the emotion of pain. Evil is the shadow of God, and perhaps our own shadow that we project onto others. Perhaps it is a collective identity turning good people evil.

Does evil seem clearer to you by now?

Or does it all seems a bit confusing and foggy? It seems we have no clue what evil is or if it even exists.

Wikipedia certainly has no clear definition of evil.

Only conflicting arguments.

No wonder evil is talked about less, and the concept of evil is considered an old and obsolete idea. Perhaps evil is just an illusion, a meaningless idea, a religious sin concept. Maybe it just doesn't exist or matters. Maybe it's all relative. What is evil for you might be good for me and vice versa.

Or yet, maybe there's another answer…

CHAPTER 4

DOES EVIL EXIST?

If we were to stop here in our early journey, our thoughts on evil would probably be that it's partly superstition, partly human nature, with the idea that we all have a shadow and evil inside us. So let's not judge and instead accept who we all are. It is all natural. And if evil is natural, should we fight it? Why would we fight something that is natural?

Thinking along these lines, how would we react if someone tells us, "I want to fight evil"?

Would we perhaps feel they were attacking us and tell the person not to be judgmental? That they should not be fighting "evil." That fighting what is natural, could be a form of hate, and in itself...evil. And so, we might end up wanting to silence those who want to fight evil?

But would this be good?

Is it true one should silence those who try to fight evil?

Or perhaps, Wikipedia's chosen hypotheses have left us with a fog and are misleading us?

What are your thoughts right now as you take in these ideas? Have the Wikipedia theories touched an inner truth in your gut? Have the theories made a clear picture for you of evil? Or have they made a fog?

For me, Wikipedia gave me a fog that covered up the trees in the forest. I always ask simple questions, and if the answers are too complex, I question them. I'm not saying answers can't be complex, but when it comes to life, often the complex answers are made by people who don't see, won't see, or who seek to create fog for those who want to see.

So let's not stop our early journey. We have just begun entering the forest. It is early morning, and the fog hasn't cleared yet. Just because the fog is covering up the trees and we cannot see them doesn't mean they are not there.

Let's wait for a moment and allow the fog to clear. Forget what the Wikipedia theories were and ask our question again.

What is evil? Does evil exist?

For us to know, we must examine ourselves. Then examine the world. Finally, we must examine if there's any difference between us and the world.

CHAPTER 5

EXAMINATION OF OURSELVES

OUR MIND, AND CONSCIOUSNESS.

Who are we? Do we have evil inside us?

Each one of us is different with unique personalities and unique lives. Even twins who start from the same little egg end up living unique lives. But at the same time, we are very much the same. We are human. We have feelings: We have sorrows, happiness, fears, and joys, a whole range of human emotions and experiences. And being human comes a long list of challenges. Life is difficult, and even when it isn't, we are rarely content.

When it comes to examining ourselves, I can only truly examine myself. Theories from psychologists and reading endless true stories can give a glimpse into someone else's world. But even then, when it truly comes down to it, I can only be with my own mind. Not yours or anyone elses. So I will do my best to open up and tell you how I see my mind and who I am as a human, which includes how my mind seems to operate. And if you can, do the same and see where we are similar and where perhaps we differ. As we examine evil and ourselves. Let's not be afraid to ask uncomfortable questions. Let's look inside and analyze our own minds and thoughts as honestly as we can.

So for us to look at ourselves, we need to think about the brain and the mind. Some neurologists believe that they are the same, a machine that makes up our consciousness. Other neurologists separate the brain and the mind, acknowledging that we know very little about our consciousness and that our mind may be non-physical. Both could be right. We are learning and continue to map the brain with names for every part as we observe how neurons activate during experiments in amazing ways. We watch this dance of neurons and try to understand our incredible brain's chemical and physical nature. Most who study neurology will tell you we are just beginning to understand this incredibly complex and beautiful part of our body. Who we are and how it all works is very much a mystery. The more we learn, the broader the view of our biology spans. Without going into the fascinating and important world of science, the point is to realize how little we truly know. Yes, we know more and more on the surface, but our inner understanding of it all is in its infancy.

We do not know if the brain is our consciousness or if a non-physical consciousness controls the brain. This is important to remember as we journey into our own thinking. Let's look at the mind. I'll try to be as open as I can. It's not an easy journey. For one, it's hard to actually analyze your own thinking. Second, it's even harder to express it in words. But I'll do my best.

As I type this, I am thinking of my own consciousness: my pattern of thoughts. It feels like I am watching myself typing. Most things are done automatically. I do not have to take action. They are done for me. The typing is automatic via my hands and my fingers. Even the thoughts come fast. I just watch the words being picked. I think about the chosen words and judge, decide, and watch.

This is my mind in action:

Judge, decide, and watch.

As I watch, I can choose where I put my focus from second to second. I'll be reading as I type. Then I'll make a mistake and consciously send my hands to delete. Whenever my mind needs to adjust the body's automatic actions, it takes a lot of time. I can choose to stop my hands from typing. I can pause and think (judge) and then change focus (decide) and then watch.

The first thing I want to theorize is that our mind is; Judge, decide, and watch.

With my mind, I can watch the outside world, but I can also go inside my mind, where my mind watches my thoughts. My conscious thoughts can be directed and used to construct concepts and complex ideas, which I can use for the outside world. In my early years of philosophizing, I would try to catch my own line of thinking, like a dog trying to catch its own tail, watching your own thought of watching your own thought. It can feel strange trying to catch your thought pattern. But the key word is "*trying.*" Because ultimately, you realize you never can. You are always behind.

But in this exercise lies the next hypothesis.

When I construct concepts and create complex ideas from my thoughts, I notice a curious thing. Some initial ideas seem to come from nowhere, and I cannot backtrack to find the roots of the idea. The idea seems to appear from nothing. It seems these ideas are separate identities apart from my conscious mind. They come to me, and I analyze and judge them, then choose if it's an idea that I want to use. Like a sentence I want to type or an action I want to take. Like a musician finding those first keys for a melody. If the musician is good enough to play the instrument and doesn't struggle technically, the melody can arrive in almost complete form into the hands of the musician.

The second thing I want to theorize is that some ideas are separate from our minds. And like the ideas, its the same with thoughts. Some thoughts come to you from nowhere, and the really interesting part of it is that they often have a decidedly negative or positive nature to them. Have you read those stories where there's an angel and a devil on each shoulder? The angel is trying to make you do the right thing, and the devil is trying to tempt you. It was often used in stories in the past, but I rarely see this analogy used nowadays. Disney made a great short film in the 1940s using the angel and the devil to discuss the difference between the man and the woman. Both the man and woman had their angels and demons talking to them. Each was tempted by the demon, and each was advised by the angel.

Those stories ring true to me today as I can relate to negative and positive thoughts that seem to come from nowhere. The part that especially makes me feel they are separate from me and my mind is that the negative thoughts are often something I do not agree with, do not like, and do not want to do (or something I would like to do, but know would hurt myself or others in the long run). And with the positive thoughts, they are often something I fear to do or that takes effort, time, and courage. In the last few years, I have started to consciously notice them more. The negative ones I try to push away, and the positives I try to listen to more. Many of the positive ones have given me greater insight and moments of happiness. There is often wisdom in the positives and often trouble in the negatives. But where do they come from?

Are they part of me? I feel strongly the answer is no.

Why? Because I do not have a say in creating the positives and the negatives. I do not get to shape them or create them. They come to me as whole sentences and complex ideas in my head. What they are or where they come from is for us to perhaps find out at some point in science, or perhaps we will never find out. But in the end, it doesn't matter. What matters is what I do with those thoughts. What matters is which thoughts I listen to and which thoughts I ignore. That is all that matters because that is the only thing I can choose and decide upon with my conscious mind.

This is where I think our journey wants us to head as we are going down a road journeyed by many past thinkers. There's a truth to the angel and demon on your shoulders. Thoughts of dark or light for us to choose from, and in this lies an answer.

Those thoughts are not you, but what you decide to listen to and choose to do, is WHO YOU ARE.

You are your choices.

You can listen to or ignore the negative thoughts.

You can listen to or ignore the positive thoughts.

Often, the negative thoughts are the easy, tempting paths, and the positive thoughts are the harder and more courageous paths.

Who we are, are the thinking, judging, deciding part. We have control over what we do, but those thoughts and ideas that our conscious mind did not create and yet arrived in our mind cannot and should not be judged as us in my opinion.

But what we do with them...should, however, be judged.

What about those dark thoughts? Doesn't that mean we have evil inside us? That anyone has the potential to be evil, like Dr. Zimbardo theorizes in his book *The Lucifer effect*.

Let's look closer at those negative thoughts. They seem to divide into internal and external directions. The internal hurts our conscious perception, telling us we are bad or putting us down. One theory is that these thoughts might come from past memories. The externally directed thoughts often tempt us into the seven deadly sins: anger, greed, sloth, pride, lust, envy, and gluttony. In the past, they talked about these as sins, but that word is so rarely used nowadays and often disliked. I remember learning as a young adult that sins were just silly religious words and beliefs that were used to control us. But as I have grown, learned, and studied, I have come around and found them to be a great source of wisdom from the past. They are sins, not because someone wants to control you, but because they will lead you into unhappiness and can ultimately destroy you.

I can also say that the journey into writing this book and the search for the Knowledge of Good and Evil has opened my eyes to God and to a much bigger spiritual world that I never saw or understood before.

It is human to have these thoughts that can lead us astray. If we listen to them and make them run us, we can do many bad things. We can hurt others. We can become obsessed. We can neglect others. We can injure others, even in extreme cases, murder others. And it will destroy our lives and others' lives: our wives and husbands, our children, our parents, our friends, and strangers. Look around, watch the lives around you. We are not perfect. We are far from perfect. Our envy can make us forget what is right and lead us to do terrible things to others.

But what happens at the end when the day is over and our anger subsides? When our pride or envy has been followed. In that quiet moment after we have stolen or taken? After we have hurt and injured? How do we feel? Are we stronger? Are we better? Are we happier? Or are we numb? Depressed? Remorseful? Sad? Do we run to self-medicate with drugs and alcohol to forget? Does a sense of guilt cut us cold? Do we look in the mirror and feel proud? Or do we hide from the mirror?

Yes, humans can do bad things. Humans often make mistakes. Some pay with their lives. Some pay in prison. Others pay with lost love, and some finally wake up. But all of us pay with guilt and our consciousness. That is what makes us humans. We do not escape our own judgment because we know what is right and what is wrong. We know what we did was wrong.

And in this lies the truth.

We own our decisions, actions, and pay with our consciousness and guilt. And should we not wake up, ultimately we pay with our soul.

But some might think, those bad ideas and thoughts are still ours. They are our subconscious. You might be right. But let's be clear that the word "subconscious" comes from a theory of Sigmund Freud. It is a word for his theory of the mind.

I'm not saying he couldn't be right. I'm just saying that he is trying to describe the same mystery and put words to something we don't understand. The very meaning of the subconscious is something that is beneath the conscious. It is hidden. Something we do not know what is. It could be chemical. It could be neurons. It could be spiritual. It can be our soul. We do not know yet.

But with what we can observe, it does not matter since either way, we cannot control this subconsciousness.

With these thoughts on who we are and how our mind works, let's turn our attention from within ourselves to the outside world.

CHAPTER 6

EXAMINATION OF EVIL

THE WORLD

Open your eyes and imagine a forest before you. A thick, deep forest where no sunlight reaches and only darkness reigns. Let's venture for a brief moment into its darkest parts and see if evil is just an empty word. A superstitious fear of the weak. A relative moral judgment that is based on who you are and what you believe. What's bad for you might be good for me.

Perhaps you yourself are very familiar with these dark parts of our world and know, all too well, what lies beneath its fake surface. Or maybe you have never experienced it personally but have been close to someone who has. Perhaps you have been blessed to never experience it but want to know the truth. Either way, I think it's vital for us to occasionally look at the darkness from hopefully the comfort of our lives, so that we may never forget what it feels like to not have a choice, to not have safety, and to have no say in what happens to ourselves or our loved ones.

It's never easy to look at. It's never easy to recognize this part of our world. It frightens us, makes us sad, and it is too easy for us to go back to our own lives and ignore the ugly realities. But we cannot do that. I struggled to choose which stories to tell. So many stories that each had its own horrors. But this book is not a history of evil. Instead, it is about the search for knowledge and for the truth of evil. In the end, two people's stories were chosen. They are perhaps not widely known stories, and sadly there are without a doubt endless like them, that are much worse. But I believe these two stories can put a light on our question about our world and evil.

There's one thing I want you to do when reading these stories. I want you to imagine yourself as the victim and not allow your mind to drift away from the unpleasantness of the story. I want you to instead go into yourself and imagine yourself being the victim. Go as far as you can with your imagination. How would it feel? Every little pain and every big pain, physical and psychological. When your mind says, "Ok, I get it," don't stop. Keep going. Imagine what you would do. Imagine HOW MUCH you would wish for it to end. Then go further, you have no say in it stopping. You have no control and are 100 percent helpless. It is not stopping. Then imagine it is 100 percent real. Not something you are reading or imagining, but something you are experiencing with your own body, your own nerves. You feel the pain of your own desperate feelings.

Imagine it being your present true reality. Find that truth in yourself of THAT MOMENT of HELPLESSNESS, PAIN, and DESPAIR. KEEP IT IN YOUR MEMORY. In it lies a true lesson of evil.

The Story of Gulsoma

The first story comes from Kevin Sites, a war-zone journalist who traveled around the world for one year visiting the different hot zones of war and trouble.

Kevin encountered Gulsoma, a twelve-year-old girl, in Kabul, Afghanistan, with the help of his friend and fixer, Haroon.

As a tragic child bride, Gulsoma was married away at the age of four by her mother to a neighbor's son. From the age of five, the family forced her to take care of not only her "husband" but also his parents and all twelve of their other children. She would do everything from household chores to laundry. This little girl was beaten constantly when she couldn't keep up with the workload.

> "They beat me with electric wires," she said, "mostly on my legs. My father-in-law told his other children to do it that way so the injuries would be hidden. He said to them, break her bones but don't hit her face."

Let's stop here for a moment and really understand this. Imagine you are six years old and live as a slave in a house where the man of the house tells his own children to not only beat you but to hide the beatings. That it is okay for them to break your bones but not your face. Imagine being beaten over and over with electric wire from this man and his other children. Try to understand the pain- even worse, the utter terror. The psychological trauma of being utterly helpless, not knowing any other life, and growing up as a child in constant fear. Gulsoma was not allowed to sleep inside the house unless the family had guests over. Otherwise, she would sleep outside on a piece of carpet without any blankets. For our own understanding, Afghanistan's average winters get well below freezing. She would have to sleep outside when it was raining and when it was snowing. After not having a night's rest, she would have to carry on the family's chores as a slave for fear of being beaten.

But this story doesn't end here. It gets worse. Sometimes the family's abuse of her would turn into cruelty that is hard to imagine. On occasion, they would use her as a human tabletop, forcing her to lie on her stomach and then start cutting their food on her bare back. Gulsoma showed her back to Kevin and Haroon, revealing endless scars and keloids from the repeated cuts, bruises, and boiling water.

Let's try to take a moment and step into this house in Afghanistan when this was happening. On the floor lies a little girl on her stomach with her bare back. The father-in-law puts food on her back with his family and kids around. Taking his knife, he begins to cut food on top of her, making deep cuts into her flesh, opening bleeding wounds. She would be screaming, crying, or maybe deadly silent from the terror and fear.

The torture of this little girl was done for what reason?

She wasn't tortured just once. From the scars of Gulsoma's back, it would seem to have been done endless times. This was not an act of anger or frustration from a father-in-law to a young child. This was done with calculated thought on hiding the abuse, to not be caught by neighbors, while hurting and torturing an innocent child.

Gulsoma tells us that there was one boy her age named Atiqullah who refused to take part in her torture. "He would sneak me food sometimes, and when my mother-in-law told him to find a stick to beat me, he would come back and say he couldn't find one."

Let's pause and allow ourselves to think about this boy. He lived in the same house, and though he was not treated as a slave, I have no doubt that he also was abused by his father. Yet he saw what his family did to Gulsoma was wrong, and with his limited ability, he resisted and tried to help her. Imagine the fear he had for his own father, who would think nothing of breaking the bones of a child, and yet, he found the strength to say no. This is important for us to remember as we continue our journey into the darkness and reflect on light and dark.

One evening, Gulsoma's father-in-law saw a neighbor give her some food and a blanket. He took it away from her and beat her ruthlessly, then locked her in a shed for two months. "I would be kept there all day," she said. "Then at night, they would let me go to the bathroom, and I would be fed one time each day. Most of the time, it was only bread and sometimes beans." She prayed and dreamt each day for her parents to save her, but then she would remember that her father was dead and her mother was gone. "Why don't you die? I imprison you, I give you less food, but you still won't die?" her father-in-law asked.

When he finally let her out of the shed, he bound her hands behind her back and beat her unconscious, only to revive her with scalding water from a tea thermos.

"It was so painful," Gulsoma told Kevin. "I was crying and screaming." Five days later, the father-in-law couldn't find his daughter's watch and gave Gulsoma a vicious beating. "He thought I stole it," she said, "and he beat me all over my body with his stick. He broke my arm and my foot. He said if I didn't find it by the next day, he would kill me." That night, left outside where the family made her sleep on a thin ratty strip of carpet, Gulsoma crawled away and hid underneath a bicycle rickshaw. When the owner of the rickshaw found Gulsoma broken and bleeding underneath his rickshaw, he took her to the police, who hospitalized her immediately. It took a full month for her to recover, but thankfully, the story has a good ending with her being brought to an orphanage in Kabul away from the family. The father-in-law arrested and put in jail.

But even so, in the orphanage each night, Gulsoma was often afraid the family would come back and pick her up. And when the sun went down, she often began to shiver involuntarily, a reaction to seven years of sleeping outdoors, sometimes in the bitter cold of the desert night. It is vital for us to remember this part because in it lies clues to our own society. Her seeing the sun going down was enough for her to experience her body shivering as if she was back outside on the thin, ratty strip of carpet. Her body REMEMBERS. Whether it's in her brain, in her cells, or both, the pain is not just remembered but experienced again and again with trauma so deep that it physically manifests with her shaking and shivering all those cold nights many years before.

Let us remember Gulsoma's story and imagine we were her. Try to imagine how it would feel to lay on the thin, ratty carpet on the ground outside in the cold desert night. Feel the wounds of the torture and your fast-beating heart from the terror just hours earlier. Imagine you dreaming of your mother and father coming for you and realizing that your father was dead and your mother had left you. There was no one to take you out of the torture and no one to love you. Imagine how dark your world would be? Allow your imagination to truly feel the darkness and despair of Gulsoma's experience. For us, it is an imagination, but for Gulsoma and endless lives like her, it was and is reality.

So what do we call this father-in-law? What word would best describe him and his choices?

Would not the word "evil" come to mind?

But let's remember Wikipedia's definition of evil with words as *moral relative*, That we all have evil in us. Would you want to do what he did to Gulsoma? Were his actions against Gulsoma's relative? Was it perhaps good for him and the family? Would someone think his acts were relative? That for some, this would be okay? Or perhaps he was insane and did not know that what he was doing was wrong?

But no, he knew not to hit Gulsoma's face and show the abuse to neighbors and guests. He knew harming her mercilessly was wrong, yet he did it anyway. Not only that, but he forced the whole family to do what he did, thereby making them guilty and part of the crime, which probably made him think no one would tell.

It is obvious that what he did was evil. But it seems Wikipedia's chosen definition of evil does not fit in any way to our story and sense of morals. Or am I wrong? I encourage you to go back to Wikipedia's definitions and see if they make sense to you in relation to this story as an example.

Let's go to the next story and see if we can find out more about the possibility of a relative moral evil.

The Story of Soon Ok Lee

On June 21st, 2002, Ms. Soon ok Lee testified before the U.S. Congress as a political prisoner from North Korea.

Her story hit me in the gut and gave me insight into true horrors that are happening in today's world right now. I've taken parts of her testimony, but I encourage you to look her up and read it in its entirety. She was sentenced to thirteen years in prison but served five long years before being released. She explained how the camps were set up and what the living conditions were like in them.

Meals for prisoners would be a salt soup and 100 grams of broken corn as a full meal. This was all they received for the whole day. Their sleeping areas held eighty to ninety prisoners in a flea-infested chamber about six meters by five meters (19 feet by 16 feet). During summers, it was so stuffy with the sweat and stink of the prisoners that they preferred sleeping at the work site even though it meant more work. Because they were only allowed to go to the toilet twice a day, the prisoners often urinated or defecated while working because they could not wait. In all the factories, there were glass boxes for prison guards to sit in while supervising prisoners at work. The glass walls enabled them to watch the prisoners while avoiding their terrible stench.

The prisoners were divided into units and teams and always had to act collectively by the group under the slogan, "All Actions by Unit and Team!" Prisoners would get up, line up for roll call, proceed to work, take meals, go to the toilet, finish work, and go to bed collectively and at the mercy of the prison authorities.

> *"A prisoner has no right to talk, laugh or look in the mirror. Prisoners must kneel on the ground and keep their heads down deeply whenever called by a guard. They can say nothing except to answer questions asked. Women prisoners babies are killed on delivery. Prisoners have to work as slaves for 18 hours daily. Repeated failure to meet the work quotas means a week in a punishment cell. A prisoner must give up their human worth."*

The punishment cell is one of the most dreaded punishments. The cells are usually sixty centimeters wide and one hundred ten centimeters high. Therefore, the prisoners have no room to stand up, stretch their legs, or lie down. They cannot even lean against the walls because they are too jagged. There are twenty such cells for female prisoners and fifty-eight cells for male prisoners. They are usually detained for seven to ten days as punishment for certain offenses, such as leaving an oily mark on clothes, failing to memorize the president's New Year message, or repeated failure to meet work quotas.

Ms. Soon ok Lee had a friend, Hun Sik Kim, who was the principal of Pyongyang Light Engineering College and was sentenced to five-year imprisonment. Her crime? To suggest to the city education board that they reduced the students' labor time for more time studying.

In the camp, her work was to measure fabrics to produce jackets. One time, she miscalculated the imported nylon fabric, and though she quickly corrected the error and no fabric was wasted, she was detained in a punishment cell for ten days for "attempting sabotage."

When Hun Sik Kim was released from the punishment cell, she was crippled and partly paralyzed. She needed two prisoners to help her walk to the worksite and back. The camp officials claimed that she was faking injury and yelled, "You bitch! Who do you think you are fooling?" She was kicked around like a soccer ball by the guards but withstood the insults and beatings for about a month. She suffered injuries all over her body while pulling herself up. The sores began to badly ooze from the infections. She often fainted. She was sent to the sick room, but she had to continue her work in the sick room.

> "*I was in the same room because I was a paratyphoid patient. The camp doctors burned her with heated stones to see if she could feel pain. I could smell flesh burning and felt like vomiting and fainting. She never felt any pain when her flesh was burning. From that day on, she could not control urination and defecation. I was suffering from a high fever myself but tried my best to caress her burnt wounds with the dirty cloth the doctors gave me.*"

She said to me, with a twittered tongue and tears in her eyes. 'I want to see the blue sky. You know my children are waiting for me.'

"The next few days, I felt very sick and was unconscious myself, so nobody looked after her as she kept moaning. A few days later, I came to myself, crawled to her, and removed the cloth from her wound. I was shocked to see the wound full of maggots!"

Hun Sik Kim died that night...

"I shouted to a guard through the small door hole, 'Sir, somebody died here.' The reply was, 'So what? You bitch! Don't panic. Wait until morning!' I found the floor full of maggots the following morning. I had to brush the floor with my bare hands and pick up the maggots into a vinyl bag. I told myself, 'You must not die like this. You must survive and tell the whole world about it.'"

Ms. Soon ok Lee was also tortured throughout her years in the camp. One of those tortures took place in a torture chamber that she had never seen before.

"I saw a big kettle on a small table and a low wooden table with straps, about twenty centimeters high. By surprise, one of the two interrogators tripped me with his leg. They strapped me onto the table and forced the kettle spout into my mouth. The spout was made so that it forced my throat wide open, and I could not control the water running into my body. Close to suffocation, I had to breathe through my nose. My mouth was full of water, and it overflowed from my nose. As I began to faint from the pain and suffocation, I could not see anything but felt sort of afloat in the air. I had been through all kinds of torture, such as whippings, beatings with rubber bands or hard sticks, or hand twisting with wooden sticks between my ten fingers, but this was worse. I do not remember how long it lasted, but when I woke up, I felt two interrogators jumping on a board that was laid on my swollen stomach to force water back out of my body. I suddenly vomited and kept vomiting with terrible pain. I had no idea how much water ran into my body, but I felt like the cells in my body were full of water, and water was running out of my body through my mouth, nose, anus, and vagina. I faintly heard somebody saying, 'Why doesn't this bitch wake up. Did she die?' I could not get up, so I was dragged to my cell that day.

"From that day on, I suffered from high fever and often fainted. My whole body was so swollen that I could not open my eyes. I could only urinate a few drops of milk like liquid with blood and felt severe pain in my bladder. I was able to get up and walk again in about two week's time. I cannot explain how I could have survived such an ordeal. I would have died if that had happened to me in my ordinary life.

"They subjected me to all kinds of torture there. Once, I resisted when they tried to undress me. One of the torturers punched me in my face so hard that I fainted to the floor. Sometime later, I woke up to find my mouth full of something. They were my broken teeth. Obviously, I bled terribly because the floor was full of my blood. My face was so badly swollen that I could hardly open my eyes. I spit out the broken teeth only after holding up my lips with my fingers. Four teeth from the upper jaw were gone. I began to feel terrible pain in my other teeth. Usually, I was taken to the torture chamber at five o'clock in the morning and remained there until midnight."

The torture was a regular occurrence in the camps, all day and all night.

Ms. Soon ok Lee spoke of one older man who no longer could withstand the tortures that continued daily. When the investigators tore off one of his ears and began tearing off the other, the old man decided to please the investigators by claiming to be a big thief. The bigger, the better. So he told them that he stole a locomotive from the city railway station. He acquired the nickname "locomotive head" from the laughing police investigators.

I want you to notice how the investigators **FOUND HUMOR** in this man's desperate plea to avoid further torture, even giving him a nickname for the entertainment.

Sometimes Ms. Soon ok Lee was sent to the medical room to report. She would witness pregnant women awaiting delivery. While she was there, three women delivered babies on the cement floor without any blankets.

"It was horrible to watch the prison doctor kicking the pregnant women with his boots. When a baby was born, the doctor shouted to kill it. The women covered their faces with their hands and wept. Even though the deliveries were forced by injection, the babies were still alive when born. The prisoner/nurses, with trembling hands, squeezed the babies' necks to kill them. The babies, when killed, were wrapped in a dirty cloth, put into a bucket, and taken outside through a backdoor.

"I was so shocked with that scene that I still see the mothers weeping for their babies in my nightmares. I saw the baby-killing twice while I was in the prison."

Public executions are standard practice in and outside prisons in North Korea. At each public execution, all the prisoners, some six thousand, are crammed into the prison square to watch. The victims are always gagged, so they cannot protest. They are tied to a pole in three parts: chest, sides, and knees. Six guards fire three bullets each into the chest for a total of eighteen bullets. With the top ropes having been cut by the bullets, the upper part of the body hangs down, bleeding, like a rotten log broken in half, still tied to the pole by the lower ropes. Then, all the prisoners are forced to march around the dead body and watch.

The executions included those who pleaded for death during torture, stole food, or simply wept over the fate of two small children left home alone. The charge was a lack of confidence in the mother party. Also included were those who were branded as "anti party elements" or "reactionaries." The public execution ground would be so crammed with prisoners that the women in the front watched the killing from a distance of only a meter or so and often got blood splashed on them. Some women prisoners were so shocked that they vomited, fainted, or developed mental illness (like sudden singing or laughing hysterically). They were sent to punishment cells for being "weak in ideology" and "showing sympathy to the people's enemy." Those who become completely insane simply disappear, and nobody knows what happens to them.

I have cried tears from these stories as I wrote. I sadly could go on and on. The testimony of Soon ok Lee is only one of many of the few who have survived these camps and even fewer who escaped North Korea. But their stories tell us a truth about not just North Korea with Ms. Soon ok or Gulsoma and Afghanistan. It tells us the truth about our entire world. Do not believe this cannot happen where you live. It is already happening beneath the surface. There's a reason why a country like Germany could turn so dark within a decade, and for this same reason, South Korea could have been and still can become North Korea. Some cultures are more healthy than others, but beneath too many lies the roots of evil.

Psychologist Alice Miller wrote in her book *For Your Own Good* about a distress line in the town of Aefligen, Canton Bern in Switzerland. During its first two years, the following mistreatment was reported:

"Flesh wounds: Blows that cause wounds. With bare hands, with fists, with a fork, knife, edge of knife, spoons, with electrical cord, with guitar string (used as a whip), wounds from being pierced with needles, knitting needles, scissors.

"Fractures: Broken bones resulting from children being hurled across the room, pushed over backward, thrown out the windows, pushed down the stairs, being kicked in the chest (broken ribs), trampled on, hit on the head with a fist (skull fracture), and hit with the edge of the hand.

"Burns from lighted cigarettes or cigars extinguished on the body, a burning match extinguished on the body, soldering iron used on the body, being doused with hot water, being exposed to electrical currents, being burned with a cigarette lighter.

"Choking with the bare hands, electrical cord. Hanging. Children have reported that their father punished them by hanging them from the wall by their legs and leaving them there for hours. Bending. The child is laid on his back over the father's knee and bent 'like a banana,' causing broken vertebra.

"Exposure to cold: Children are exposed to extremely cold temperatures or placed in cold water. Thawing out causes pain. Immersion. Children who splash in the bathtub are held under water.

"Eating. The child is forced to eat what it has vomited. After the meal, a finger is stuck down the child's throat to make it vomit. Then the child must eat what it has vomited.

"Torture chamber: One child and his grandmother reported that the father set up a torture chamber in an unused coal cellar. He bound the child to a 'trestle' and whipped him. The whip was selected to match the severity of the punishment. Frequently, the child was left bound overnight."

So I ask you again... Does evil exist?

Or are Wikipedia's chosen definitions right? Is it all relative to whom you ask? Are there no moral truths in any of these abuses?

CHAPTER 7

THE DIFFERENCE...

It is common sense that these true stories were about evil. But did Wikipedia's definition of evil at the time of writing this book, reflect this truth?

Before we discuss the depth of this, we must understand the importance of why we are looking at the word evil to see if its definitions are true. Why does it matter? Why be so insistent on defining the word evil? People will always differ and believe different things. It's just a word.

It matters because if the word evil becomes meaningless and thus disappears from our normal vocabulary, its concept, and with it, our thoughts, values, and ideas, will vanish as well. Words are how we define our world. We use words to understand and relate to each other. Words are the nutrients of our culture. They reveal how we view the world and give us the ability to see or to be blind. Words can nourish our thoughts or starve us to death. So we must define the word evil and make clear what it means. Only through clear understanding can we begin to communicate properly. Thereby, get the majority of the people to understand and finally awaken our knowledge of good and evil.. and make good people stronger.

So we must define and defend the word evil.

Avoid it becoming meaningless.

Any word that stands for ideas and truths that challenge people and puts a light on darkness is at risk of being manipulated and changed.

By changing a word's meaning, little by little, they can confuse people and can take away its power. This is happening with the word evil. They can either make it stand for nothing (it's all relative) or flip its meaning (evil is good, cool, etc.). Slowly, over time, the word will no longer stand for any truths. Once that happens, the word loses its meaning and can disappear from most people's used vocabulary and thereby their thoughts and thinking. From this, and through no fault of their own, more people will become fools–and fools are fuel for evil.

So let's closely compare Gulsoma and Ms. Soon Ok Lee's experiences with Evil against Wikipedia's definitions and theories and look for the truth. One of the first quotes in Wiki to explain evil was from a book by Caitlin Matthews called *Walkers between the Worlds*:

> "Evil remains a name for something unbalanced, something whose origins rest in expediency, selfishness, ignorance, or neglect."

Though her book is interesting, I want us to think about if these definitions make sense. Without going into depth on where she found these associated elements, I think we can still look at them from a basic perspective. Is evil expediency, selfishness, ignorance, and neglect? Let us briefly explore them and see if they make sense.

"Expediency" is a fancy word for "suitable" and "appropriate with urgency." Which, in the context of the concept of evil, makes little sense. What does this have to do with evil? Let's not forget the horrific, cruel moments of torture of the girl Gulsoma. What did that have to do with expediency? Was it suitable for the man to torture Gulsoma?

"Selfishness"...Yes, that is a negative trait, behavior, and feeling. Evil is no doubt selfish. But haven't we all experienced selfishness? Especially as children. Since we are all guilty of this, does it make us all evil? Really?... evil? Selfishness is a bad human behavior present in evil, but it is not exclusive to evil. Decent people know selfishness. We all struggle with it, more or less.

"Ignorance"...I'm not sure how to even respond. How is evil related to ignorance? Did the father not know that Gulsoma was hurting from his torture? Perhaps the Korean guards were also ignorant about the pain they gave the prisoners when they tortured them? Of course not. They knew very well what they were doing. One could say many people are ignorant of evil and, because of that, allow evil to happen. But evil itself isn't ignorant. On the contrary, evil is highly aware.

"Neglect" is a very negative action certainly. And like selfishness, evil can be done through neglect. But like selfishness, an act of neglect can also be done by someone who cannot properly take care of the person. It is not exclusive to evil.

So far, these words seem to confuse rather than clear up what evil is. I don't know about you, but I start zoning out, trying to follow these ideas. Their theories act as a blender of confusion that kills my curiosity. I cannot say that is their intention. But the fact that these unclear ideas are the chosen ideas to represent 'evil' in our times is rather troubling.

Next, We could go into Spinoza, Nietzsche, and Jung's statements in detail. Still, they seem from my perspective so far from reality that we will just quickly ask these few questions. Is the reason for cutting Gulsoma's back because she hinders the father from possessing anything good? Are the Korean guards that torture children and women just non-good and resented by weak prisoners? Perhaps it's the prisoner's fault, projecting their own shadows onto the guards, making them evil? These questions seem to be nonsense. Perhaps I am missing the point of these philosophers and psychologists. That is certainly possible. But one thing I think is clear. Their thinking has not defined evil clearly. Yet, they are the chosen quotes on Wikipedia for us and our world to define evil.

Finally, let's look at Zimbardo's hypothesis on evil.

I want to take you through this important experiment and spend a full chapter on it because I believe it has had an ill effect on our society and shaped too many people's views of evil today. Its hypothesis puts on trial goodness and good people. And as good people often do... they feel guilty and stay silent while their integrity is questioned. Making their voices, opinions, AND values not just meaningless but part of evil. So in the end... who would listen? if we are all evil.

So who is Phillip Zimbardo, and what is his hypothesis?

THE DIFFERENCE...

Dr. Zimbardo suggests that people act in evil ways as a result of a collective identity. This hypothesis was published in his book *The Lucifer Effect*. Understanding how good people turn evil and is based on his Stanford Prison Experiment. Before we go into the details, let's look at his book title for a moment and allow its meaning to settle in our minds and hearts. He is stating that there's a Lucifer (Satan) effect that can turn good people evil. Let's note he didn't say people in general but specifically good people. That's quite a statement because common sense would tell you that good people cannot be good if they do Evil. I guess his point is that we are all evil. That there is an effect or situation that would make you or I take a five-year-old girl as a slave and enjoying cutting meat on her back as torture.

This sounds preposterous to me, but this professor is taken very seriously in the academic world and has received much acclaim for his studies. So I think we should dive into his world with an open mind. Perhaps there is something to it? I certainly want to know how this "Satan effect" could affect me if it's true.

Before we go back to 1971 with Zimbardo's experiment, let's look briefly at the man and what Zimbardo tells us about his childhood. He grew up in the ghettos of the South Bronx, New York City. As a part of a gang, he witnessed and experienced the urban ghetto life with crime and brutality. As an initiation, he had to steal, fight kids, and intimidate Jews and girls. None of this was considered bad, according to Zimbardo. It was obeying and conforming to the gang. Instead, the real bad ones were those with "systemic power," as Zimbardo calls it. The janitors who kicked him off the stoops, the heartless landlords who evicted families who couldn't pay rent, and the cops who would take his bat for playing on the streets. Zimbardo wrote in his book: "I never trusted grown-up, in uniform until proven otherwise."

We can already tell his experiences and viewpoints were shaped at an early age. Like all of us, we develop a worldview from our experiences and influences as our brains begin to understand the social world.

At an early age, between six and twelve, your own experiences and challenges will affect your views and perspective. Zimbardo grew up on the streets in gangs and a tough neighborhood. I grew up in a safe town but was often very sick in hospitals and saw at home my father being mistreated by strangers. All this shapes our perspectives and motives, which is good if it becomes a positive force that drives us. But we have to be mindful not to be blinded by it. To stay honest in the search for the truth no matter where it brings us. Even if it challenges our own early shaped worldview.

One of Zimbardo's main conclusions of his experiment is that situational forces can create subtle powers that will dominate people's will and seduce them into doing things they would have never imagined. Through obedience, rationalization, and deindividuation, good people do evil. He questions what he calls assumptions that inner determinations guide our paths of good or bad (thoughts, feelings, and actions). That most of us hide behind egocentric biases that create an illusion that we are special. That we do not know who we are. When we are outside our familiar settings, we start a job, go on a date, get arrested, enlist in the military, join a cult, or volunteer for an experiment. You might not be the person you think you are when the ground rules change. So in his book, he asks the reader to ask themselves "me also?" when they read about evil and its atrocities. You, the reader, and all of us possess evil. As he explains it, "Upholding the Good vs. evil concept takes 'good people' off the hook." It separates and frees them from the responsibility they have in contributing to rape, torture, and violence, with their "what can I do to change it?" attitude. Instead, he believes in a concept that explains evil in incrementalist terms. That we all are capable of evil, we all hold it inside to greater or lesser degrees. We can learn to become evil regardless of genetics, personality, or upbringing.

Together with the incremental concept, Zimbardo explains that as a social psychologist, he avoids the traditional view of the dispositional question, which means to look for a guilty person and ask "who" questions like "Who did it?" Individualist cultures have a bias looking at motives, traits, genes, and pathologies. They underestimate the importance of the situation when looking for causes of people's behavior. Zimbardo finds it much more important to look at the "What questions." What situation contributed to certain reactions? Though we think we have consistent personalities across time and space, it is likely not true. We are not the same person at home, school, or work. People's characters often transform when they are caught in powerful situations.

Zimbardo has a clear definition of evil. "Evil consists in intentionally behaving in ways that harm, abuse, demean, dehumanize or destroy innocent others." It's a good, short description, and I believe he is close to the answer. Only a one key element is missing. This element will be addressed at the end of the chapter as we look at the bigger picture with hopefully a deeper understanding of the conclusion.

But right now, how do you feel about yourself? Are you beginning to doubt yourself slightly, feeling a sense of guilt? Do you maybe wonder if Dr. Zimbardo is right? Maybe you are thinking of things you have done that you regret a long time ago or perhaps recently? Hold those thoughts and feelings, and we will soon return to Zimbardo's hypothesis to analyze it all in-depth. Quotes from Zimbardo's experiment will be referenced, but a lot will be shortened, so I encourage you not to trust my words and do your own research and see for yourself. Read his book, watch online clips of the experiment.

But for now, let's dive into Dr. Zimbardo's experiment because it raises some interesting questions.

The Stanford Prison Experiment

The government-funded experiment took place in Palo Alto, California, in 1971 in the basement of Stanford's Psychology Department. Zimbardo had put out an ad in the *Palo Alto Times* and *The Stanford Daily* offering fifteen dollars per day to be part of a two-week psychological study of prison life. About one hundred men replied to the ads and were interviewed for an hour to filter out those with medical or mental problems: Twenty-four young men from the Bay Area, some students of Stanford and some Berkeley, were selected from the group to participate. The idea was that twelve would become prisoners, and the other twelve would be guards. Zimbardo says that they randomly assigned which volunteers would be prisoners and which ones would be guards in the book.

THE DIFFERENCE...

> "We randomly assigned all the volunteers to each of the two conditions, like tossing a coin. If it came up heads, the volunteer was assigned to be a guard; if it was tails, a prisoner."

He goes on and states:

"We went out of our way to select young men who seemed to be normal, healthy and average on all psychological dimensions we measured.

"By preselection, our subjects are generally representative of the middle class, educated youth. They are a homogeneous group of students who are quite similar to each other in many ways."

Zimbardo goes on to say that: "Our research will attempt to differentiate between what people bring into a prison situation from what the situation brings out in the people who are there."

"By randomly assigning them to the two different roles, we begin with guards and prisoners who are comparable, indeed, are interchangeable. The prisoners are not more violent, hostile, or rebellious than the guards, and the guards aren't more power-seeking authoritarians."

Is that true?

After some research into his original papers and looking at the three personality tests he used, Comrey personality scale, F scale, and the Machiavellianism scale. His subjects were within 40 to 60 percent of the American male population. He certainly didn't invite any who were psychologically unfit. But at the same time, the tests show there were differences between the students, which he briefly mentions in his paper but does not go into in his book. Instead, he shows the mean/average scores of all combined prisoners and guards, which removes the ability to see patterns of the individuals. I was unfortunately not able to analyze it closer from the original papers because the names had been blacked out. Since fake names were used to protect identities, one wonders why he would black them out. If it was me and I had to prove that it was mostly the environment bringing Evil out in good people and not what they brought into the experiment with their personalities. I would make sure to highlight their individual tests first and then show the overall results.

Since we cannot see the results and make our own decision about the truth, we need to go deeper into the story and find out more to find out if it is indeed true that the environment can make good people evil.

For that, Let's go back to 1971 in Central California. It was a Sunday morning in August and the first day of the experiment. A basement had been transformed into a prison with three cells with three prisoners in each. The cell doors had a window with bars, and the hallway simulated the yard. Guards had been given their orientation the day before with uniforms, whistles, reflective sunglasses, handcuffs, and billy clubs.

The prisoners were about to be picked up by the real Palo Alto Police as Zimbardo had worked out a deal with the sheriff to make it as real as possible.

Let us look at how different each volunteer reacted during the fake arrests. Zimbardo described three of them in his book: Hubbie, Tom, and Doug.

THE DIFFERENCE...

The first arrested was Hubbie. He followed the orders of the officer, trying to comfort his mother while taken to the police car and handcuffed. "Momma, Dad knows all about it, ask him. He signed the release, it's all right, don't worry."

The next one, Tom, was a well-built young man with a crew cut, was cooperative and ready to go with the officer: "I'm Tom Thompson, sir. I am prepared to be arrested without any resistance."

The last to be picked up was Doug.

Unlike Tom and Hubbie, he became aggressive and confrontational. "The fascists can't push us around" He continued, "Prisoner, huh, so that's the game? I prefer it, didn't go to college to become a pig (cop)."

Without knowing the details of the other volunteers, we can still observe that the three in the book had very different personalities.

Upon arriving at the prison, the prisoners were given mocks and rubber clogs. Attached to their ankles were locked chains. They were not allowed underwear. Everything was done to dehumanize them as much as possible. Seventeen rules were given with a warning that failure to obey might result in punishment. During this degradation ritual, the prisoners were stripped naked and sprayed with lice powder.

This was the first exposure to the environment that Zimbardo would be testing, and there was great attention given to the details. At the beginning of the first day, both guards and prisoners showed a sense of awkwardness. This changed quickly though, as different reactions began to show.

The guard, John Landry, felt guilty and left the "yard" when he could. The guard, Arnett, on the other hand, felt they were too polite. Especially to the prisoners Doug and Stewart, who did not take it seriously and found it amusing.

But the amusement did not last long. When the night shift guards came, two of the guards turned abusive. With a big grin, Hellmann would start the "count" where each prisoner would yell his number out. Hellman's orders soon turned into a game of push-ups and ridicule.

Their night shift partner George Landry, on the other hand, did not feel comfortable being a guard. He tried to compete with Hellmann's authority, but it was obvious that he did not find it enjoyable as Hellmann. That first-night prisoner Doug was put in the "'hole." The hole was a closet meant to be an isolation and punishment cell. Doug had laughed at Hellmann, which turned into a scuffle and got him put in the hole for a couple of hours.

After this first night, Hellmann, Burdan, and Landry would discuss how to be better guards.

Hellmann found it fun and games and wanted to act like "hot shit' and be more domineering. Interestingly, Zimbardo used the same words, "fun and games" about the prisoners attitudes during his guard's orientation speech. He told them to get "into the mood of the joint." He continued this by saying, "We cannot physically abuse or torture them.... We can create boredom. We can create a sense of frustration. We can create fear in them, to some degree."

Unlike Hellman, other guards like Landry found it upsetting and tried to be the nice guard.

THE DIFFERENCE...

At the morning shift, the new guards.-Ceros, Vandy, and Mike.-took over. During the instructions of the toilet rules, the second prisoner, Stewart, was put into the hole for laughing.

As the mild yet still emotional humiliation continued to escalate, the prisoners began to get more rowdy. The guard, Vandy, didn't like Doug's bed and ripped off his blanket, throwing it on the floor. Doug yelled back: "You can't do that!" Getting very emotional, Doug lunged at Vandy but missed and was put in the hole again with Stewart for some time.

Angered by the rebelling prisoners, the guards got the blankets from Cell 1 and Cell 2 and dragged them through the brush outside. Dirty with pin needles, the prisoners were then ordered to clean up their blankets. The anger at this action escalated into Stewart, Paul, and Hubbie tearing off their number IDs on their mocks. Which then resulted in the guards punishing them by stripping them naked and taking away their mocks.

I think it's easy to understand how psychologically uncomfortable this would be, even for a healthy person. It ignited the beginning of a group effort for Cell 1 and 2 to rebel. When the morning came, the day shift guards saw the door for Cell 1.-with Paul, Glenn, and Hubbie.-had been blocked with their beds. In frustration, the guards retaliated at Cell 2 and rushed in, pulling their cots out into the yard.

Stewart screamed at them: "This is an experiment, leave me alone. Shit, let go of me, fucker!"

Doug yelled, "It's no prison. It's a fucking experiment. Fuck Zimbardo!"

The guard Arnett explained in a calm voice that once Cell 1 behaved properly, their beds would be returned.

The naked Doug began to yell: "They took our clothes! They took our beds!".

He yelled at Cell 3 to block their door. "Get your beds in front of the door! Don't let them in."

For the first time, Rich joined in.

"Fight them! Resist violently. The time has come for violent revolution."

In response, the guard John Landry took a fire extinguisher and shot bursts into the rebelling Cell 2.

Cell 3 (Tom, Jerry, and Jim) didn't rebel as their beds were taken out into the yard. This made Doug angry, especially at Tom, who had helped his cellmates obeying the guards.

The guards prepared a special lunch for Cell 3 to eat in front of the other [less-well-behaved] prisoners. Cell 3 refused to eat but cooporated with chores given.

During the count, Jim and Hubbie were quick to say their numbers. Glenn and Stewart were slow and reluctant. Watching the guards do the counts, Zimbardo found that Arnett didn't seem to enjoy it. In his book, Zimbardo wrote, "Arnett doesn't seem to take nearly as much **PERSONAL PLEASURE** in his performance as the other shift leaders do."

Without going into details, this is a hint we need to remember for our later conclusion on the definition of evil.

Zimbardo was not happy with Arnett as a guard, but there was someone even more inactive as a guard. Markus stayed away from being involved with the yard and jumped at the opportunity to do chores outside. His body posture wasn't what Zimbardo wanted either. His head was down with dropped shoulders. Not the macho image that Zimbardo needed. So Zimbardo got his assistant and "warden" Jaffe to talk to him.

"Guards have to be tough. Our experiment rides on the guards' behavior".

Markus challenged him, saying that he had found that tough, aggressive behavior was counterproductive. Jaffe became defensive and explained that they needed to show how prisons changed people when they were faced with situations of guards with Power. Jaffe:

> We need you to play the role of the tough guard. We need you to react as you imagine the 'pigs' would. We're trying to set up the stereotype guard. Your individual style is a little too soft."

Markus agreed to try harder at being tougher.

For the night shift, Hellmann and Burdan kept becoming more verbally abusive, and as things got more volatile, Zimbardo had the warden Jaffe announce that the prisoners should elect three who would represent them all and talk to "superintendent" Zimbardo.

Wearing his dark sunglasses, Zimbardo met with the three and heard their complaints about the verbal and physical harassment and abuse. He promised them to change as much of what he could as long as they represented the will of the others and there were no rebels. The three representatives reported back to the others. Doug didn't buy any of the goodwill and kept disobeying orders and was finally thrown into the hole again, handcuffed until the lights were out and a very emotional Doug was taken out. Soon after, Doug went into a panic attack, screaming.

"I mean, Jesus Christ, I'm burning up inside. Don't you know? I'll do anything to get out! I'll wreck your cameras! You have no right to fuck with my head!"

At the time of Doug's panic attack, Zimbardo was out having dinner. A fellow student, Craig, was overlooking the situation and interviewed Doug. He was uncertain whether Doug was acting or truly disturbed. It had been thirty-six hours, and Doug was acting worse than they had expected any would in the two-weeks experiment. Craig finally made the moral decision to release Doug.

Afterward, when Zimbardo came back, Craig, Curt, and Zimbardo analyzed the decision, and though skeptical, they agreed it was the best option. It left a big question for them. Why did Doug break down so quickly? Did they miss something in his profile? His personality tests had revealed no hints of mental instability. For a minute, they agreed he must have been very sensitive and overreacted to the simulated prison experience. But as Zimbardo explained in his book, he thought this was "groupthink" and just a mistaken belief. Because that would mean Doug's internal influences, his emotions, and possible adverse experiences had been the cause of his "overreaction" to the mistreatment... instead of the situation causing it.

As Zimbardo said in his book: "It was only later that we appreciated this obvious irony, that we had dispositionally explained the first truly unexpected and extraordinary demonstration of situational power in our study by re-

THE DIFFERENCE...

sorting to precisely the kind of thinking we had designed the study to challenge and critique."

Let's hold that thought and remember Zimbardo said his study was to challenge and critique theories that looked at the person instead of the situation as a cause of the behavior. It is ironic that his students would indirectly challenge Zimbardo with what I believe was the right answer. It was obvious that Doug could not take the mistreatment as well as others. Zimbardo did not want to see the possible truth that Doug had a panic attack and needed to get out because of his internal emotions about the mistreatment that Zimbardo had caused by directing the guards to "act brutal, assertive, like a pig" throughout the experiment.

The following day with one prisoner less, it was visitor day for family or friends. Stewart's parents were the first to enter the yard. Coming up to him at the end of the yard, both his father and mother shook Stewart's hand but kept the talk short. Rich's parents, on the other hand, seemed warmer and animated. His mother was very worried about his appearance and told Rich, "Now you be good and follow the rules." Afterward, Rich's parents went straight to Zimbardo's office and expressed their concerns. Rich's mother let out her fears. "I don't mean trouble, sir, but I am worried about my son. I have never seen him looking so tired." Worried that the mother might raise trouble, Zimbardo tried to put the blame on Rich. Zimbardo explained this is what any authority would do to protect the system and its procedures. Without being able to convince or manipulate the mother, Zimbardo changed to the father and, as he writes in this book, to put his masculine pride at risk. "Don't you think that your son can take it?" Seeing this did the trick. Zimbardo stopped listening to the father and quickly closed the conversation by promising he would make sure to keep an eye on their son and winked with the handshake to the father.

Zimbardo expressed in the book of his thoughts on the father: "We silently acknowledge that we will tolerate 'the little lady's overreaction.' What swine we are, and we do it all on automatic masculine pilot."

I want to pause here and make a few notes. Zimbardo seemed to take satisfaction in manipulation. He justifies it by saying he was acting as those authorities in prison, yet there's a strong arrogance in his words. He doesn't know what the father is thinking, yet he attributed his maleness to being a swine, tolerating his wife, and being on automatic masculine pilot. Sure, perhaps Zimbardo was right, but maybe the father was polite. This father could have thought many things, yet Zimbardo saw only a dark and cynical side.

Back to the experiment.

Zimbardo had a priest visit the prisoners and talk to them. Among them, Stewart was particularly upset. He was feeling sick and depressed after his parents' visit. The parents felt they had a great talk with him (only five minutes), but Stewart felt they didn't seem to care at all about his condition. They had talked about a play they had seen instead of listening to him. Stewart finally broke down and cried deep tears in front of the priest and Zimbardo.

Zimbardo's response to Stewart: "You're going to have to be less emotional."

THE DIFFERENCE...

Zimbardo promised Stewart he would get some good food and get to rest outside the yard for a while.

The priest explained to Stewart: "Maybe you are responding to the smell of this place. The air is oppressive. There's an unpleasant smell... You have to get your balance. Plenty of prisoners learn to handle it."

The basement had, over the days, began smelling from the urine and feces odor because of the five-minute rule of the toilet a day.

After the meetings with the prisoners, the priest told Zimbardo that the study was working as a real prison and what he had seen was the typical "first offender syndrome." They both agreed Stewart needed counseling, and Zimbardo explained his thoughts on Stewart:

"I think that he cannot accept the idea that he is chickening out, that his masculinity might be threatened, so he wants me to insist he leave as a way to save face."

Chickening out? Save face? Maybe so, if one does not think of the emotions triggered by the treatment that Zimbardo's experiment was causing. Zimbardo seemed obsessed with machismo and walked a fine line of ridiculing his volunteers over showing emotions and pain.

Maybe it wasn't about saving face but about trying harder even though one is scared and feeling overwhelmed. There's a certain "put down" in Zimbardo's line of thought I find disturbing. Sure, you can say "save face," but you can also say "try harder." One is a putdown, and the other is an uplifting thought. That being said, I can appreciate Zimbardo's openness about his thoughts since it helps us also understand him while absorbing the information.

Because Doug had been released, a new prisoner, Clay, was added to the group to fill in. He was quickly singled out and harassed. Zimbardo suggested perhaps there was something about Clay's shabby and scrawny appearance that was offensive to the guards since they tended to be meticulous. Again, Zimbardo's words implied a strong dislike for men who did not act or look macho and strong. Because of the harassment, Clay decided to go on a hunger strike and, with his first meal, refused to eat. This angered Hellmann, making him order every prisoner to tell Clay how much they disliked him. But for Tom, Hellmann wanted more. He ordered Tom to say, "Tell him he is a pussy." Tom refused to use obscenities, and Hellman spent an hour yelling at him.

The next day was parole day. During this day, three important quotes can help our understanding and clear up conclusions of the experiment.

Zimbardo used his new friend Carlo Prescott, a convicted felon of armed robbery, as his parole board officer. Zimbardo questioned whether Carlos would have compassion towards the prisoner's requests for parole as he had been there himself many times. This did not happen. Carlos was aggressive from the beginning, questioning the first prisoner, Jim, about what he did to cause the arrest.

Carlos: "What did you do? Shoot them or stab them or bomb them? Did you use one of those rifles?"

Jim tried to plead not guilty. Since this was all made up, most of what Jim thought up reflected his naivete and clearly showed he was not a criminal. On the order hand, it was quite clear that Carlos was, and his questions felt almost biographical. If it wasn't so sad, the contrast in language between the "prisoners" and the "parole officer" could almost be seen as funny. The second prisoner, Glenn, was put up against the parole board. He tried to justify his release. Jaffe, the warden, jumped into the discussion and argued against him. As Zimbardo writes: "Warden Jaffe cannot resist getting in his licks."

Let's pause for a moment and reflect on Zimbardo's chosen words. Unless I have missed something and this description of Jaffe was actually expressed by Jaffe, there's a certain troubling enjoyment in Zimbardo's language "getting his licks." Its as if he enjoys getting people riled up and verbally abusing each other.

Later, during another parole hearing, prisoner Rich opened up about how the experiment had helped him.

Rich: "I've gotten to see a lot of people's different reactions to different situations, how they handle themselves with respect to other people, such as speaking with various cellmates, their reactions to the same situations. The three different shifts of guards, I've noticed the individual guards have small differences in the same situations."

Here we have the first quote that's very important.

Rich saw how each cellmate and guard behaved and reacted differently to the same situation. Let's remember this for the later conclusion of Zimbardo's experiment.

Tom, was the last prisoner to be interviewed. Carlos asked Tom why he had never asked for parole before.

Tom: "I would have requested parole the first time only if not enough other prisoners requested it."

Tom felt that other prisoners could use it more than him, and he didn't want them to lose out if he got it. Both

Zimbardo and Carlos were at first skeptical but realized he was sincere. Carlos asked more details about Tom's life, and Tom explained that he was living in his car and didn't have a girlfriend. The food and shelter in this experiment were actually a step up for him. For Zimbardo, Tom seemed to be a contradiction. He saw Tom's actions as one-dimensional and mindlessly obedient yet also most logical, thoughtful, and morally consistent throughout the experiment. In his book, Zimbardo expressed his worries that Tom might "have a harder life than the rest of his fellows."

Why would Zimbardo think that? This is an important point since Tom probably handled the experiment the best out of them all. Zimbardo felt Tom's abstract principles might cause him to live ineffectively with other people and make him unable to seek out help—financial, personal, or emotional.

This is the second important quote.

The principles that Tom lived by were abstract to Zimbardo. He did not see them as wise. On the contrary, he looked at them with foreign eyes and thought they would make him weak. Rebelling was for Zimbardo being strong-willed, not obeying the authority.

Without going into Tom's future, which we do not know, we can look at how Tom reacted and see whether his actions were good or bad for him and his cellmates. And here lies a vital argument against Zimbardo's hypothesis. Tom came from a tough life, yet he was grateful, respectful, and hardworking. He accepted the terms of the experiment as a prisoner. With a military-style language, he followed the guard's order as long as they were in line with his morals. But when the guard's orders became

THE DIFFERENCE...

abusive and pushed him to do something against his cellmates or put them down, he would avoid the order, even when it meant harassment towards himself. His cell was the one that was calm, and we can likely assume his demeanor affected his cellmates in a positive way. While the other two cells quickly deteriorated from the other prisoners' emotional reactions to the guards.

Would you not find these qualities good and noble? Something to look up to? Yet Zimbardo thought these principles were not only abstract but that Tom would suffer through life because of his strong commitment to them.

If it is true that the "situation" is the cause of evil, then wouldn't Tom have become selfish, violent, and evil? The prison experiment and situation certainly succeeded in becoming abusive for most of the participants. But why did it not change Tom's personality and actions? Could it be that Tom's principles helped him understand what was going on and that he, as a person, had a very strong will and strength? Perhaps he was less emotional. We do not know his past and what he had gone through. But we know how he chose to live with respect towards himself, respect towards others, and being there to help others and not to hurt others.

And that is what he did in the Stanford Prison Experiment.

Tom did not turn evil...

During the morning count, a fight broke out between the prisoner Paul and guard Ceros. Paul was put into the hole for refusing to do his sit-ups, and after breakfast, when Paul was let out of the hole, he tried to strike at

Ceros. After the scuffle, Paul complained about his foot hurting and asked for a doctor.

During an interview, Paul explained: "I ate alone but did apologize to Varnish, who was the least hostile toward me. But the guy I really want to crack is 'John Wayne' (Hellmann), that guy from Atlanta. I'm a Buddhist, and he keeps calling me a communist just to provoke me, and it does. I now think that the good treatment on the part of some guards, like big Landry, is only because they were ordered to act that way."

Here's the third quote to remember.

See how Paul looked differently at the guards. He apologized to Varnish because he was less hostile than the others and expressed his anger towards Hellmann (nickname John Wayne). Later, he changed his view on why some of the guards were good and thought it was because they were ordered to act good. Yet isn't the opposite true? Did Zimbardo tell the guards to be polite and respectful? As far as the book and the research shows, it was the opposite. Zimbardo clearly asked the guards to act like pigs. We all know what that means. He even pulled guards that were friendly into a meeting to emphasize how they should act and to be more aggressive. So why were there still guards who were good and not hostile? Why did their mirror sunglasses, uniform and billy club, and situation not change their behavior? Why were Landry and Varnish so different from Hellmann and Ceros?

Neither the Landry brothers nor Varnish turned evil.

Zimbardo finally realized it had gone too far when he brought his girlfriend, Christina, to help to conduct more parole interviews. Arriving at Stanford's psychology de-

THE DIFFERENCE...

partment, she went down to the basement and into one of the rooms for the guards.

In this room, she met one of the guards. "He was very pleasant, polite, and friendly, surely a person anyone would consider a really nice guy."

She was told by the research staff that she would meet the new late-night guard shift with 'John Wayne' (Hellmann). Christina explained, "John Wayne was the nickname for the guard who was the meanest and toughest of them all. His reputation had preceded him in various accounts I had heard. Of course, I was eager to see who he was and what he was doing that attracted so much attention. When I looked through the observation point, I was absolutely stunned to see that their John Wayne was the 'really nice guy' with whom I had chatted earlier."

She described how he transformed into someone else. "He not only moved differently, but he talked differently, with a Southern accent. He was yelling and cursing at the prisoners as he made them go through "the count," going out of his way to be rude and threatening. It was an amazing transformation from the person I had just spoken to. A transformation that had taken place in minutes just by stepping over the line from the outside world into that prison yard. With his military-style uniform, billy club in hand, and dark, silver reflecting sunglasses to hide his eyes, this guy was an all-business, no-nonsense, really mean prison guard."

Did Christina really believe that putting on a uniform and sunglasses would turn Hellmann into "John Wayne"? I'm surprised that she didn't contemplate the idea that the real Hellmann was the "John Wayne" and his mask was the "really nice guy" she first met.

Instead, we see how she described the "transformation" as if going into a room changed Hellmann. Christina would later describe the experiment and what happened as "the power of the environment."

The power of the environment? This is Nonsense.

An environment has no power unless it is referring to nature with earthquakes, tornadoes, or gravity, etc. The basement of Stanford's psychology department was just that. A basement. Dead Walls, ceilings, and doors. That dead environment got its power from the actions and plans of Zimbardo, and this power grew in some guard's hands like Hellmann, as they were allowed to unmask their desires and find enjoyment in abusing the prisoners.

Even Zimbardo admitted "I was simply wrong. Boys were suffering. As principal investigator, I was personally responsible for their suffering. They were not prisoners, not experimental subjects, but boys, young men, who were being dehumanized and humiliated by other boys who had lost their moral compass in this situation."

He was right, except for the last part. I would state that those boys (Hellmann, Ceros, Burdan, and Arnett) who humiliated their fellow friends had not lost their moral compass.

They did not have it from the beginning.

How can I prove this? By the fact that the very first day, we could already tell who became the worst offenders. At NO point did any of the guards change their personality and moral compass. Some had one, whether it was weak or strong, and some had none. Those who had none could be picked out from their comments and actions on the first day.

THE DIFFERENCE...

Now you might say it's a bit strong to say they had no moral compass. Yes, I would agree I'm simplifying it to keep it brief. But when someone steps over the line and finds **JOY**... or what guard Arnett calls, **ELATION** from it. This is someone without a moral compass and also someone who hints to us a key element in defining evil.

This difference between the guards' actions was also expressed by one of the most rebellious prisoners, Stewart.

Stewart: "I developed a strong resentment of the fascist guards and a strong liking for the compassionate ones."

This is a clear statement that the guards' actions were different.

The guards in their reports also expressed different feelings towards their jobs and what they were doing. Guard Vanish was bothered that he wasn't told what the limits on the force were. He was frustrated with the prisoner Stewart who acted with indifference towards his fellow inmates but felt torn on how to handle him in the best way.

Guard Vanish: "Stewart didn't seem to care that his actions caused trouble for them. I felt I was uncertain as to the amount of force we could, in fact, use, and this bothered me as I felt the limits on this case were not clearly defined."

Guard Vandy expressed a different opinion. "I enjoyed harassing the prisoners at 2:30 a.m. It pleased my sadistic senses to cause bitterness between us."

Zimbardo found this statement remarkable, yet isn't he the one who had been pushing the guards to be authoritative and act like pigs? Also, there's something odd about

Vandy's words that seem, unlike Hellmann and Ceros: "my SADISTIC senses to cause BITTERNESS between US." It feels like he is trying to say what Zimbardo wants to hear. What is sadistic about causing bitterness? Someone sadistic would never say "bitterness between us." First, They would never consider the other person. Second, "Bitterness" is such a mild word I think it would make a sadistic person laugh. I question if Vandy was trying to please Zimbardo and used words he had heard in the orientation. I could be wrong, but Vandy's words seem odd.

Guard Arnett expressed that he was surprised how he never felt any anger except for one incident. "I felt quite relaxed. I never experienced any sense of power or elation when pushing people or ordering them around."

Watch how he describes it opposite to Vandy.

His choice of words is very interesting and especially one word: "ELATION." Let's remember that for our conclusion later. He said he did NOT have any sense of elation, but why did he mention elation? It's a very strong word for pleasure. Other synonyms for 'elation' are ecstasy, euphoria, high, great joy. He could have said, "I didn't feel any sense of frustration, irritation or anger." This I would have understood. Instead, he chose ELATION. Let's pause and think about that. Whether or not he felt this in the experiment is less important (though he might have felt it and was lying to us).

What is important is that he thought of using this strong word in connection with a sense of power.

That means for him, having the power to push people around COULD mean elation. This bears repeating. Pushing people around could make him feel **GREAT PLEASURE**.

THE DIFFERENCE...

He goes on: "I am aware from my reading that... aspects of prison life can be exploited to make people feel disoriented... by punishing all prisoners for bad behavior by individuals, demeaning perfect execution of trivial demands. I tried to heighten alienation by using some of these techniques. I could use it only in a very limited way because I didn't want to be brutal."

He didn't want to be brutal? Yet, he remembers in great detail these techniques he had read about. Together, with the fact that we know he found great pleasure in power, we can see how these two things fit together well. Now let's check and see where he fits in among the guards. Was he the friendly or the abusive guard? I think we all know the answer to that... Indeed, he was among the abusive like Ceros and Hellmann.

Ceros was similar. Guard Ceros spoke of enjoying bothering the prisoners. "I **ENJOYED** bothering them. It bothered me that Sarge prisoner 2093 (Tom) was so very sheepish. I did make him polish and wax my boots seven times, and he never complained.". He continues, "I am tired and disgusted at times. This is actually the state of my mind. Also, I make an actual try of my will to dehumanize them in order to make it easy for me."

Let's focus on what he said and the feelings of disgust he expressed. Where do these feelings come from? Is it the experiment and how the prisoners behaved? There seems to be a conflict between what he did and what he said. He said it took will to dehumanize the prisoners. First, using the word "dehumanize" doesn't seem likely to come from an eighteen-year-old but more likely copied from someone he heard, perhaps from Zimbardo's first-day explanation for the guards.

Rich, the prisoner, would express that the most disturbing thing he noticed was when some guards gave him the feeling that they were really their true self and it wasn't just a game. "Some guards seemed to really enjoy our agony."

The vital point, "**Some** Guards."

Not all, but **some**.

Another clear proof directly from the prisoners that the guards did not take the same actions.

CHAPTER 8

CONCLUSION

DEFINITION OF EVIL?

Zimbardo's conclusion: Because his selection was purely random between guards and prisoners and that neither group had any history of crime, emotional disability, or social disadvantages from his three psychology tests, it could not be that the young men imported any pathology that then subsequently emerged. Instead, he concluded that the pathologies must have come from the set of "situational forces constantly impinging upon them in this prison-like setting."

Zimbardo: "Neither the guards nor the prisoners could be considered 'bad apples' before the time when they were so powerfully impacted by being embedded in a 'bad barrel.'"

Zimbardo: "Good people suddenly becoming perpetrators of evil as guards or pathologically passive victims as prisoners in response to situational forces acting on them."

Zimbardo: "We invest human nature with God-like qualities, with moral and rational faculties that make us both just and wise. We simplify the complexities of human experience by erecting a seemingly impermeable boundary between good and evil. On one side are us, our kin, and our kind; on the other side of that line, we cast them, their different kin, and other kind. Paradoxically, by creating this myth of our invulnerability to situational forces, we set ourselves up for a fall by not being sufficiently vigilant to situational forces."

Zimbardo: "ANY DEED that any human being has ever committed, however horrible, is possible for any of us—under the right or wrong situational circumstances."

So for Zimbardo, ANY of us (not some or a few), can from our own will, pour boiling water over a seven-year-old girl or torture a woman and cut her head off. And one person's morals and rationality to act just and wise is a myth.

Is this really true?

What a frightening world of non-good and cruelty. What value would we have as humans if this is true?

What a sad conclusion.

But fortunately, there's another conclusion.

Like a magic trick that didn't fool, I have a feeling you might have guessed this all along. There is no lucifer effect, and good people do not become evil from dark sunglasses, a uniform, billy clubs, and a given authority over a group or individual. It was an interesting story and an insightful experiment. But not for the reasons Zimbardo gives. Even he had to twist his own logic and deny the obvious. Each person brought in their own psychological and moral makeup, which determined whether guards became abusive or passive and if prisoners could cope or

CONCLUSION

break down, rebel, or obey. Each person reacted differently to the situation of Zimbardo's prison experiment. In a later BBC documentary from 2002, Even Zimbardo uses the term "good guards" yet is able to spin it around again for his main point.

Zimbardo: "There were few guards who hated to see the prisoners suffer, they never did anything which would be demeaning of the prisoners, the interesting thing is, none of the good guards ever intervened in the behavior of the guards who gradually became more and more sadistic over time. We'd like to think there's this core of human nature that good people can't do bad things and that good people will dominate over bad situations. In fact, a way to look at the Stanford prison studies is that we put good people in an evil place and we saw who won, and well, that sadness, in this case, the 'EVIL PLACE' won over the good people."

Do you see where he flipped it around? First, he turned around the fact that there are good guards who are not abusive by changing the focus to the fact that they did nothing to stop the bad guards. This doesn't mean the good guards are sadistic. It means they lack courage. And last, he uses "Evil place" to again focus on an abstract "situational system."

What comes first for a "situational system" like Zimbardo's?

The system or the planner of the system?

If a situation can cause evil in good people. Don't we have to analyze who or what caused this situation? If a storm goes through a town and wrecks and kills half of its population, wouldn't the situation be because of the storm? And if Zimbardo set up the prison and its rules and the situational system, doesn't that fall on Zimbardo and not empty words like situation, system and what?

Shouldn't it be who?

After all, the prison didn't make itself on its own. It had people chosen by Zimbardo and rules made by Zimbardo. He does admit this in brief parts, but like many lies, it's not whether there are sprinkles of truth here and there. It is about the direction of the main points.

Zimbardo created an environment that unlocked what is not morally accepted and allowed masks to come off from some of the volunteers.

If it was the system of power and situation only, all volunteers would have reacted in a similar way, maybe not completely the same but similar.

They clearly did not.

Some wore masks to hide their real selves, and others did not. Those who did not wear 'masks' did not turn abusive. But those who had something to hide about who they were inside, did.

By telling the guards to act like a pig and follow the seventeen rules, it indirectly encouraged psychological abuse. All in the name of simulating the "man's prison."

The underlying message was clear.

As each day progressed, we saw some guards at first feel uncomfortable being a guard, then later some of those faded into the background, avoiding to act, and a few others began trying to copy the abusive guards, but it was always clear it was not their nature.

CONCLUSION

The abusive guards showed hesitation at first, but once their harassment was not stopped and encouraged, they quickly began raising the level of abuse.

Little by little, those who wore masks in real life started taking them off.

So it was not really an experiment of good people turning evil.

History shows us it's more common for people to deny evil than to face it. But why has the idea of "good people being evil" resonated with our society? Besides being associated with Stanford University, which gives the hypothesis credibility, I believe there are at least two reasons why Zimbardo's hypotheses have been able to take hold of our society's view of evil. One, because the press and academia never questioned his hypothesis. Like most lies, it was partly true. Some guards were abusive, but Zimbardo conveniently forgot to mention others weren't.

Second, and this one is more troubling, is because I believe some people wish for the world to be blind to evil. Who are they? Obviously, those who have a dark side (in various degrees), but sadly also many who are victims of evil. They are often trying to survive or stay in denial because they are either biologically related, benefit from the action of evil, or are in love with someone dark. Both types have a stake in the world being blind:

One is doing evil. The other is protecting evil.

Maybe Zimbardo unintentionally or intentionally mistook anger for Evil. If his book title was "good people becoming angry," this would be true. But his book is *The Lucifer Effect*. Anger does NOT equal evil. To feel anger is human, and depending on the situation, it can come from a bad or good place. On the contrary, Evil might have gotten its start in the deepest valleys of anger, but it does not come from a gradual increase of anger in the present. evil is already ever-present in those people who are evil.

During the experiment, I suspect that some of the neutral guards (Varnish, Vandy, and Landry) might have felt anger towards their predicament and some of the prisoner's actions. They probably even followed the abusive guards, putting this anger out on the prisoners. Though this was wrong, it is very human. It takes courage to stand up against the norm and the more aggressive guards. But was this anger or lack of courage... or evil?

In this lies a truth and a hypothesis.

Did they enjoy it? Would they have done it if the other guards were firm yet fair to the prisoners? I say no. I think they were followers. Anger does not equal evil. I believe there is not a gradual line of anger that leads to evil. If a person is evil, he/she will be evil from the beginning. They will only show it through subtle hints until they have enough power to show more and ultimately take off their mask. The mask is always there. It doesn't develop. It's always been there, hiding. Anger, on the contrary, is a human emotion that we all can feel, and it can blind us from truths and make us do bad or wrong things. But anger can also be a source of goodness and used as strength to fight or survive.

I generally believe that behavior has reasons. If someone is acting a certain way, there are reasons for his actions. Doug, for example, was an anti-war activist. From the very first moment he was arrested by the local police, he was cursing and using the typical words "pig" and "power to the people" Words that Zimbardo used himself.

Couldn't it be that Zimboardo had an attraction to revolution fantasies and saw authority as 'pigs'? And this attraction, unintentional or intentional, blinded Zimbardo's view of the facts? He seems to have set out to prove good people are evil, and surprise, he found empirical evidence for it. Yet, none of the facts in the experiment I have seen, proved any of it... On the contrary.

It made me distrust his book.

Another part that stood out to me, was Zimbardo's pick as the ULTIMATE example of evil power, which was likened to George Orwell's 1984. One could guess he picked the National Socialist Party of Germany (Nazis) or perhaps Lenin and Stalin's Soviet Union or even Mao's communist China. All these tyrannical states were, and some still are, great systems of power. Ruthless powers guilty of killing over one hundred million of their own people, not including World Wars.

one hundred million! Let that sink in...

These State powers did much greater harm than the worst wars in world history. World War II killed half of that... fifty million worldwide.

So what did the professor, whose main studies are the social psychology of evil, pick as the ULTIMATE example of an evil system of power?

"The Military-Corporate-Religious complex of The United States."

I have been through certain things in life. I have seen things and felt things. Though I have never truly been in the hands of evil, I have been very close. I have felt the deep fear of helplessness with utter terror in my stomach till I wanted to throw up. During this time, I could no longer be entertained at horror movies in the same way as I had prior. I remember being at Disney at the haunted mansion. Even the slightly dark entertainment was no longer fun or funny. There was nothing funny about it. Because when you have been close to true evil or, even worse, felt it personally, you know it's not a game. You know it happens every day around the world to endless innocent people. There's nothing to laugh at or take lightly. And if you should ever get close to it personally or with someone you love, pray it's not within a system of power as a government. Because your voice means nothing, your cries mean nothing, your life means NOTHING. There will be no escape.

To call the United States military, the greatest evil is a sick lie.

It is the opposite. The United States has fought evil for decades. It has saved countless lives and been the savior of innocent people from true evil when no other countries would. Young American men and women have died to protect innocent lives. But because some soldiers do wrong, the American military is often generalized as evil. The fact that American soldiers who do evil, are reprimanded, is ignored. On the other hand, true evil countries are ignored, even when it is a fact their general orders for power are done with terror, torture, and murdering as their main tactic, especially towards civilians, children,and women.

That does not mean it cannot change. I pray to God America's constitution and covenant with God never

CONCLUSION

changes and that its military power is never used for evil. Against its own people or good parts of the world. Because I am highly aware that there is much darkness in America, just like in the rest of the world.

Decent people in America must stay vigilant.

To be a light for the world. A city upon a hill.

Okay, I think we are ready to define evil.

It is time to define it clearly.

CHAPTER 9

THE DEFINITION

WHAT IS EVIL?

So what is evil?

I believe it is finally time to compare what we know and put it together. How did the Wikipedia definitions of evil compare to the real-life stories of evil? Did the Stanford experiment and Dr. Zimbardo's hypothesis explain evil?

Did the puzzle come together for you?

It didn't for me. All the definitions were at best unclear and at worst lies and upside-down theories. None of them spoke to the horrific true-life stories.

So here we are, deep in the forest. We have ventured into the darker parts and listened to the stories of survivors who told us of the true nature of evil. Yet the selected wise men of our society are telling us it is all relative, our imagination, or our fault.

There's no light to lead us out.

Perhaps it is best not to seek answers and instead close our minds, eyes, and soul. Maybe it is for our best. Maybe the dark forest is meant to be our home. After all, perhaps it is true. We are the darkness we have tried to find. Perhaps the light inside us is just a myth.

Or perhaps… This is not true.

Perhaps we are being lied to, and perhaps there is a way out. Maybe the survivors are giving us hints of the truth. Maybe there is, after all, a faint light. A light that can lead us to the truth. Out of the darkness. First, let's see if there is anything that can link the stories together.

Did you notice words while reading that were all in bold? **JOY, PLEASURE, POWER,** and **CONTROL**. These words I put in bold for you to notice and remember. Why? Because in them lies a path that will lead us to an important answer. An answer that holds the key for us understanding evil and finally lead us to its possible origin.

Let's go back to Zimbardo's definition of evil slightly shortened: "intentionally doing harm, abuse or destroying innocent people."

Is this true? Though this does partly cover evil, it is only partly true.

For it to be true, only evil can fit its definition. No acts from a decent and flawed person should be able to fit. Yes, evil does abuse, destroy, and yes, it can be intentional, and is often done to the innocent. But why was it done? Are there never reasons when one chooses to do something very bad? Both intentionally and to someone innocent? And this is key. Does the person regret it later? Something that might even haunt one for the rest of one's life?

THE DEFINITION

Going back to our mind and our thoughts. We have these thoughts that are often dark. Don't we sometimes listen to them? Don't we sometimes even act on them? Maybe we are tempted by greed, lust, pride, and anger. Don't we sometimes harm others for selfish or self-righteous reasons and say or do something that hurts others?

Wouldn't that fit into this definition?

I will speak for myself and say I know I have done things with regrets. Times where I turned angry and did something stupid. I have hurt and harmed people I love, by my actions. Perhaps Zimbardo meant his words only to be thought of as "major harms." But even this doesn't fit. Because though I have never majorly harmed someone, I do believe there have been times I could have chosen it. That innocent friend or stranger might have been hurt greatly by my actions or words. It can happen to us all. Not because we have the drive to do it, but because we're human and make bad decisions.

But the key thing is, we have a consciousness.

Some people will struggle more with their consciousness than others. Some will feel a deep burden. Others might lie to themselves and only feel little. Like courage, our moral consciousness is different from person to person. Some find ways to convince themselves that it was okay. But the point is, it takes energy and effort to fight our guilt. Even if we have successfully lied to ourselves over decades, being led by temptation, weak will, and bad ideas, deep beneath the surface, the guilt lingers. We can hide from it or face it, but it's there. Given a mirror, we know it to be true. Because of this, we would not be evil. Perhaps bad, flawed, wrongly self-righteous, and lost, but not evil.

So then, what is missing?

I think the answer is within our Stanford experiment. Though subtle, it was there. An answer that is rarely mentioned in stories like Gulsoma and Ms. Lee because many authors and victims are not consciously aware of it. Ask yourself, Why would someone torture someone? Why would someone humiliate someone? Why would someone laugh at someone hurting?

Could it be because it feels good?

Could it be because it gives them not only power and strength but pleasure and joy?

I believe this is the path we have to take and look into. I believe this is the key part of evil that our society is looking away from. Thinking back to those days where caretakers were giving my mother and father trouble and getting my mother to cry, I vaguely remember them smiling. As if they were getting a kick from seeing the tears of my mother. Looking at Gulsoma and Lee's stories, we don't have enough details to verify this conclusion, but with the Stanford experiment, there were many signs of this.

So I think you are ready for a clear description to define evil...

THE DEFINITION OF EVIL:

"EVIL is CONSCIOUSLY and INTENTIONALLY harming others without remorse... COMBINED with getting PLEASURE from HARMING OTHERS."

That is it. This is evil, universal evil, and yes... it exists.

As goodness, it can be big, or it can be small. The key part missing is realizing that deep joy, pleasure, and relief can come from harming others. It is what drives evil. It is its fuel, its need, and is a strong force.

Perhaps you think, How could one find joy in killing? Find pleasure in the pain of others? And if so, why? Maybe it's not true. How could there be joy or calm in evil? To answer this, we must go deep into the darkest parts of the forest and open our eyes. We must not be afraid of what we see. We must not be afraid to question everything. We now know the path to take and what to look for.

Let's see if we can identify and verify our new definition of evil.

I want you to be brutally honest with what you read and your own judgments. Some things might get uncomfortably close to home. Some things might bring taboos up. But we cannot afford to look away because this will keep us blind. We must not be afraid of the truth, should we find it.

Evil is always counting on us to stay blind, stay passive, stay ignorant. Let's not be its slave. Goodness can and will overcome darkness. I know because I believe there is an answer to the origin of evil. Not to a perfect world, but a better world.

But it all depends on you and me.

Do you want to see or remain blind?

CHAPTER 10

DO MONSTERS LAUGH?

Is there JOY in EVIL?

Do monsters laugh? Do they find pleasure in cruelty?

Where do we find the proof that this is true?

For most, cruelty gives us a gut-wrenching feeling. It's difficult to comprehend how some people get satisfaction from the destruction of others. Yes, I understand jealousy, anger, righteousness, and the spectrum of negative human feelings. But pleasure in seeing others truly hurt is foreign to me. It was only through my journey in life, meeting people, and finally studying darkness that this became clear. The forest I knew became larger and also darker. Much darker.

You saw the bold words of "Joy" and "pleasure" from the stories of Gulsoma and Soon Ok Lee. They were your first introduction to evil in this book. But we need to explore more and go on a path across history and the world to see more examples. Follow my path and through this, remember to reflect on your own life and see if you can find any connections. Truth is often right in front of us, but it is so easy to miss when we do not know what to look for. We find ways to ignore it, to excuse it. But once you know what to look for and you see the truth, you cannot unsee it...

Evil does not only harm and destroy, but it finds joy and pleasure in its cruel acts.

I want you to enter into a world that is perhaps foreign to you. A world that you might not even know exists. If you have been on the other side as a victim and gone through abuse and manipulation in your life, you will recognize the actions of these people. Still, there's a chance you never understood the true nature of these people. When one does not understand, one is blind to its reality. This blindness leaves you vulnerable and our precious world vulnerable to suffering and cruelty. You cannot afford to be blind. Yes, there's some comfort in being blind. If you are lucky to have never been touched by the hands of evil, you can live in bliss, ignorant of the pain of your neighbor. But unbeknownst to you, you'll be helping evil choke out the life of your neighbor. If not your neighbor, your neighbor's neighbor. Your ignorance will help darkness spread its lies because you will not even know they are lies. Be brave and learn of a world that has been raining poison on humankind for as long as we have known. Learn it, understand it, and only then can we fight it together. The world of cruelty. A forest so dark that its trees bare rotten fruit. The skies are always dark, and light cannot shine in. Do not let the darkness stop you. Open your mind, your eyes, and ears to this darkness. Let your own inner light shine, and over time, if enough of us gain the knowledge of evil, we can bring the darkness to light.

Forget your taboos, forget your own beliefs for a moment and enter a world you should pray never reaches you. The world of viciousness and laughter.

The first path takes us into the past with a man named 'Marquis de Sade,' a French Aristocrat born in 1740. Sade's writings shocked the Western world as he openly expressed the darkest sexual desires hidden from society. He showed that for some, pleasure came from torture and seeing others in pain. Normal arousal did nothing unless it involved inflicting pain. His stories like *Justine* and *Juliette* were so upsetting his name ended up being notorious and used as the very meaning for sexual cruelty. The word "sadism."

Let us start with his book 'Justine,' where the leading character Rodin doesn't just find slight pleasure from beating his daughter. He is utterly transported.

> *Rodin ties her to the stake as he tied his scholars, and while one after another and sometimes both at once his domestics flay him, he beats his daughters, lashes her from her ribs to her knees, utterly transported by PLEASURE."*

> *The whips are picked up... The child bursts into tears, Rodin is in seventh heaven, but new PLEASURES call, he releases the boy and flies to other sacrifices."*

Notice the chosen words and how they express great joy. Were we to remove words like "whip" and "child" could you have guessed what Rodin was doing? Would you have thought he was whipping a child until they burst into tears?

> *"Dear heavens!... How can one find PLEASURE in the torments one inflicts?"*

Yes, that is the question. How can this be? Though Sade was honest enough to ask this question, he does not give an answer. In one of the last lines from the book, he goes into great detail to explain the suffering of Rodin's victim:

> Rodin is beside himself. He snatches up a cat-nine-tails that has been soaking in a vat of vinegar to give the thongs tartness and sting. 'Well there,' says he, approaching his victim, 'prepare yourself, you have got to suffer'... Julie emits cries, piercing screams which rend me to the soul, tears run down from beneath her blindfold and like pearls shine upon her beautiful cheeks; whereby Rodin is made all the more furious... Rodin begins again, not a cut he bestows is unaccompanied by a curse, a menace, a reproach. Blood appears. Rodin is in an ECSTACY. His delight is immense as he muses upon the eloquent proofs of his ferocity."

Did you catch the word? A word describing emotions so strong they produce a trance like dissociation. The word "ecstasy." Few paragraphs could express more clearly the connection between violence and pleasure. But maybe this is just fiction, his imagination? Not quite. Looking at history, we can see Marquis de Sade was jailed for rape and torture against women. His stories, though mere fiction, came from the real man's own acts. In the late 1800s Germany, these stories would inspire a psychiatrist Richard Von Kraftt-Ebing to create the words "sadism" and "sadist." It's not clear if Richard Von Krafft-Ebing truly coined the words, but in his published book *Psychopathia Sexualis* he went into detail about the complexities of abnormal human sexuality and under the cases labeled "sadism" showed how the libido mostly worked through desires for cruelty. One of the first cases he talked about was a thirty-year-old soldier who came under legal investigation and confessed that he gradually had thoughts about how PLEASURABLE it would be to stab a young and pretty girl in the genitals. When he then started the violence, he found he took DELIGHT in the sight of the blood running from the knife. In another case, a man would attack young girls on the streets by stabbing them in their arms. When stabbing the girls, he would get ejaculations. The case did not mention pleasure, but let us consider what an orgasm does to our body. It releases two hormones called oxytocin and serotonin. Oxytocin is, from what we know, a hormone that plays a big role both regulating social bonding, especially maternal and infant bonding, but also sexuality and orgasms. It is also linked to memory and reading of emotions. The other hormone is serotonin. This hormone has been named the "happy hormone." It is produced mainly from the gut but also in the brain. It is thought to regulate mood, social behavior, libido, and sleep. Without going into the details of these hormones, which we still know little about, we can look at them from a bigger point of view. First, they do have a connection with pleasure. Second, there is a link which we will soon look at, that leads to another big insight. And this is the oxytocin's link to maternal and infant's bonding.

Remember that... Maternal and Infant bonding.

Going back to Dr. Richard Von Krafft-Ebing's cases, he had a wine merchant who, at the age of fourteen, had the fantasy to cut girls. Because of no opportunity and no courage, he did not act on these desires until he was nineteen, when he cut a girl for the first time. During the act, he experienced intense pleasure, and from that time, the impulse grew constantly more powerful. This case brings to light something we should be aware of. Lack of COURAGE and OPPORTUNITY hides many people in our society who, given the chance, would bring their dark fantasies into life. Like Zimbardo's experiment where a situation was created that encouraged cruelty from a few. When this happens, it should not be a surprise that the majority of hidden people who hide darkness will come out.

But there are complexities also. Dr. Krafft-Ebing would label these cases ideal sadism because they were much milder and mostly fantasies. One patient was abused with spankings from the age of four to eight. When he was twelve, he convinced a friend to whip him, and the patient found great sexual pleasure in whipping his friend. But when his friend whipped him in return, he found no pleasure. The impulse to beat others was never very strong, though, and going forward, he found more satisfaction from his imagination of whipping than in the real acts. After associating with girls, these fantasies disappeared almost entirely, and he went into adulthood with a mostly normal sexual life. As we can see, the spankings gave him pleasure, yet it was not strong enough for him to act it out again.

This is where it becomes important for us to ask the question. Was this man evil? Did he fit the criteria? As a child, he spanked another friend and got satisfaction from it, but what was the harm? He made a consensual deal to have a fairly innocent child's play. It did not seem cruel. There is little doubt there is a connection between his early punishments and the whipping, but it did not create someone evil. Perhaps what happened to him was not severe enough to make him a monster. Let's compare that with a case that was a married man with two children who came from a family of an alcoholic, bad-tempered father and a mother who suffered from hysteria and seizures. As a child, he remembered he took particular pleasure in witnessing the slaughtering of domestic animals, especially swine. The killing gave him lustful pleasure and ejaculations. He would later continue visiting slaughterhouses to get delight in the sight of flowing blood and the death throes of the animals. When he could find the opportunity to kill the animals himself, he would do it. It always gave him a vicarious feeling of sexual pleasure.

Similarly, in Case 46, another person would also enjoy seeing animals suffer. But for this patient, it was more about the torture. He would visit prostitutes and have them purchase living birds or rabbits to make them torture the animals in front of him. He particularly reveled in the sight of cutting off the heads and tearing out the eyes and entrails. If he found a girl who would agree to do it his cruel way, then he would be delighted and paid her without asking anything more or touching her.

We can see how each case gets worse, going from the mild pleasure of whipping, to great excitement over animals killed, to the cruelest torture of animals.

For every case, there's a strong connection to pleasure, sexual dysfunction, violence, and torture without disgust.

What normal people would find revolting creates for them feelings of desire, pleasure, and orgasm. We can see this pattern repeat again and again.

Let us follow this pattern into history and look at a few more stories.

The first road leads us to the Balkan country of Wallachia in eastern fifteenth century Europe. A man named Vlad III would come to power. A brutal time and place in history where his father was killed by being face-scalped. A method of killing by cutting the edges of the face and then peeling off the skin while still alive. Vlad's life and his actions would take this brutality a lot further, leaving a great terror over the land. Though it's likely doubtful he killed over 100,000 people as rumored. he did kill in great numbers, creating a legend as a monster. From burning, skinning, roasting, and boiling people and feeding them to their friends and relatives. From cutting off limbs, drowning, and probably the one he's most famous for, impaling. His method of impaling was by having the stakes rounded and not too sharp while covering them in oil so the victim's inner organs would not be pierced too quickly. Their legs would be stretched wide apart, with each leg tied to a different horse. The horses were then sent in different directions while attendants held the body and stake in place. Judging from several ancient prints. Men, women, and children were also impaled through the heart, navel, stomach, and chest. As Vlad was often present during punishment, One can speculate that this was for the enjoyment of Vlad. But there are more stories to support him finding joy and humor from it. In 1458, when a nobleman of Polish origin tried to negotiate with Vlad, he was met with a scene that could only be described as gruesome.

In Vlad's castle, he was ordered to sit by a table surrounded by impaled dead and dying people. In front of him stood a large stake covered thinly in gold. Vlad asked him, "Tell me why did I place this stake here?". The frightened ambassador summoned as much courage as he could and said, "Lord, It appears that some great man committed some crime at your expense and that you wish to reserve for him a more honorable death than that given out to humbler men."

Vlad replied "You spoke well. For you are the representative of the great king Matthias and I have reserved this stake for you!" The ambassador contended, "Lord, If I have committed some crime which deserves the death penalty, do what you think is just, for you are an impartial judge and it would not be your responsible for my death but I alone." Vlad burst out laughing. "Have you not answered me properly you would be on that stake now!"

A true monster's laugh...

The same year, Vlad would order any Saxon merchants who didn't comply with his laws impaled on the spot. The German writer, Michael Beheim, from the fifteenth century, wrote that Vlad had six hundred such merchants impaled and some assembled in a huge cauldron adapted with holes so that their heads could peer out. Boiling water was then poured over the cauldron, boiling them alive. If this is true, the cauldron was made for this purpose only. A cauldron with holes big enough for heads is useless for anything else. Why holes for the heads? So the victim's expressions and suffering were seen by Vlad. Perhaps he had been frustrated with other cauldrons that didn't show enough of the suffering when boiling people?

During the cold winter of 1459, Vlad organized one of the worst raids in Transylvania to seize Prince Dan III and his supporters. He pressed against the vicinity of Brasov, burning villages, forts, and towns. Capturing as many as he could, he would impale them lengthwise and crosswise, according to Beheim's narratives. While bodies were strung on the hill above a chapel, Vlad sat at a table having his meal while his butchers cut off the limbs. Though not reported to practice cannibalism himself, he would compel others to eat human flesh. Beheim tells us that he would "dip his bread in the blood of his victims, since watching human blood flow gave him courage." During this "festivity," a member of the highest rank had the misfortune to show revulsion from the terrible smell of rotting bodies. Vlad immediately ordered an unusually long stake prepared and had him impaled with the words, "You live up there far, where the stench cannot reach you." During the following spring, Dan III tried to bring an offensive against Vlad and invade Wallachia. He soon found himself at Vlad's mercy after his defeat. With his creative cruelty, Vlad forced him to read the mass of the dead and then dig his own grave. Whereafter, Vlad cut off his head and stated, "I reserved for Dan a death worthy of 'The Prince' he styled himself."

Are you seeing the connection of cruelty and pleasure? His laughter, his humor, and festive mood around the most horrific acts.

Still, let us look for more evidence on the connection between evil and pleasure.

From the ancient country of Wallachia, let us venture further east. Over the hills and mountains into the twentieth century and the mind of another brutal ruler, the emperor of China... Mao Zedong.

Though Mao's usual practice was not to keep records for posterity, let alone proof of torture, there is plenty of evidence of his character and brutality. One such evidence we can find in his writing during his student years of 1917-18, in a book called *A System of Ethics* by the German Philosopher Friedrich Paulsen.

Mao:

> *I do not agree with the view that to be moral, the motive of one's action has to be benefiting others. Morality does not have to be defined in relation to others. People like me want to satisfy our hearts to the full, and in doing so, we automatically have the most valuable moral codes. Of course, there are people and objects in the world, but they are all there only for me... I do not think these commands like 'do not kill,' 'do not steal,' 'do not slander' have to do with conscience. I think they are only out of self-interest for self-preservation... For the Elite, everything outside their nature, such as restrictions and constraints, must be swept away by great strength in their nature... When great heroes give full play to their impulses, they are magnificently powerful, stormy, and invincible. Their power is like a hurricane arising from a deep gorge, like a sex maniac on heat and prowling for a lover. There is no way to stop them."*

Consider the thought of Mao's character with his view of people and objects. They are all there for him... ONLY.

He goes on:

> "Human beings are endowed with the sense of curiosity. Why should we treat death differently? Don't we want to experience strange things? Death is the strangest thing that you will never experience if you go on living. Some are afraid of it because the change comes too drastically. But I think this is the most wonderful thing. Where else in this world can we find such a fantastic and drastic change?... We love sailing on a sea of upheavals. To go from life to death is to experience the greatest upheaval. Isn't it magnificent!"

Knowing the fate of China during his rule and that at least forty million and some say up to eighty million of Chinese died from starvation and killings, these comments are chilling and bring to light a very cold and evil person. It also shines a light on the fact that we humans don't all want the same. This was an illusion for me for a long time where I thought humankind and people all wanted pretty much the same but had different ideas on how to get there. A good life, peace, happiness, and love. But I've come to realize that there are those who do not want this.

They want chaos, destruction, killing, and death for others. The opposite of our dreams.

This truth is in Mao's next words...

Mao:

> "The country must be destroyed and then reformed. This applies to the country, to the nation, and mankind. The destruction of the universe is the same. People like me

> *long for its destruction because when the old universe is destroyed, a new universe will be formed. Isn't that better!"*

These comments are Mao's true nature. We saw how he took them into action during the early Chinese revolution. At thirty-two years old and founding member of the nationalist Peasant Movement Committee, Mao started working to bring down the social order. On his inspection tour as the leader of the Hunan countryside, he reported how he saw the thugs loved to toy with victims and break down their dignity. They would use their victims arbitrarily with the idea, anyone who has land is a tyrant, and all rich are bad. They would strike down the landlords and stump on them.

Mao:

> *"A tall paper hat is put on the victim, and on the hat is written landed tyrant so and so or bad gentry so and so. Then the person is pulled by a rope (like pulling an animal), followed by a big crowd. This punishment makes victims tremble the most. After one such treatment, these people are forever broken."*

In a report he wrote afterward in March 1927, he said he felt "a kind of ECSTASY never experienced before." The brutality made him flow with an adrenaline rush as he'd exult, "It is wonderful! It is wonderful!"

Here is it again... brutality strongly connected with pleasure and joy.

After taking over the red army and working with the Russians and Stalin, Mao would purge many of his fellow party members. Mao's goal was to become Party Emperor. Though Moscow knew of this, it did nothing because it looked out for the hardest people and sided with Mao. With this encouragement, all work was stopped in order to slaughter. Everyone lived in fear. All those who were not demonic in striking against The Jiangxi Reds were treated as them. With one hundred twenty kinds of tortures like "Sitting in the **PLEASURE** chair," "Toads drinking," "Monkeys holding a rope" and "Angel plucking zither."

Notice the funny-sounding names and the chosen words like "pleasure chair." If you let yourself imagine how they came up with the names, what do you think their mood was? Serious? Or were they laughing coming up with these names? I think it's safe to assume they were having a good time with making the most funny name for each torture.

Now that we know the silly names, let us take a closer look at what they were. I know it's unpleasant, but it's important we understand what these funny names refer to. The tortures included some having a red-hot gun rod rammed into the anus, others a wire run through the penis and hung on the ear of the victim, and having the torturer pluck at the wire as a zither which is a Chinese musical instrument. When the torture turned into killing, there were reports of the stomachs being cut open and scooping out the heart... and this was just the beginning. During the later years and during the Cultural Revolution, Mao would start photographing the torture. One senior official, who Mao hated because he had complained about the great leap forward, was exhibited in front of organized crowds and had his arms twisted ferociously backward in the form of torment known as being "jet planed." He was shoved onto a bench, bleeding, shirtless in a temperature well below freezing, while thugs rushed to cut him with knives. Finally, a huge iron stove was hung around his neck, dragging his head down to the cement floor where his skull was bashed in with heavy brass belt buckles. During all this, photographs were taken. Photographs for Mao to see, and we can guess it might have been for his own pleasure, just like Vlad III sitting at his table watching men die.

Are you beginning to see it now?

Do you see the MONSTERS that laugh?

For another angle, let us go from China and Mao to the Middle East and the country of Iran. A true story that teach us how one has to act in an evil organization and gives us a hint to what evil people look for in others to know they are evil also.

The story is about Reza Kahlili. In his book *A Time To Betray*, he details his life and how three of his young student friends were taken in the middle of the night and thrown into the Evin Prison, a notorious prison located in the northern section of Tehran. Trying to help them get out, he approached his friend who had hired him into the Revolutionary Guard. Going to the prison, Reza saw in the hallway a dozen girls. One of them was his friend's sixteen-year-old sister. Blood caked on their skin, all of them mentally and physically broken with hopeless and resigned faces. Minutes later, they were all executed, and days later, so were his other two friends. In deep sorrow, Reza tried to reach out for answers about the prison and the Revolutionary Guard. He would find a young woman named Roya who would write him a letter detailing what she had seen and been through. Her beloved husband, Hamid, had been killed and returned to the family with his arms and legs broken, bones protruding out. Cigarette burns all over his body. Thousands of young girls had been held there. She herself had been in a room designed for a few but which held more than thirty women. Each day, names would be called, and those named would be shot that day. They would hear the cries and screams only to wait for their turn. Rape was routine. Every time she was tortured, she'd think of her husband. For every crack of a broken finger, she would think of the good times with him. Shortly after she had sent the letter, she hung herself.

Through the book, Reza talks about how he had to mix in and convince the Revolutionary Guards he was one of them: "I needed to keep a bright expression on my face through this. Only God could know how sick I felt at this and every other moment when I had to pretend that I was **ENJOYING** the killings, betrayals, suicide bombings, and martyrs."

And there we have how MONSTERS verify each other. They viewed him as one of them as long as he enjoyed the horrors.

I ask you now... Are you beginning to see it? Do you see the evil? I hope the fog is clearing. I hope you are beginning to see evil and recognize it. It is more than bad choices and our flawed human nature. It is something very different.

It is evil... and it enjoys giving pain and suffering.

CHAPTER 11

KNOW THE MONSTER

BIG or Small

All the stories so far have been about immense evil. An evil that should be obvious but sadly is not in today's times. But I believe we must also ask ourselves about lesser evil. Can it be smaller? Does evil start small and grow? Or is it just serial killers, dictators, and mass torture that defines it? For this question, we must look at the smaller bushes in our forest that are so easily ignored and not seen. Didn't those big trees start small? And though some bushes will never reach the sky like the trees, could its thorns not be as poisonous?

To this question, let's look at humans. We all come in different sizes, colors, intellects, and talents. This is no different with evil people.

I learned this lesson myself while I was studying the larger evil in society and its psychology. It cost me fifty dollars and was perhaps the most worthy fifty dollars I've spent because it gave me insight that I would never have realized otherwise. It involves the people you never read about. Those people who rarely achieve anything. They are unseen by society, yet I believe they do a great deal of damage because they are unseen and underestimated and, most of all, pitied. This lesson started when I was moving to a new place. I needed a few extra hands, and my best friend offered to help. He asked me if I wanted to hire a guy where he worked. The owner's son didn't have a job nor much to do, and my best friend believed he could help out and earn a little extra money. I thought it was a good idea since we did have some heavy furniture and a lot of boxes. So my friend asked if he would help out for fifty dollars. It would be a couple of hours of work. He agreed. When my friend arrived with his van, a young guy in his mid-twenties stepped out. He looked healthy, average build, but had a timid look to him. My friend and I quickly started to hustle, moving things out as quickly as we could. I noticed the guy, let's call him Tim, sitting on the stairs. I found it odd but grabbed a few boxes and kept moving stuff. My friend began organizing the van while I went back and forth. After a couple of runs, Tim was still sitting on the stairs. He was quiet and didn't say a word. He seemed extremely introverted and shy. I'm not the kind of guy who will yell or force people to do things. In my mind, I thought he might be a little slow mentally, perhaps shy, so I started guiding him and told him in a friendly way to take a certain box and bring it down to the van. I grabbed another box. When I came back, he was still in my living room and had not touched the box. At this point, I began feeling angry and used. He was there to help, but I also got this feeling of helplessness from him that made me feel guilty. So I told him that the kitchen had some things that needed to be put in boxes, thinking this might be easier for him. I then watched him walk around the apartment each time I came up for another box, and a few runs later, he was back on the stairs. At this point, I had given up on him and was not happy. Finally, my friend's van was full, and I said I'd take it from there. Reluctantly, I gave Tim the fifty dollars though I felt he had been dishonest and of no use. He didn't look me in the eyes. Unemotionally, he grabbed my money and got into the van with my friend.

Feeling I had just wasted fifty dollars, I gave myself the positive thought that Tim had learned something and at least I had kept my promise to pay him. Yes, I was naive.

That is, until I couldn't find a couple of photo frames. I began looking until I ended up outside by the trash, and found them inside the trash all smashed up. The photos were ripped, and the frames were broken. There was only one person I could think of who had the opportunity to do this. It was Tim. I was shocked and angry. I had given him fifty dollars! Why would he do such a thing? Jealousy? Perhaps. How I could be so dumb? But that was not my lesson... The lesson came when I called my friend that evening. Before telling him I suspected Tim to have trashed my photo, my friend told me about the trip back. Driving back, Tim had turned to him and said with a big grin and laugh that they should do this more often. They could make a lot of money this way.

It was then that I flashed back on the stairs to Tim as he sat there timidly and made me feel bad for him. The reality was that he was aware of what he was doing. He had played me. I had allowed him to sit there while I did all the work and then paid him the money afterward. His shyness and timidness was an act, a mask.

He found pleasure in fooling me, doing nothing, while playing for pity.

We don't think of the timid as evil. We think of the strong, those who do great evil in history. But what about those like Tim? Some might say he was jealous. His act was just part of being human. Someone flawed who we can pity and say they are filled with resentment because of what they lack. Perhaps Tim saw me with a girlfriend he didn't have. How can just broken frames and torn photos be evil? Small nothingness compared to our other stories of horror. You could say so, and you would be right if it weren't for one thing. There are some people who could have done what he did out of jealousy, who are not evil. They could even do it against someone innocent. But there's one thing that makes it different. Yes, Tim was not likely to hurt me more. He will probably not do much in his life except small things like what he did to me. But the clue we have to evil was his reaction. He had no guilt. He was very aware of what he had done, and he was EXCITED, LAUGHING.

Doesn't that ring a bell from our other stories?

My question is, what would happen if Tim was put into a situation of power? What if Tim was a guard in North Korea, born into a powerful family? The same Tim, still with no courage and few skills. But this time, in charge of his own cell and its prisoners. What would he be capable of? With no sense of guilt and seething to break a photo frame. Only this time with all the freedom and torture devices to do what he wanted. Do you see it now?

Do you see Tim's potential?

It is "Tims" like him that makes it possible for the bigger sociopaths to conquer and grow. They need people like him because they know he will do anything to keep his power. He will not fight them but will be an extension of their brutality. Like most people, few reach the heights of success. The majority of evil people are not murderers but people with normal jobs. They are part of the fabric of society, and depending on how healthy a certain society is, there will be more or less of them. They remain hidden until such time that they can show their true selves and take off the mask. They are the unnamed mob, the misfits, that are used to overthrow a decent society and create chaos. So before society breaks down, it's not kings, emperors, and dictators who do the greatest evil. No, it's from somewhere else. Somewhere more familiar. It's within families and friends, where those with masks, the less courageous, and the less ambitious, do their damage to those closest to them. Evil flourishes among the weak. In the home, mothers, fathers, uncles, aunts, grandfathers, and other family members or friends and acquaintances. Whoever they have power over…

But we have a problem. They look like us all.

If my best friend had not told me what Tim had said, I truly would not have seen him for who he was. He was not easily detected. He fooled me. Because I could not imagine someone doing nothing, sitting on the stairs, going through my things, trashing pictures and then looking so pitiful and feeling a sense of joy behind the mask. His mask was new to me, and I fell for it, as we all do, and continue to do because it is so hard to see through the mask.

CHAPTER 12

TRAPS & ILLUSIONS

So how do we learn to know evil? How do we learn to see through the masks?

This is one of the hardest things to do. Those who are evil are masters at deception. Masters at hiding their true inner selves. It is scary to truly realize they act normal and look just like you and me. They can act kindly, be friendly, do good things, and be even your best friend.

The Austrian psychiatrist Victor Frankl gave us insight from surviving a Nazi concentration camp. In his book *Man's search for meaning* he said:

> "We may learn that there are two races of men in this world, but only these two, the 'race' of the decent man and the 'race' of the indecent man. Both are found everywhere, they penetrate all groups of society. No group consists entirely of decent or indecent people. In this sense, no group is of 'pure race' and therefore one occasionally found a decent fellow among the camp guards."

This other "race," the indecent, wears the masks of the decent.

Artists often find ways to express complex truths with their stories, and I think of the film *They Live* by John Carpenter, where alien life forms arrive on Earth and try to take over the human race. The film uses the visual concept of a pair of glasses that gives the lead character the ability to see the aliens' faces as they truly are. But only through the glasses. Otherwise, they look just like regular people. In real life, without fictional glasses, we must learn to see through the masks. I believe we possess this ability, but we are fearful of using them. Why? Because we all wear masks and engage different personas. It's part of human nature. Evil uses fear and guilt to twist the truth, stopping us from seeing its true nature.

But we cannot let that happen. We must open our eyes, and to do that, we must learn to judge. Without judging the person, we can never see through a mask, and here lies the problem. It is painful to judge. We are often told in our society never to judge. It is not polite to judge. It is bad and selfish to judge... it is even evil to judge. Does any of this ring familiar? Do you have a hard time judging someone else? Do you feel guilty doing so? You might do this because people often condemn others if they judge. And for good reasons, because many people judge unfairly, judge with contempt. Because of this, it makes sense to think that judging is wrong. But this is a half-truth. Because if the judging was always wrong, judging those who judge unfairly would be wrong, leading to a more unfair world. It ignores the basic truth that those who are dark do not care about others. They despise them. They seek a world of no judgment because they do not want their cruel actions caught. They do not want to be seen. They do not want you to point fingers and for their masks to crumble. They condemn judging while simultaneously judging all the time, so they can decide over others what is right and wrong and what is a lie and what is "true." It is very dangerous for them if others are free to judge.

Thus you must learn to judge. But judge fairly.

To do this, you must bear the pain because it is not painless. We all wear masks. We have different masks for different people and occasions. Not masks of malignancy, but masks to protect ourselves. To be accepted, feel worthy, be loved, and even hide jealousy, anger, or perhaps resentment. Some have more masks than others. The more healthy you are, the more loved you were, you'll likely need fewer masks. Still, even the most healthy person has them, and because of this, it is painful to see through others masks because we must look in the mirror of ourselves at the same time. To see means you have to first see through you, and it is rarely easy. It is often disappointing. We rarely are the heroes we wished we were. Our ego has a hard time accepting the truths of our flaws. The term "Ego" was invented by psychologist Sigmund Fred, who tried to explain the very unexplainable thing called our consciousness. The part that links to our pride and our self-worth. The ego does not like to be wrong. It attaches itself to anything and everything it can to make itself big and important. The ego most likely develops in the early years of childhood and is part of our consciousness that separates "me" from "others." It is like a child. It gives us confidence, and it gives us much strength. But it is also one of our biggest flaws because it's like a child that won't let go of their toy.

But why do we need to look at ourselves to judge? Because to be able to judge fairly, and FAIRLY is the key idea, we must be as close to the truth as possible, and we can only do that when we are honest. Our masks/personality/ego and righteousness can and will blind us to the truth and make us unable to judge fairly. So when judging others, you must at the same time judge yourself. Look at your ego and make sure it does not interfere with the truth.

This leads to the next problem and pain. What is the truth? How can we know it? Some truths are apparent, some are learned, and some are unknown to us humans as we learn about the complex world. Because of this, we need to seek wisdom and knowledge and accept the challenge of being wrong, be open and question everything and listen to others as we search for the truth. Know and realize that searching for the truth in a pure and honest way is one of the noblest things you can do in life, both personally and socially.

Because the truth has to be found, each person is on their own quest and at different stages in life. This means what is learned for some is unknown to others, and here lies the danger. For those who do not have access to learning, those who are told lies, and sadly for those who do not care to know, the truth stays unknown and leaves them unable to make a fair judgment. Evil people know this. This is why they fight every day, every hour, to deceive the world. To destroy the truth. Make it relative, make it confusing, make the truth false, or, even better, nonexistent. Where they can, they attempt and, in some places, succeed in making the apparent truths seem false and make it highly accepted by the mob. I say "highly" accepted because those with egos that know little and question nothing will be the ones with the strongest need to fight the real truth because they fear the most to be wrong. They have never faced themselves, looked the ego in its "eye." Deep within, they know this and are afraid it would destroy their false importance. They are, as philosopher Eric Hoffer called them, the true believers.

Don't be one of them. It's okay to be wrong. The ego will not die. It is like a child. It does not like to give up its beliefs and "toys." But know the ego's pain is short-term, and once you start exchanging old beliefs for new beliefs that are closer to the truth, your ego will begin to learn to accept the pain of changing toys. The pain will be there, but you will be the master of it, not the slave of it. Eventually, it can learn to accept the pain of changing toys when needed if learned truths were wrong. Be disciplined and teach yourself to question everything and learn the wonderful feeling of curiosity and the high of getting closer to truths. You will be wrong often. Your ego will be hurt over and over. But your beliefs will become stronger because they get challenged, and the chance they are true will be more likely each time. Searching for the truth will make you weak often in the short term, but in the long run, it makes you strong and wise. Growing stronger will give you confidence, but you will be a threat. Evil isn't about to let you go and spread truths. It must confuse you, make you fall, and make you weak. To do that, it must tempt you with lies and deceive you.

So we must be aware of how evil will trick us and the traps we can fall for and so often do. The traps are many, but I've found four that are especially important. They are how WORDS are used and understood, your EXPERIENCES, your SOCIETY, and you YOURSELF... your human nature. We must ask questions about these traps and consider their effects on us, understand them, and become braver in avoiding them.

The Trap of WORDS

WORDS and language are evil's way to get into your heart. It's not a coincidence that the Bible says the devil is the father of lies. It is through words we comprehend ideas. Language makes us human, and through it, we can conceptualize people, time, and our reality. It helps us build an inner world, verbalizes the reality we see, and understand it. It is, in essence, a big part of what makes us human. What separates us from animals. Language reveals our complex consciousness. The wonderful inner world of who we are. Without it, we would not be much more than animals. We would have our instincts and be able to hunt and stay alive, but evolving would be hard, and we would stay ignorant about the wonderful complex truths of our universe. Some might say that would be good, and I do see the qualities of living a life in simpleness. But I still believe we were given a mind and the ability to speak for a reason, and one of them is to figure out this mysterious world. To find, bit by bit, its truths and, eventually, *the* truth. To do that, language is essential. This might not be apparent, but they cannot be separated. It is easy to take what we know for granted, but if you and I were born and grew up without parents or people around us talking a language, we would lack all basic ability to understand most of the world.

To illustrate that, we can look at the jungles of Brazil's Amazon where the American linguist Daniel Everett had gone to study a small tribe called the Pirahãs. Daniel and his wife first came to the tribe in the 1970s as missionaries to learn their language to translate it to the Bible. He would stay with the tribe initially for a year as he would point at things/actions and learn nouns and then verbs. Within the next couple of years, he had learned the language and found out just how unique it was. They only used three pronouns. There were no words for time, colors, or numbers. This gave him and other scientists the opportunity to study what kind of influence and understanding of numbers the tribe could have. Psycho-linguist Peter Gordon visited them and tested their mathematical abilities. They were asked to repeat patterns between ten small batteries and remember how many nuts Gordon had placed in a can. The fascinating results were that they did not get the concept of numbers. The tribe only had the concepts of "a few," "more," and "a lot." This meant that without words of numbers 1,2,3, etc., the concept could not be communicated or understood. A concept so basic to us yet unimaginable to them. This supports Benjamin Whorf, another linguist, who hypothesized that people are only capable of constructing thoughts for which they possess actual words, and this rings true. Everett himself would later try the same and see if he could teach them to count. He tried for eight months to no avail. In the end, not a single adult person in the tribe learned to count to ten.

Another interesting fact is that the Pirahãs language is based on verifiable truths. Even without a concept of time, they have a firm foundation and rule to know where a story or fact comes from. Every word spoken has to have evidence and point to whether they themselves saw it, they overheard it, or they deduced it. These three rules are wise and very useful for setting our values in learning to judge fairly.

So what can this teach us? It speaks to the extreme importance of words, language, truths, and their connection to our ability to think and understand the world. If we cannot see and share certain truths because we lack the words to understand them, we stay blind. And here lies the point. If one can change the meaning of words, one can change people's ability to understand and mass hypnotize people's perception of the truth.

But changing words takes time and a lot of organized effort. It is happening every day, but in between this, there are other ways to manipulate and hypnotize people.

A large portion of people never learn to question their own thoughts or analyze simple statements. Some are, by nature, very trusting people. So to hypnotize them, changing the meanings of words can be very effective. It's an interesting pattern I've noticed with manipulation, and it works well. If one states a truth but adds a negative verb, people will likely believe the negative statement, even if the opposite truth stares them in the face. Those with masks can say precisely what they are lying about, in the most upfront way but with a small but significant change. For example, using the word "not." "I am NOT lying about this."

I learned this lesson from one specific event. An insignificant marketing lie that probably was ignored by most but which stood out to me and made me realize this widely used manipulation.

I was in an art store looking for a briefcase or portfolio case. While going through the cases on the shelf, I noticed a small black case made from plastic. A sticker with big, bold letters said: "STAYS OPEN and CLOSES SMOOTHLY." I thought to myself that would be a good thing. I tested the book but had a hard time keeping the page open. It would keep closing from the poor plastic bend. For a brief moment, I ignored the opening part and looked at it. It was the right size and quite nice. I tried a few others but kept coming back to it because of the nice design. I almost caught myself thinking this one is good, the right size, AND it closes nicely. Wait! No, it didn't. I allowed myself to look at my own judgment and picked up the case again. I read the sticker again and then opened and closed it. It kept closing. I asked myself if it was really true that it did not stay open well. In my mind, I had to spend energy on telling myself that the sticker was clearly lying, and when I realized this, my eyes were opened. It was the worst case of them all to stay open. The sticker had almost gotten me to believe the opposite because how could someone have the arrogance and dare to put in bold letters the exact problem with it. And my reaction told me how my mind had taken the message and ignored the reality in front of me. From that day on, I noticed this over and over with people manipulating others. They would say "I'm NOT this" or "I WON'T do this" and then do precisely what they had just said they wouldn't. This plays to people's doubtful side. It is hypnosis for vulnerable people. Too many people don't trust their inner self, and once they have a "he is NOT going to do this", without an inner strength to challenge it, they will ignore the truth and what really happens.

So watch for WORDS and question the statements. Especially if there's a NEGATIVE promise in it, words can be used like magic and pull your attention from the truth to a false perception and experience, which leads us to the next trap we often fall for...

The trap of EXPERIENCE.

With our inexperience, they can fill our heads with preconceived half-truths and lies. Carefully and cleverly, they will entangle your ego with these beliefs and, in effect, chain your thoughts to them, making it very hard for you to unchain yourself and see beyond.

On the other hand, you are the total sum of your experiences. The memories of your life that have shaped your mind's view. How you see and understand the world. It is very hard to understand what you have not experienced yourself. We can try our best, but it will always be put into our own box and made into analogies. This creates opportunities for those who wish to deceive.

Evil people will look for weaknesses. They will get us to open up to learn about our deeper vulnerabilities, which they can use to exploit us. They will look for traumas that they sense. Traumas that give them the power to manipulate you. The danger lies in that we are often not aware of these traumas ourselves. They are hidden from our consciousness, yet they affect our decisions and our mind in deeply emotional ways that leave us blind to manipulation.

Why are we sometimes not aware of these traumas?

We can have traumas in our childhood that are too painful to realize and truly feel. Our brains and our body keep the memories hidden so we can live. But they do not go away. They are still within us, which can be seen through the signs of our bodies. The body never lies, and it is those signs that dark people pick up on. These experiences will keep us partly and sometimes completely blind to important truths that at the moment were impossible for us to recognize but, as adults, are vital to know and understand. To learn to see the masks of evil, we must learn to look into our own abyss. The places we do not want to go but which keep some of us in the role of infants/children in personality and actions. I have, over time, learned to recognize signs of these experiences in people's body language, and I see them as I know dark people see them.

I had some tough experiences as a baby and young child. Most of the trauma is beneath my awareness, but by listening to my body, I can feel and remember it. When I am around threatening people who have power over me in small ways, and if I'm unsure what will happen, simple situations can trigger my body. It is as if my whole body is connected to a powerful battery, and electricity is flowing through my spine, making my heartbeat extremely fast and giving me a hard time breathing. I cannot stop the feeling myself. My heart feels like it will burst with my whole body shaking. This is how it feels on the inside. On the outside, if you looked closely, you'd probably see my eyes slightly more open, slightly shaking hands, and my body movements fast or slow, not coordinated. All of it is very subtle; none of it is exaggerated. On the outside, I would just look upset and nervous for most people. But for those who enjoy hurting other people, they would see more. They would recognize the weakness and feed upon it in their own ways. My reaction likely comes from the months in the hospital as a child. I was very close to dying from an illness, and I suspect there was a connection to a person hurting me on some level. Perhaps a nurse or doctor. Maybe it was not intentional, but it was traumatizing from my point of view as a child. I can analyze my body's reaction and understand it is showing signs of extreme distress, which is not reflected in the reality of my adult moment and situation. So why does my body overreact like this? What triggers it? I believe it comes from memories that are not clear to me because of their intense, painful nature. Like the way, we can go unconscious and faint when we experience sudden, great physical pain or in other situations when the pain is shut off and is not felt. It's a form of self-defense. When I try to remember, I have only vague memories of nurses struggling with me as a small child, putting me into a tar bath with most of my body being open wounds. I do not remember much else, but I know I was close to dying at an early age from reading my medical journals. This gives me enough knowledge to understand why I react the way I do. Because of this, I can prepare and know to separate the past from the present when I'm triggered. It is partly an alarm that helps me, but it can also hinder dealing with certain manipulative people, and I have to be aware of that.

So be aware of your inner traumas. Know that these experiences might be seen in your body language by those who seek to deceive you, even if you try to hide them. Evil people often see your traumas better than you do yourself. They seek victims like predators seek prey. They are experts at noticing people's movements and weaknesses, traumas in particular. In an interview from 1985,

Ted Bundy, the serial killer of many young women in the 70s, would explain how he could tell a victim by how she walked down the street, the tilt of her head, how she carried herself. Dr. Angela Book, an Associate Professor at Brook University, did a study where she videotaped a random sample of people walking down a hallway.

One of them had been a victim of a violent crime, rape, or mugging (she does not identify which). The people who scored higher on psychopathic traits that relate to manipulation and lack of empathy were more accurate in telling who was a victim and who was not, just from watching a fifteen-second video. Watching it myself, it was also clear to me who the victim was. Each person walked across the hallway in different ways. Most stayed in the center. What was different with the victim's walk was a few things that stood out. One was her path and that she was closer to the wall, especially towards the corner. Second, her movement was asynchronous, where her left arm was not swinging at the same speed as her other arm and legs. When it comes to our bodies and healthy movement, there is a lot of symmetry. Similar to beauty in nature. So I was not surprised when I found out who had been the victim. But I will go further and say that there's more to the story than a violent crime. I do not know, and I could be wrong, but I believe her particular walk is not from a mugging or one-time rape. The odd walk was strong, and I would sadly guess earlier trauma cut off her natural walk. And this is where it is sadly true that abuse victims are often in a vicious circle because they invite more abuse from their telltale signs.

Now what explains this?

What is going on with our bodies and trauma?

Psychoanalyst Dr. Wilhelm Reich and later psychoanalyst Dr. Alexander Lowen did some groundbreaking studies on the human body and our emotions that reflect the body and mind/trauma connection. This first insight happened while Dr. Reich was working with one of his patients. The patient was talking and free-associating while sitting with his back towards Reich, when suddenly, he stopped in the middle of a sentence. The traditional analytic method would be to ask the patient to keep talking so he would avoid blocking himself. You can notice this with others speaking, and even yourself when you begin talking about something and emotions suddenly come up. The response is to stop, avoid the feeling, and quickly change the subject to escape the feeling. Maybe to cough or hold your breath for a moment. Reich noticed just that. The patient hadn't just stopped talking, but his breathing had stopped briefly. Listening to his instinct, Reich told the man he wasn't breathing. He asked for him to start breathing, and out came the tears from the man. He started crying. This moment made Reich realize the deep connection of breathing to emotions and how we hold our breath to avoid feeling certain emotions. It is a way for us to avoid listening to our bodies. To block the natural flow. Our tensions in our muscles and body can often reflect our psychological problems. A healthy person has a body that is alive and vital, with open eyes. If an area of our body has a great deal of unconscious trauma, the muscle tensions will, over time, show in our body movements. It can be subtle or more obvious, like the woman in the hallway study.

What happens with our body, the same happens with our mind. Our mind and our awareness can be blocked to protect us from past trauma. This can put us in danger of being blind to deceptions. We might miss small signs of lies in a person's mask. We will look away or quickly forget the sign to not feel the pain of the truth.

But there is another much worse experience. It is taboo in many societies, and it is one of the greatest obstacles in fighting evil. It is the blood of evil. Our personal connection to darkness... the parent bond. The experience of having an abusive mother or father. This experience is complex and dark. It can make us vulnerable to false masks in society. To believe the false mask with every fiber of our being. Why? Because one had to grow up and love the false mask. I noticed across my research on evil, biographical or psychology book authors mostly avoid the subject. Even with the most horrific evil, they will speak of a happy childhood or, in some cases, admit discipline and some abuse but quickly refer to other factors such as genes or leave it as a mystery. This topic is very delicate. This is understandable because it affects us all. Raising children is very hard in much of the world, especially in our Western world. We all feel sensitive to any judgment on parenting. If we have kids ourselves, we don't want to be accused, and we don't like to think of our parents in a bad light. But for us to see better and recognize darkness and evil, we cannot afford this taboo. Though painful, we must start opening ourselves up to the past and our parents. It is true we must be careful and to be aware of just how hard it is to raise children. We must be mindful of our own flaws and how our parents' own childhood affected how they reacted to being parents. Parenting is hard. Life is hard. We are flawed as human beings, and children are at their neediest and most difficult when they are in their early years, needing the love of their mother and father.

So it's a balance of compassion towards parents but also to have the strength to ask the tough questions to get an idea of the truth. It is not easy because those who didn't have loving parents sometimes have blocked out the bad and have trouble seeing beyond the false mask of the parent. This can also make us attracted to the false mask. As the former psychiatrist and author Alice Miller reflects in her book *For your own good*:

> *We often ask how a marriage can last, how, for example, a woman can go on living with a certain man, or vice versa. It may be that the woman endures extreme torment in this relationship, continuing it only at the cost of her vitality. But she is mortally afraid at the thought of her husband leaving her. Such a separation would probably be the great opportunity of her life. Yet, she is unable to see this as long as she is forced to repeat in her marriage the early torment, now relegated to her unconscious, inflicted on her by her father. For when she thinks about being abandoned by her husband, she is not reacting to her present situation but is re-experiencing her childhood fears of abandonment and the time when she was, in fact, dependent on her father. I am thinking here specifically of a woman whose father, a musician, took the mother's place when she died but often disappeared when he went on tour. My patient was much too little at the time to bear these sudden separations without a feeling of panic. In her analysis, we had been aware of this for a long time, but her fear of being abandoned by her husband did not subside until her dreams revealed to her what had hitherto been unconscious: the other—brutal and cruel—side of her father, whom she had until then remembered only as loving and tender. As a result of*

> *confronting this knowledge, she experienced an inner liberation and was now able to begin the process of becoming autonomous."*

For some, this part might be hard to read, and if you sense this, I kindly ask you to take it step by step and give yourself time to think this through. Listen to any conflict in your mind, any tension in your body. If you feel a motivation to not think about it, give yourself space. Allow it to be a question. Watch yourself and allow yourself time to absorb the feelings and questions. Do not be hard on yourself. The thoughts alone can still help you with seeing better and judging better. With time and courage, you can learn the truths, whatever that may be. It's okay not to know right away.

Which leads us to what we don't know.

The trap of our INEXPERIENCE.

We must be aware of our limited experience. Without realizing this perspective, is it easy to become self-righteous and believe blindly and judge blindly. To see through masks, you must acknowledge where you come from. Are you talking from experience, or are you dealing with a person and a subject matter you do not know? There might be similarities that you can recognize and use to understand. But know they can be wrong. You will be much more vulnerable to deceit and lies. In these situations, allow yourself to be more cautious. You can only understand what you know and have experienced, and to some extent, similar situations. This is where you have to be very truthful to yourself even if it hurts your ego. Your ego can put you in serious trouble. Be strong and ask yourself, How ashamed am I to not know things? Are you afraid to be aware of your own limits and ignorance? Be careful of the temptation to fool yourself into thinking you know more than you do. Because if you are dealing with indecent people, they will detect it and use it against you. It is better to be humble and quiet than loud and boastful. Accept when you are wrong. Accept when your ego gets in your way and ahead of you. Step back and acknowledge the mistake publicly. It will balance you and keep you on your footing even if you are outside your experience. Listen and know, if you are dealing with a sociopathic person, they are mixing truths and lies. Take everything with a grain of salt, but know it's too early to judge. You might be dealing with someone honest. You might be completely wrong, and you might be right. Know that you don't know. It's not a nice position to be in. The good news is that there is an antidote. It is to be curious in life. Grow and learn, and life will reward you with wisdom, little by little. Open up to questioning everything, even your own beliefs, and your inexperience will become experience.

Truth and wisdom are connected and, in many ways, the same thing. You will see this through time, which leads to the idea of time. It takes time to grow wise. It takes time to learn to see. Society gives us early in life a direction that can help or hinder us. But it is vital we learn to reevaluate our values given by society. They might be good, but some can also lead us astray.

And here comes the next possible challenge for us to learn to judge fairly...

Our SOCIETY.

When born, we first enter the world innocent and ignorant. But soon, lessons are learned of rights and wrongs through your family, mother, father, brothers, and sisters. A mini-society that often reflects the bigger society. As you grow older, you get exposed to more rights and wrongs through education, friends, and media. You begin to learn the social rules. Rules that are shaped by society and the foundation from which you learn. These values can become a blessing or a curse. A trap of lies or a springboard of wisdom. Because we all come from ignorance, we depend and rely on our society to tell us how to live. To tell us about the world and why things are the way they are, how to fit in and understand the world. To tell us the truth as far as we know it.

As we grow older and get into our teens and young adulthood, much of our society has been integrated into our own viewpoints. But few of us realize that these values did not originate from ourselves. We are too young to have shaped them from a deeper experience yet. Yes, we can begin to question things as children from a child's point of view, but only if our culture allows questioning. If our world around us tells us not to think and never to question things, and we do not see our own parents do it either, then we are unlikely to do it. In many ways, we are the product of our culture and environment. If our culture is curious and free, it will encourage us to think and question. If our culture is authoritarian and closed, it will discourage any descent and punish thought.

To understand this profoundly is to ask yourself about the idea of freedom? Ask yourself how self-evident this idea is? Imagine you are in a prison camp. You have witnessed multiple public executions a year and extreme abuse and rape daily. You live on a tiny diet of corn, cabbage, and salt. You wear the same clothes for a whole year, which is hard as cardboard from the sweat and dirt. Hard labor is forced on you twelve to fifteen hours a day until you die. How strong would you want your freedom? What would freedom mean to you? Now imagine you were born into this camp. You had never experienced life outside. The only world and society you knew was the camp. Would freedom mean something different? From the book *Escape from Camp 14* written by Blaine Harden, you will learn about someone for whom this was reality.

Before going into the details, I want to mention there is some controversy around his story. When a video of his father from Camp 18 emerged, people questioned what was true. Did he grow up in Camp 18 or Camp 14? Shin told Harden, the book's author, that while he was born at Camp 14, he spent part of his youth at another complex, Camp 18, escaping twice before landing back at the first camp. He explained, "When I agreed to share my experience for the book, I found it was too painful to think about some of the things that happened, so I made a compromise in my mind and altered some details"

So keep this in mind reading the next part.

But I have still decided to tell his story because his trauma and example still give us insight. Whether or not, some facts have been changed.

Shin Dong-Hyuk was born a slave into a North Korean camp surrounded by a high-voltage barbed wire fence. He bears visible signs from years of torture. His arms are bowed from childhood labor. His lower back is scarred from burns. The skin around his pelvis shows puncture scars from the hook used to hold him in place over the fire. His right middle finger was cut off from dropping a sewing machine. His ankles were scarred by shackles from hanging upside down in solitary confinement. He was different from prisoners who were born outside the camp. He had no concept of the world outside. Like Blaine Harden writes, "No hope to lose, no past to mourn, no pride to defend." He did not know any other life.

It was not until he met two older men at different times who spoke to him about the outside. Shin wasn't interested or cared for a lot of it. The concept of money, countries of wealth, and technology was too foreign for him to perceive. But there was one subject he took delight in. The subject of food. His first friend, Kim Jin Myung, who wanted to be called Uncle, took care of Shin in their prison cell after Shin had gone through the worst kinds of torture by being burned above a tub full of burning coal. Uncle would care for Shin's wounds, help him up when he had to go on the pot, and massage his arms and legs so the muscles would not atrophy. Not being allowed to speak, Uncle would whisper to Shin when they were lying next to each other. He would explain in a loving way how food outside looked, smelled, and tasted: boiled chicken, eating clams at the seashore. For the first time, Shin learned to trust and learned what love meant from seeing Uncle's kind actions. Something he had never felt towards his parents. Shin would never forget this kind man and his stories of food. Years later, back working in the camp factory, a new prisoner named Park Yong Chul arrived. The guards ordered Shin to befriend him and report back what he said. Park opened up to Shin, and his decency to Shin would change Shin's life forever. Like Uncle, Park would tell detailed stories of the world and its food of chicken, pork, and beef, especially the grilled meat. These stories became dreams for Shin, fantasies of a better life. He wished for the freedom to taste just one bite of grilled meat before he died. For this, Shin decided to risk his own life and betray his order to report on Park, and months later, with great paranoia, he made a plan to escape with Park.

To say the food was the only reason for Shin's wish for freedom would make Shin's decision too simple. It was a combination of everything he experienced, combined with two kind men and the contrast. The stories of almost fantasy-like lives and then the fear of death, seeing people disappear each day, people being tortured, and public executions.

But the food was what Shin understood and what finally drove him to risk his life for freedom and a new society. Even though he was in hell on Earth, his lack of knowledge of the outside world and simply not knowing any other way of life made him a prisoner in his own mind. He could not imagine another world. He could not judge the guards, the camp, the life as a man who knew freedom. He could only react to his experience, and it was void of any love. He saw his mother and father as competition for food. It wasn't until he saw someone who showed care and affection towards him and who brought stories of a completely different society that he was able to begin to imagine another way. Even then, it was mostly through the food, which he had some experience with.

So we can see how influential society is to our minds and ideas. It's our foundation to understand the bigger world. You stand on the shoulders of your society and generations of civilization building. For better or worse, you are the society until you decide to open your eyes, venture outside, and see for yourself if what is taught is true or not.

But too often, we don't go outside. We believe we shape society and its views, and not the other way around. The views and ideas are ours. But if we try to think back, we can rarely remember moments that shaped our view of the world. It took me personally until my midtwenties before I could begin reading on my own and open my eyes to completely new and different ideas. Suddenly, I was bombarded with new viewpoints, theories, ways to understand the world. Through learning different sides to history and through reading philosophy, psychology, and politics, I began to question everything and slowly form my views based on what both felt right but, more importantly, what reflected the truth around me. I looked back at long-held beliefs and started seeing they were influences from my education as a child and my culture growing up. Had you asked me when I was fifteen or even twenty years old, I would have fought for each belief without being able to explain why I believed it. I had not yet gone through my views from different perspectives, and my ego and knowledge only knew the simple dogmas and ways to see the world. As I've gotten older, some views remained the same. I found them to be true from my experiences. Others I found to be lacking in truth because I lived long enough to identify them as wrong.

This is where one can get into a deep discussion on what is true or not, and this is the battle for each society. This is where we shape the future. It all starts with each of us accepting that our early beliefs are mostly from the mountain of knowledge below us. Its mistakes and its successes. The iceberg beneath us from the past thinkers and doers. the theologians, scientists, artists, writers, philosophers, politicians that gave us their views and understandings to shape society. Most ideas died with time. Few ideas evolved into bigger ideas and became the values and principles we use today. It's vital to be aware of this. To know why we believe what we believe. We must judge those beliefs and judge our own motivation for believing them. Not until we do that can we fully trust our own judgments. To do that, we must learn history, not only our own but others' as well. We must learn to expect doubt and have the courage to be wrong. To seek the truth with the utmost earnestness. But also to learn and better understand other people we share our society with and the land we stand on. To know if they will stand in our way of the truth or if they will lift us up and shine the light on the truth, wherever it may lead us.

But seeking the truth is hard. It is sometimes right in front of us, and sometimes it is hard to comprehend as we expand our knowledge. So what do we do? One way is to also seek falsehood and lies. Lies are more easily detected, and for each falsehood you realize, you get closer to the truth.

But this is also where it gets dangerous. Because you enter the realm of evil when you begin to unravel lies and untruths. You will put light in places where some people only want darkness. Just how dangerous this is, depends on your society. It is certain death in many countries across the world and in others, still a precarious choice. Because even in the freest societies, as we've read in previous chapters, dark realities lie in wait. Realities that are taboo and if talked about have real consequences.

For this, a mostly unspoken story comes to mind that's well over a hundred years old but still relevant. It reminds us just how difficult it can be to open society's eyes.

On the evening of April 21, 1896, the now-famous psychologist Sigmund Freud gave a paper before his colleagues at the Society for Psychiatry and Neurology in Vienna, entitled *The Aetiology of Hysteria.* Freud realized that in giving this paper, he would become one who would disturb the sleep of the world. The address presented a revolutionary theory of mental illness. Its title referred to Freud's new theory that the origin of neurosis lay in early sexual traumas, which Freud called "infantile sexual scenes" or "sexual intercourse in childhood." This would later come to be called the "seduction theory." Namely the belief that these early experiences were real, not fantasies, and had a damaging and lasting effect on the later lives of the children who suffered them.

In the book *The Assault on Truth* Jeffrey Moussaieff Masson would seek out the truth of Freud's paper and this important event. He had looked for reports about it in the psychoanalytic literature and the medical community but found zero references. It was as if it didn't exist. Being very thorough, he went to Vienna and looked through the historical medical journals to find a startling discovery. In Vienna's clinical weekly paper from May 14, 1896, three papers were reported in the normal practice of summarizing the paper's content and then an account of the discussion afterward.

But in the last paper with Freud, it only said,

> *"Sig. Freud, Lecturer: On the Aetiology of Hysteria."*

There was no summary or mention of discussions.

None of the audience members left any account of what happened that evening. Only silence. But thanks to history, Freud would write a letter to his closest friend, Wilhelm Fliess, about that important night. According to Freud, his paper was met with an icy reception, especially from a certain head of the department of psychiatry at the University of Vienna, a Richard von Krafft-Ebing. Does that ring a bell? Remember chapter eight where Krafft-Ebing talked about sadism? The psychiatrist who studied abnormal sexual behaviors and who we used as references to understand better the acts of violence and pleasure. If someone would have been interested and even understood Freud's paper, it should have been him. But what did he say to Freud's theory?

Richard von Krafft-Ebing's response was:

"It sounds like a scientific fairy tale!"

A fairy tale?

Richard von Krafft-Ebing knew exactly the sexual mistreatment of children from studying his patients who were perpetrators of such violence. But he mocked Freud, and so did his colleagues. They were so afraid of his paper that they went the extra mile to remove any mention of it, trying to erase it from history.

Freud's courage to speak up must have given many of his colleagues sleepless nights. From the fear that his paper would light up dark corners of homes in European society. I would not be surprised if there were plenty of perpetrators among the evening's audience. But their power was great. They could and did silence him. Freud was left with a decision. Continue with his findings or ignore them and change his theory. Understandable as a flawed human, Freud sadly chose the easy path and gave up on his theory, and publicly retracted it in 1905. A decision that has had an enormous influence on psychology, our world, and the truth. Even today, I've found that most psychologists and universities do not know or do not mention Freud's first theory. The one that was closest to the truth.

So you can see how society's taboos and going against them is a big challenge. Both on a large scale with a country's culture and on a smaller scale with your town, family, and friends. It can and likely will break you from speaking the truth if you are not prepared. You have to realize that many will not want you to see the world the way it is and, much worse, do not want you to share these ideas and truths with others. Sadly both perpetrators and victims work together to silence the few who dare to speak up. You might ask yourself why victims often join the perpetrator's side. It's a complex problem, but they often depend on those who abuse them or fear their punishment. Also, they often feel guilty and especially ashamed of what happened and sometimes, if it was in early childhood, might not be consciously aware of them. So expect sometimes to fight both groups when you expose uncomfortable truths. Take comfort that most victims do not speak up out of fear. Courage is contagious, and the silent victims can ultimately find strength once more people speak up. Like Hans Kristian Andersen's famous tale about the emperor's new clothes. It was not until a little child spoke up, "But he hasn't got anything on" that the townspeople started crying out, "But he hasn't got anything on!". People were afraid until a few people spoke the obvious truth that the emperor had no clothes. The same is true in real life. It shows us that it can take just one individual who is brave enough to speak up to overcome a crowd's ridicule and wake people up.

But in Hans Kristian Andersen's tale, it was a child that spoke first. Why a little child and not an adult?

Because all of us, as adult humans, have an Achilles heel, and here comes the last trap that I want us to consider. A trap that will stop you from judging and seeing.

The one in the mirror... You.

Afraid of society's eye and tempted by the world's vices.

Learning to judge fairly and to unmask evil is a road only for those willing to fight their inner selves. What broke Sigmund Freud was not only his colleagues and the medical society around him. It was also himself. He saw the hard road ahead. He probably tried, and we know he wrote to his friend briefly after the event, "To hell with them!"... but eventually, he decided to deny his own work and instead continue the lies of his society. It does not matter whether he convinced himself he was wrong or if it was an act. There can be little doubt he did it to avoid the pain of being ostracized and to keep his status and wealth. It is easy to blame him. But not until we experience this can we know how we would react. It was not an easy choice. We are our biggest enemy. We are often more blind than seeing, and sometimes we choose to be blind even after seeing because it is easier.

Life is hard. Surviving the world and living is hard. Each day is a challenge for us. Even the heroes among us walk a conflicted line of temptations and hard choices. The more flawed, which is most of us, me included, fight the daily battle of desires, needs, and wants. We inhabit a world we can only understand from our own limited viewpoint. Emotionally it is very hard to open up our minds and look at different viewpoints. We are constantly being challenged, and we do not like to be wrong. Anger, jealousy, fear, and other negative emotions are our Achilles heel to know the truth and stand up for it. As I write this, the society I see is glorifying vices. There is a disturbing amount of silence around the increasing medical tyranny. The world is becoming noticeably darker. Films, books, and shows. Narcissism is played to and lifted up. Responsibility is put aside and ignored. You are encouraged to indulge without any thoughts of consequences. You are told it is the fault of others. You are a victim. It is these "people or groups" that are the cause of your misfortune. Tempting you to take the "easy" path.

But it is vital you ask yourself if this is true. Are you truly a victim? It is so easy for our human nature to point fingers. It speaks to our inner cowardice and fear of being wrong. "It's those people!". For it to be true, it must be real experiences. It cannot be in the abstract. If it is, be very careful in how far you attach your ego to those beliefs. You are likely believing lies and being used.

Yes, the world is full of innocent victims, true victims, who are not at fault for their situations. We must honor them and defend the word 'victim' for them. Think of the democide of innocent human beings who were slaughtered and torture during the regimes of the 20th century. Think of the domestic abuse and children used in slavery. These are victims. I do not know your history, but it is rarely good to think of yourself as a victim even if you have been through a lot. It is much healthier to think of yourself as a survivor. It puts you in power, to choose, to change paths. To be your own defender. Otherwise, you put others in charge of your happiness and path in life, which is rarely a good choice.

So, again. Don't take the "easy" path. Though it is tempting to listen to words that say you are a victim, fight it. Be a survivor. It makes you responsible for yourself and your choices in life. It will be painful and scary. You will have to face yourself in the mirror. Look at your actions and lack of actions. Battle different parts of yourself. The lazy part, The fearful part. You will be up against all your flaws and especially your ego, which often shows up as self-righteousness. But do better and fight it. The "easy" path is often a deal with the devil. He will give you the illusion of comfort and happiness, but it is all lies. He and his followers will devour you... or worse, you'll join his followers and devour others! and be in hell... on earth.

So fight yourself and your own flaws. There is one guide and compass you can always use for this. It is not easy to use, but it is simple...

To serve the truth... That is it.

SERVE THE TRUTH...

Not "your" truth, but the truth.

Over yourself, over your ideas and beliefs. Ask yourself over and over, are you serving the truth? As the insightful American comedian Owen Benjamin said, "I might be wrong, but I'm not lying."

As you attempt to find the truth, you might be wrong, but as long as you honestly seek it, you will get closer than if you didn't. Listen to new opinions. Slowly you will learn and become wiser. You will begin to love growing. To serve what is right. You will thank each lesson when you had it wrong and be grateful for what you know but not be blind to it.

If you consider all this… consider WORDS and LANGUAGE, your EXPERIENCES and INEXPERIENCE, Your SOCIETY and finally you, yourself.

You will be ready to learn to judge…

To judge fairly.

CHAPTER 13

TO JUDGE...

Judging is the way to clear the fog in the dark forest of life. It is your shield when you are attacked. It is your sword when you defend those you love. It is, by far, not perfect. It is as imperfect as you are, and we all are. But it is your right and your duty for your own sake and those around you.

You must learn to JUDGE. But with both the gentleness of a good mother and ruthlessness of a curious child.

Depending on your experience, society, and personality, it will be challenging and against your nature or fairly easy and second nature.

For those who will have a hard time, you need to know you cannot light up the dark forest without it. Judging can be a light... A light that can show you the real world.

For those who have an easy time, ask yourself what kind of judging you do. Are you seeking the truth or hiding the truth. We discussed the traps. People can use judging to put others down and make themselves feel better. It can be a way to manipulate and lie. Be careful. Judging is like a fire. It can light up the world, but it can also destroy the world.

So I will say it again... always try to judge fairly.

If you do, it will help you see situations and people better. It can protect you from evil. Without it, we are often like boats without paddles. Unable to guide our own lives and see the world for what it is. We can be the best person, but without judging, we will not defend goodness. We will be at the mercy of our society and whether it is healthy or not. Sure, We can be lucky to be born into a loving family, and in theory, we can live a good life protected by others. But we will not know why life was good. We will not understand why our society was decent. With love, we could continue our healthy society and be an important part of future generations but should this society change or be affected by outside influences. We will not have the ability to see whether this would be good or bad. And thus, we could become guilty of letting something decent and good be brought to an end.

It often happens in history, both with countries and cultures and on a smaller scale with families and relationships.

So learn to judge others...

Perhaps, you are feeling a sense of guilt? You might be saying to yourself, judging others are wrong. Who are we to judge someone else? It is all relative. We are all deep down good. What right do we have to judge what others think or do? We cannot say we are better and know the truth more than someone else. What we judge depends on what our society tells us. Cultural beliefs are relative...

Perhaps...

Believing this is certainly a powerful force in our society today, influencing many people.

TO JUDGE...

Truth is often looked at as relative, especially in today's world.

It's an idea that gave life to relativism and postmodernism. Two philosophies that believe there are no universal truths about the world. Only different ways of interpreting it. The idea that everything is relative. That people have their truth. I have mine, and you can have yours. Well... you can have it as long as it is not about the real truth.

Without entering too much into the dark valley of postmodernism's madness, We must look at it. Because it is gaining popularity making people confuse cultural opinions and beliefs, with the truth. They are mixing truths with lies to deliver an ideology that kills people's ability to see.

People are becoming more blind, not less, and it troubles me.

If you are curious, look into postmodernism yourself and make your own judgment. But notice your pattern of thinking as you read writers like Michel Foucault or Martin Heideggeror. Notice the flowery words and grandiose sentences that lead to nowhere. It is the modern jazz of philosophy. No melody, no meaning, no substance. Empty but with a lot of pretense and big words. It sounds impressive as long as you do not think twice. With their words, they spellbind you and your natural ability to see. They offer an escape from reality for the price of your soul, hypnotizing, like a virus to the mind, making us question our logic and instinct.

Making us believe 2+2=5.

Postmodernism is smart and has a purpose. It is meant to fog people's view of the world and hide lies right before us.

It is effective and dangerous because it can easily imprison us. These ideas stop our free minds. We risk believing nothing. That everything is relative, and nothing matters.

You might say, I'm missing their points. You could be right. Perhaps it went over my head, and I lack the intelligence to understand their wisdom. Certainly, postmodernism is very popular. Why would someone intelligent as Faucoult write something he didn't believe? What would be his motive? and the same for all the other postmodern philosophers and followers? Why do they spend so much time philosophizing about a world that has no meaning? Why spend so much time trying to convince others everything is relative and thus meaningless?

What is their ultimate purpose? If not to show us the truth... To show us the truth that there's no truth.

See the blaring paradox? If there's no truth, then the truth of there being no truth cannot be true. See the nonsense? Don't be fooled. It has nothing to do with that. Their motive is much more simple and easy.

It is to stop you from thinking and... JUDGING.

Remember the first chapter where we talk about our consciousness? Where I analyzed my thinking patterns, judge, decide, and watch.

If they can remove your first thought pattern of judging, you become highly vulnerable to their manipulation. They gain power over you, and you will accept anything and become a pawn in their game as you have nothing to decide and are left to watch them control you. To some, this is comforting since they are no longer responsible for their actions. Like infants, they can do no wrong. I believe some of the attraction to these ideologies boils down to some of this psychology. The world can be a scary place, and there's so much to judge and decide as an adult and endless ways to fail and do wrong. Some choose to believe in postmodernism or relativism and give power to those who want to control them. Like a cult, postmodernism removes all responsibility for actions. As long as you follow their dogmas, you will be accepted.

Just be open-minded, they would say. Same with society. We are told more and more to be open-minded. To be tolerant. But what do they mean with Open-Minded?

On the surface, it seems to be about accepting other people's opinions and lifestyles, which seems like a beautiful idea. A way for us to grow and accept others.

But is this true? Ask yourself... is an open mind good?

Initially, most would say yes. It is easy to be close-minded with our human ego and not listen to other opinions. It can be scary to be open. But we need to ask ourselves. What is it that we are asked to be open to? What is an open mind? A mind that accepts all? That accepts anything? Is that good? Is anything good? If everything is relative, perhaps. In a naive world, it would be. But as you've been through this journey with me, you've seen true darkness.

Would an open mind not be convenient to a dark world?

So think about it again. Observe those who want us to be open-minded. Watch them. Remember words can act as a spell.

Anyone who is empathetic and wants to please others can be hypnotized with those two words; open... mind.

They will take it to show their goodness and allow in darkness because they do not want to be seen as bad, wrong. It stops them from prejudging other people's words and actions. It stops them from judging and defending themselves. Like a snake, the "open-minded" group has bitten the receiving person with poison, blinding their ability to see. Like zombies, they will keep the words 'I am open-minded' circle in their minds as they are abused... over and over.

So when a group is saying they are open-minded and asking you to be open-minded, Remember, the first statement could be a lie, and the second could be a way for them to control you.

Look at their actions. Ask them something opposite to their own beliefs and see if they are truly open-minded or if they react briefly with anger or fear. I'm not saying the latter means they are dark. It is human to be fearful of opposite views. But it does mean you should watch out because it could mean they want to stop you from judging them. For you to be open to their viewpoints and, more important, actions of power over you.

Know accepting to be open-minded, without knowing about what, leaves you blind to evil ideologies, groups, or people. It makes you perceptible to being open-minded about evil.

So though being open-minded and not judgemental sounds good, it helps evil and puts good people in a difficult situation to protect themselves.

An open mind is not good, nor is a closed mind.

Why? Because it makes us blind.

Evil never shows its true face unless it has absolute power. Instead, it puts on a good face. It takes judging to uncover that mask.

So you must judge others. Judging and truth go hand in hand.

But it is not easy. For both the religious and those who are not, a famous quote from Jesus is often used to stop people from judging.

"Judge not, that you be not judged."

He continues with, "Condemn not, and you shall not be condemned." Condemn is not a light word. It is the ultimate and harsh judging of someone. It ends with forgiving, and you shall be forgiven.

This had always been a very hard concept for me as I looked at evil. Until I wrote this book. Jesus's quote does not condemn fair judging, in my opinion. He does not say 'never judge.' Instead, I believe there is a great lesson in it.

To be better at judging fairly, we must learn to accept others to judge us.

This is the wisdom. To give others the freedom to judge us and to accept their views. To be critical of us. It is not easy to do because it hurts our egos. We all like to think highly of ourselves. We like to believe we are the hero that will save the elderly lady in a burning building. We like to think we will be the courageous ones in hard times. But the truth is, most of us do not live our lives with the utmost effort. We can be lazy, tempted by things that are not good for us. It is difficult for us to allow others to look at who we truly are. We are afraid that they will see what we are trying to hide. We fear they see the person we are ashamed of. So we do not like others to judge us.

Evil knows this... Darkness uses this to silence us.

Do not be silenced. Look at yourself in the mirror. Yes, you have flaws. We all do. But you have a choice... Be afraid and ashamed of your flaws... or acknowledge them and live each day to become a more humble man or woman.

So, learn to judge yourself.

Judge yourself in a healthy way. Be kind and loving to yourself but look at the things you know you can improve. When you do, you will be able to judge people more fairly. Why? Because you see yourself in them. You will see their flaws, their humanity, and their fears. The same fears that you have. Because of that, your judgment of them will be softer and more honest.

And when you learn to judge yourself fairly, you will learn to allow others to judge you as well.

You will learn that you cannot control what others think. But it's ok, because you are more aware. You will be less afraid of criticism because you have learned to look at yourself. If you sense their honesty, you can ask for their observation and determine if they see things in you that you have not seen yourself. It is never easy to see our behavior when we are occupied in our own minds. Their feedback can help you discover new qualities and flaws.

Which sets you up for the next thing.

Lies and Unfair Judgement against you.

A thing that happens to you every day and will happen for as long as you live. Being unfairly judged. Gossip and lies against you from a world full of resentment and envy. There's plenty of judgment in this world, and a lot of it is dishonest and cruel. It is one of our human flaws. Self-righteousness and projecting our past, fears and anger onto someone else. Putting others down, lying about others. Look at kids in kindergarten and watch the little bullies.

But because you have stepped outside your inner perspective and began looking at yourself, You will be able to better see if someone is lying. You should still entertain the idea that it could be true what they say. But if it is not, you will be able to cope better with hurtful feelings from being judged because you know yourself much better.

When we are afraid of being judged, we cannot hear and see these lies the same. We are absorbed by our inner guilt. But when you have judged yourself and are growing, you will not be afraid of other judgments. Instead, you will have your eyes and ears open, and here is the interesting part. Because of that, you will see and hear the lies against you, and you will be able to shield yourself from them. They will not have the same power over you as before.

That said, I want to emphasize that past trauma can greatly impact our ability to do this. If one has grown up with lies against oneself. Been psychologically abused.

There will be an unhealthy voice inside us that will judge us harshly like we were treated in the past. This endless well of pain will not go away and make it much more challenging for you to accomplish a sense of peace with loving judgment. Still, if you slowly and carefully judge yourself with healthy, disciplined care and love, I believe it can be done.

We are not masters of judgment. We cannot be. It can only be as flawed as our limited perspective and knowledge. Because of this, It can never be for gossip, no matter how innocent. This is not easy. We are all tempted to speak about what we do not know completely. Try your best to be balanced with your voice. There's a BIG difference between judging a person based on their ACTS and judging a person based on RUMORS.

Those who rail against people judging others are often those who very often spread rumors and judge others by rumors.

And here lies an important truth.

Judging is only a threat to the ones who fear being judged. Live life as if you are judged. So before you judge, ask the world to judge you. And then, you can judge, even judge the judgment that comes to you.

Judge me, and I can judge you.

Judge often, but judge silently.

And always watch your righteousness, which can blind you from the truth.

To end these thoughts. What I'm trying to say is that judging is about judging fairly. It's about first being kind and gentle to the person or people we are looking at, from our own experience of judging ourselves and our loved ones. We can then begin to look at others and see them from a light of love first. But then, should we see flags that contradict their words and actions, we will be able to also see those aspects, and with time, in a quiet and respectful way, we will begin to open our eyes and see both light and dark.

With the light, we do not need to protect ourselves beyond clear communication and honesty. But with the dark, we need to shield ourselves and protect those around us and, if need be, fight back strongly.

Expose their masks!

Which is the first step to fight evil. Because evil people with masks are masters at deception.

Which leads to our next chapter and second step.

Knowing who they are, their signs... The monsters behind masks.

CHAPTER 14

A MONSTER'S MASK

It is time to learn to see the masks of monsters...

Horrific things are happening, from far lands, across the continents, poor and rich countries. All the way to your little neighborhood. Yes, evil lurks close. You have likely looked at an evil person within the last days or weeks. Each day as you go to work, go to school, meet up with friends, evil is rubbing against your shoulders, shaking your hand, and perhaps even hugging you close.

Let us not wait any longer. Close your eyes. Imagine someone is standing right behind you. A person who embodies evil. Keep your eyes closed and listen. What do you feel? Let your imagination go. Allow yourself to drift in any direction. Though there is no touch, no visuals, Are you not beginning to feel a sense of dread? Do you remember as a child being scared of the dark? Of the open closet? Of the long dark hallway?

Now, imagine this evil getting so close to you that you can hear its breath. Now, keeping this feeling, examine your thoughts as I ask for you to turn around and open your eyes. Look straight at it... the face of evil.

Are you hesitating? Are you scared to turn and look? It's natural.

But you must turn. You must look.

I will never forget this dream I had a long time ago. I was standing in my apartment looking at a painting at the end of a small hallway. A door opened right behind me, and I felt a presence, someone or something behind me. It felt like pure evil, the blackest of black. I was frozen in fear. I wanted to escape and wished for it to go away, but it did not. Then, perhaps because I spend a lot of time thinking about this subject, I wanted to fight it. I did not want it to win. Standing in utter fear, I gathered my anger to the point where I exploded. Strong enough to overcome my terror, I turned around and looked straight at it. I yelled at the top of my lungs, fists clenched. I do not remember what I saw, but I know an immense force threw me across the room and through the window. As I clung to the window frame outside the house, I woke up drenched in sweat.

Dreams can teach us. I learned a lesson. Use anger to gain strength to overcome your fears. We must learn to turn and look straight at evil. Yes, be afraid because there is a reason for the fear. Evil destroys. Monsters are real.

But overcome it. Anger is one way. Be strong and pull your head out of the sand, and fight. Are you ready? Do you want to win over evil?

Do you want to pull off its masks?

If you are unsure, I do understand. There is comfort in looking away. It is easier to turn around in bed and cover yourself until the bad goes away. But often, it does not go away. Instead, it only gets closer. Though I have an odd determination to look at evil in my life... when I go into the real dark corners, allowing myself to sit with true evil, my faith and courage go away. I do not think I have what it takes to be strong in real life. It is so easy to be a thinker but if I was in an actual situation. I doubt I would have what it takes. And it is in this contemplation I try to search for extra strength. Anger can be useful, but in the real world, it is not likely to be enough.

So, where can we find the strength?

Over the years, the answer has come to me personally. A strength coming from a source that is beyond me... The belief in God and the trust in God. Who is good and above darkness. In him, I find purpose, justice, and love.

So if you fear the masks, open your eyes. Do not give up. If you have little faith in yourself, there is a source, much stronger, that can give you strength. It is God. A belief in someone higher who is above us all. Who is above darkness, who is only light. Believe in him, and I believe you can find the courage.

Now, if your answer to face evil was already yes, You are ready to pull the masks off. Good. The world needs shepherds. Being good is worthless if there is no courage to face fears. Evil feeds off fear in good people.

To prepare yourself, I want you to think of the symbolism of three monkeys. No doubt you've seen them. It's three monkeys portrayed, each covering up either his eyes, ears, or mouth.

There's a duality in these three sculptures. From the eastern culture's perspective from which they originated, They were about protecting what is moral and good. In Confucius Lunyu XII, Yen Yüan asked the Master how one can obtain perfect virtue. The Master replies with the words: "Look not at what is contrary to propriety; listen not to what is contrary to propriety; speak not what is contrary to propriety; make no movement which is contrary to propriety." Contrary of propriety means what is the opposite of good and moral. The wisdom rings true. If we want to stay on the path of goodness, we must be careful not to see what is bad as it can tempt us. We must be cautious of what we hear, as it can mislead us. And we must be careful in what we speak, as our words can become actions. Instead, make no movement, and you will not move away from goodness.

From this perspective, the symbolism guides us to protect ourselves. It is about goodness.

But it can equally be seen from the other side, evil. If its symbolism is about evil, the meaning becomes very different. It becomes about submission and evil's dogma. Do not look, do not hear, and do not speak… of evil. Cover your eyes, cover your ears, and cover your mouth… so evil can flourish.

And this is what the masked people want. They want a world where they can do anything, and people will stay silent. They need most people to be the three monkeys. Sadly a large part of the world and its varying cultures is precisely like this. Good people stay silent from fear, and evil people rule their land.

Because of this, in my view, the Western view of the monkeys tells a more important lesson. Yes, the Eastern view is good, but it talks about perfection, and in this fallen world of ours, the search for perfection, primarily by closing our senses, will lead to our destruction.

It is better for good to be able to see evil, than for good to know no evil. Like we talked about in previous chapters, when a tree falls in the forest, but no one hears it, the truth is, that the tree still fell. Unheard, evil will tear through the life of any forest. Like cancer, it will kill each tree, and flower in its path until the forest holds no life.

So we must not be like those three monkeys.

First. Let us uncover our eyes.

CHAPTER 15

SEE NO EVIL

Wherever you are right now... look around. Perhaps you are in your living room. What do you see? A familiar room? Now, try again and look in ways you normally don't. Look all the way up around the ceiling. Look at the details around you. Look behind you. Explore with your eyes. Do you see new things? For a moment, use your imagination and tell yourself you are somewhere else. Let that thought enter your mind. You are not where you think you are. You are in a stranger's house. Does it look and feel slightly different? Your brain is reorganizing what it sees and letting in new information you have ignored for a long time. With this new information, we can briefly see an old place in a new light.

The same with people.

The closer we are to a person, the more we know them and put them in a box of expectations. This box can be familiar and comforting. But it can also blind us to things we should see clearly, but we don't. If the person then begins to change, instead of questioning it, we ignore it. Our eyes are open, but our minds are closed. Our visual information in daily life is so routine. We don't see the roads we drive on. We don't see the people we work with. If you ask yourself: What did my co-worker wear today? There is a good chance most of us would not know. Our brains filter out anything that is not needed as we navigate the day. Routine surroundings are blocked out and overlooked.

But to see masks, we must begin to undo this habit.

We must learn to see, but not only that… We must dare to see.

Because it is hard. It is very hard, once you open your mind's eye, you will see how many people stay silent. They do not want to see the ugly truths around them. Hiding behind their masks, they help evil stay unseen. They would rather attack you than look within and look out at the real world. On some level, I don't blame them. It is not easy to face harsh realities. It is tempting to stay a child forever. To keep our masks on. To avoid being seen. It is human nature. Look at the Latin word *persona*. It means "theatrical mask." The less comfortable we are, the more we wear masks to fit in and be part of a group. Only with our closest friends do we tend to let go of any pretense and be who we are.

So it is less about seeing and detecting people's masks and instead about finding out who is behind the masks and separating the flawed humans from the monsters among us.

So how do we do that while judging fairly? We must be careful and never jump to conclusions, knowing that we cannot read minds nor hearts. Instead, we can make notes and flag concerning behavivor. When you see a certain behavior, an action that hints at a possible manipulation, you need to make a mental note of it. The more flags you see from a person, the more you should be aware of his or her actions. Look for the true person behind the mask.

Before we go into some behaviors to watch out for and learn to see better, it is important to understand who monsters truly are. To see through the masks, you must know what to look for behind the masks. To know them as they know you. Because monsters know their human companions extremely well. They might not know about a good person's nature as it is completely foreign to them. But they, as predators, have studied people their entire lives. On the contrary, most healthy people are often naive about monsters because even if they have encountered them or been hurt by them, the game left them destroyed and confused. They never really saw them coming, and once it happened, they didn't learn about their true nature.

We need to turn that around.

When one is good, one often tends to trust others. It can be hard to understand or even imagine the darkness in some people.

Ask yourself these questions. When you look at people who do you suspect, is not showing their true nature. Do you try to justify their pretense? Do you defend them by thinking they might feel shame or guilt and cannot admit what they did? Or do you justify their behavivor by thinking that they probably do not know what they are doing?

If you do, you might be ignorant about the world you are walking in. Denial is easy and comfortable… but only in the beginning.

To clear the fog, it is time for us to go into a monster's mind.

Since this is not physically possible, I will paraphrase part of a chapter written by Ken Heilbrunn M.D. from Sam Vaknin's book *Malignant Self Love*. This chapter made a big impact on me, as did Sam Vaknin's brilliant book on narcissism.

A monster says Hi...

> "You might recognize me from my books, my art, my inventions, voted me into office, listened to my lectures, laughed at my jokes, excused my faults, or envied me. Don't know me? I think you do. I am sure you do.
>
> "Maybe we met privately. Maybe I am the one who met you when you were down and built you up. Hired you when you needed a job, Gave you hope when you were down, listened to you when you needed it, made you happy and excited about life. Of course, you know me. I am your inspiration, your role model, savior, and best friend.
>
> "But let's be honest, I can also break you down. First I will help you up because you need me. Then, when I want it, I will tear you down. You are used to it. You let me do it. I will not take pity on you. You are pathetic, weak, dishonest, dumb. Such an embarrassment. A selfish partner, a terrible parent, sexually impotent, and a loser. I like your reaction when I tell you. You are my toy. I can do anything with you. I act and do what I want at home and outside. It is my right because that is who I am. I lie to your face with ease. My lies are not lies. It is the truth. My truth. A truth you

> believe. Because you needed my trust, and I gave you hope, stability, and confidence. Now that comes with a price, of course. But it is worth it and much more.
>
> "Sure, you can try to escape and run. See if your friends believe you. Try to have them see someone else than the charming me they always see. No, they will see the crazy person you are. The more you beg, the more they will avoid you. You should question yourself. Your sanity. It is not me, but you. Who has done me wrong? You have embarrassed me to your friends, ruined the good things I have worked hard for. You have always been a pain to me. You disgust me.
>
> "But I have my way of dealing with that. Moments of pure rage. Those moments you fear so much. The power I have over you. Absolute power and control. It gives me a high. So does all the lying. But it all pales in comparison to when I explode on you in an unexpected furor. See that is the real reason I am with you. Sure, go ahead and tell your friends our little secrets of me torturing you. See if they believe you. Try to explain that me, the funny, friendly, and charming person, is causing your breakdown. No, don't be foolish. They will never believe you. You are mine and mine to do whatever I want with. And when I get bored or find someone better at pleasing me. I will throw you into the garbage. Because that is what you are to me, garbage."

Do you recognize this person? Perhaps you loved such a person but didn't want to realize their true nature. To fully realize some think like this is scary, very scary. They are nothing like you and me. Though they are human in every other aspect, their minds differ greatly from ours. Consciously, they feel like a different species. Like Victor Frankl said, the decent and the indecent. They carry no guilt, no remorse, and most importantly, they enjoy and find pleasure in the destruction of people, society, and culture.

They are the true monsters among us.

Anna C. Salter Ph.D. talks about it in her book *Predators* where she explains that the average person misreads psychopaths repeatedly because they think that those who betray us will feel bad about it. It is a sad and dangerous expectation. They feel no remorse in deceiving. On the contrary, they get a kind of joy and almost childlike delight in duping others. People misread this joy as honest and innocent. After all, there was no gaze aversion or nervous mannerism. The guy seems pretty straight. He looked me right in the eyes.

So you see the reason for their masks? They have much to hide. They are the masters of masks. Chameleons that prey upon any who invite them into their lives. They are real-life Vampires.

But how do we see them? How do we see their evil?

When evil exists within a culture that truly protects victims, and evil is not in control. Even with our eyes open, it is hard, very hard to see them. They look like any of us. They have neither horns nor tails. They know how to manipulate and get what they want. In interviews that Anna C. Salter set up with several sex offenders, we glimpse their methods to avoid detection. In one of them, a young man wearing a black jacket and white shirt explains how he would gain people's trust to get access to their children. It is disturbing to watch because he explains everything in such a calm and neutral tone.

> *Anna: And how did you get control of them? Was it through force and control?*
>
> *Offender: No, it wasn't violence. It was more like manipulation. It was coercion. It was like; I'll buy you this. I'll give you that. Treating them like a person but they were just objects. I was doing anything in my power to get them to give sex up. To give it up, and that's what I used to tell them. I groomed them up, and I would have done... I groomed them up, and they would comply. I would buy them beer, get them drunk, get them high. Any way, I could manipulate a woman or a girl, a child, into having sex, I would do it.*
>
> *The best way to fool people is to help them. Ask them what they want, what they need. They need any help doing anything? Do they need any money? Do they need their cars fixed, their grass fixed, do they need their children looked out for. Do they need a job? Do they need anything? Anything to get them to think that I am a decent person and want to help. Trust me. I will help. Overall that was a flat-out lie.*
>
> *Anna: Why do you think what makes people so trusting?*
>
> *Offender: What do you mean? As far as trusting? Trusting me? I thought that I could be trusted to a certain extent... but behind their back... No, I would take things from them. Steal from them. Scope out things that I could steal. Just to see what I could get out of somebody. Just get what I wanted.*

I was looking out for number one. For me. I didn't have any empathy for anybody else because, same to me, nobody had any empathy for me. I wasn't going to give anybody any empathy that didn't give it to me. And that was it, that was the bottom line. I didn't have people cry for me or asked me if I needed anything. Then you know, I wouldn't use any empathy. I would fake it. Now I would fake empathy. Like saying, I know how you feel. I have been in that situation before. But there was no empathy there. That was just a show. That was just to get the person to say; he seems like he's a pretty good fella, and yeah, that was manipulation all the way."

See how he would gain trust?

By acting kind and giving. By doing everything he could to look like the good guy.

I do not know about you, but it is troubling to see how offenders are using kindness. It makes kind acts almost seem dirty and destroys the sense of goodwill, making everyone suspicious. But in a good society, it is the only way for evil to gain control. So appreciate the hardship to see it. Because in societies where goodness and law do not rule, evil can take off its mask. No need for masks.

So accept the difficulty and remember that you should judge yourself first and allow others to judge you. Accept distrust and do not take it personally. People are protecting themselves, and we all should.

Evil is out there, and when you meet it for the first time, it will likely be the most friendly helping hand, showing you just how good they are by their first actions. And here lies the key: their actions. Look for actions. Watch and see because they will eventually show their true self. The kind acts do not continue. Cracks in their kindness will show when they deal with others or in small odd moments with you. Make a flag of that moment.

Enough flags from a person, and one would be wise to be cautious.

How far they go is all about what stage of power they are in, their ability, intellect, and drive for darkness.

Evil operates in stages. How much power or lack of power the individual or group has. Less power, it will be forced to hide behind lies and manipulation and society's norms. But the more culture shifts toward darkness, the more it will begin to show its true nature. Its natural drive is to push, pull, destroy, and lie its way to more power in a society, culture, community, family, and relationships.

Knowing the stages helps to see them better.

STAGE 1: SOME POWER

The Predator Stage

Monsters obtain control and power from an early age. As they go through life, they look for ways to establish power over others and, if ambitious, groups. This is the stage when they are actively looking to gain power. It is also the stage when they are the hardest to detect. They will be hiding almost all of their true self in public.

At this stage, they do not have the ability to abuse and control.

They are like starved vampires out for blood.

Like chameleons, they will manipulate you into their traps. Even the most knowledgeable and bright people can fall for their charm or persuasion. Like the offender in this chapter, they look like anyone else.

The most effective way to detect their fake masks is often the first impression and gut feelings. But that doesn't last long as they draw you in with their words. They are watching you closely, looking for ways to tempt you and gain control of you. What are your weaknesses, needs, and dreams? Slowly they will guide you down the path towards their cage, making your mind weak through words and promises. Like predators on the prey, they will throw out fish hooks for you to bite. Hooks of gifts, promises, and sweet flattery. Knowing about these hooks is one way to sometimes differentiate kind acts versus malignant hooks in disguise. How fast did they appear? And by how much? Was the flattery also too much? The sooner it appears and the more over the top, the more likely it is a hook. They play to your need to be loved. We all want a friend. We all want to be liked.

As we think about this, it is important to acknowledge these acts to gain influence are done by us all. All of us flatter and promise for emphatic or selfish reasons. It is human social behavior. But for monsters, their intent is very different. It is nefarious. They need a victim. They need you to follow them into the shadows where no one would go willingly.

So if you feel you are being pulled in quickly, be cautious. Protect yourself and question things. It is not easy. What they say is exactly what you wish for. They know that. It is the devil's deal. He will tempt you with the very things you cannot say no to and want to believe.

Count the flags and future actions, so you can protect yourself and hopefully avoid the bigger trap: the abuser stage.

STAGE 2: POWER OVER INDIVIDUALS.

The Abuser Stage.

You will find most monsters in the abuser stage.

No matter intellect or skills, the walls of society and taboos make it easy for them to hide while they act out intimate terror within their world. A lot of them have no criminal records and are seen in public as decent fellow citizens. You have heard the saying many times, "He was just a quiet neighbor. Seemed so friendly and nice."

The easiest position of power is to become a parent. The utter dependence of a child gives full power and control to an evil parent. No trust is needed. The masks will be on when others are present but come off once the child or family is alone.

Living multiple lives, they only show their true nature to the ones they abuse. It might be the whole family within a family, but they might also pick one or two children as targets. This helps them build walls of deception within the family unit. If only one child is being abused, he or she will not find support or understanding from the siblings. Instead, they will be isolated in a twilight zone where the truth is hidden in plain sight. This strengthens the monster's ability to brainwash. Making the victim even doubt their mind and reality.

In society outside the family, monsters might seek positions of power depending on their darkness and ability. From the bottom up, a low-skilled person might seek power within a government and bureaucracy. More intellectual individuals might seek academia or the business world. Any place where they can hide while forcing their dominance over others.

But how do we see and detect these monsters?

For many, their darkness cannot be seen. Because they never go over the line, exposing themselves. Publicly they mix in with the rest of us. One can try to read their body language and other methods to find inconsistencies. But one should be careful reading too much into these techniques as they are flawed and easy to misread.

But are there other ways? What about our culture? Have you noticed our culture changing? From good versus evil to evil versus evil and even evil portrayed as good? And worse, good as evil.

An example is Disney's *Sleeping Beauty*. The fairy tale was first made in 1959 and then later in 2014 as Maleficent. The moral of the stories became the opposites.

In Stage 2, sometimes one can recognize these people's true nature through their taste of culture. In the same way they are attracted to jobs and positions of power, they are attracted to entertainment that expresses their inner darkness. Watch and observe their favorite characters in film. Watch what they enjoy. What T-shirt slogans do they wear? Are their social media memes cruel? Do they favor villains in films? Do they enjoy sadistic horror films?

A grandmother with her whole house decorated in creepy settings for Halloween should raise a flag. I knew someone who abused their children that had a special fondness for Halloween. Their choice of costumes and favorite characters in films was not the brave hero or the funny sidekick. It was always the Disney villains. Coincidence? Sure, Enjoying Halloween has no direct link to evil. We all can be fascinated with darkness, and monsters are cool when they are not real. But it is a flag. It could mean there's a draw to the dark side, likely through experiences from real life. The question is if they are in the light or the shadow. Many victims of evil who are in the light are pulled to these dark fascinations. They know evil but are not evil themselves. Others walk the fine line between light and dark. So look for more clues. How dark are their favorite films? Do they relate to the victims in the horror film or the killer? Do they joke and find it funny instead of scary?

This is anecdotal, of course, and many of them hide behind Christmas and Angels. Things of goodness and fairness. But when they do, it is because they are not in a community that celebrates darkness. They need to protect their false masks more and hide within the relatively decent culture and accepted values.

Look for any patterns of behavior that conflict with their words. The more conflicts, the more you need to be prepared for cracks. Seeing things you weren't supposed to see. When that happens, have the bravery to look. Do not close your mind and ignore it. Evil and monsters depend on your blindness. The cracks will be brief, which makes them so hard to detect. They live a life in hiding, resenting it, resenting you, resenting the world. Wishing for freedom of more... More power and more control to do whatever they want with no masks.

Which leads us to their next stage.

STAGE 3: ABOVE THE LAW
The Destruction Stage

What if one has boiling anger inside? A superego with no restraints that thinks he/she is God but reality doesn't bow to their demands or wishes. They will feel trapped with a deep resentment of the chains of society, especially if they have extra charm or high ambitions. Going after individuals, scamming, abusing family and friends are not enough.

They want more. They want true power in society. Sadly, a large majority of the world is a playground for these people. Depending on the culture they are born into, it can be easy or hard. If it is a corrupt and authoritarian country, the world is their oyster with many options to expand their desires. Freedom to gain power without the hassle of laws and order. They will be able to stretch their hatred and destruction through tribes, government, military, or gangs where they can be pawns in the gears of terror.

But if they are in a first world country, things will be more complicated. The laws and the restraints of society will keep life difficult. But this will not stop them. Like basic human needs, these people need control. Any place that has strong individual protections will be a harder place for them to operate. Because of this, their desire to change their environment will be strong. They will support all ideological, political, or cultural movements that create confusion, distrust, and anger towards society. Anything that moves the culture away from the core center of individual liberty. They won't need to be vocal about their intentions. Those who are akin will recognize each other and know the goals remain secret and the actions wrapped in lies. Because they cannot show themselves, they can be even more insidious as the suffering they cause is behind walls and away from the public view.

They will gravitate towards all sectors of power in society: government, big corporations. All sectors that are useful for manipulation, such as media, marketing, and entertainment. Unlike Stage 2, where these people abuse inside homes or in public against smaller groups and individuals, in Stage 3, they work towards transforming society and manipulating culture. They can still operate because they function within legit systems of law, hiding behind the walls of justice, regulations, and policies. Many of them with small positions might seem inconsequential and nothing like monsters. But they should not be underestimated. They kill societies. They demoralize and divide each day, making the world less safe. One cannot do much damage, but a million of them can and do, with a million small cuts each day. Without the mob and the work of these worker ants of darkness, softening a decent society for collapse and greater evil would not be possible.

They have a deep and desperate desire for control. A lust for power. Like decent people look for love, they look for power. The more control they gain, the closer they think they get to rebuild the world in the image of their superego. It is a twisted and dark world where they are gods and everyone else, is an objects with whom they can do whatever they want.

They are the ones who give birth to the biggest monsters. The ones who make it possible for true horrors to sweep the lands with genocides, mass slaughter, and torture.

They will say they fight it, but they are the ones who will dry the fields and make the world ready to burn.

STAGE 4: ABSOLUTE POWER

The Dictator and Serial Killer Stage

The last stage for evil. Hell on Earth...

This is the one stage we all know and talk about. The grand stage. The one where true horrors come to life. A place where there is no hiding. Where masks are burned, and the ugly face of evil comes forth. Letting out all it's brutality on an individual, group, or nation.

It is a long road to get to this point. But if enough people look away and do not see, then the monsters will hide long enough to finally gain absolute power. Good societies will collapse and transform. People will be asked to kneel to evil. Chains will be put on people as they are led to the gulags, into trains, or taken to the execution camps. It will all be on display, and any fight to stop it will be long and bloody. Once chaos sets in, the benevolent order is hard to put back together. Evil knows its enemy well. I will repeat it. It sees good people clearly and reads them. On the contrary, good people too often are ignorant of evil and how dark it truly is. A monster's paradise is nothing like the films. It is much, much worse. They will have the power to control every aspect of your life except your inner thoughts, and even that, they will try to take over through brainwashing.

There will be no easy way out from this end game.

Sadly, this place is not fiction. It is not only history but the present. As you read this book, there are people in this world who are suffering in Stage 4 under the absolute power of evil, who cannot protect themselves. Who cannot escape. Who live every day at the end of a barrel if they do not obey and bow to evil. I once read about a German Jew who wrote how he was lying on the ground by the booths of German soldiers who raped and killed his wife and kids… and now was going to be executed. Utterly at the mercy of these soldiers, he had no way to fight for himself nor his family. "I could do nothing. All I could do was pray and watch them kill my family. It was at that moment. I promised myself if I ever survived, I would never, ever again, be helpless. I would never allow myself to not be able to protect my family and my own life." I do not remember the source of this writing, but I believe he survived where his family did not.

The truth of these words cannot be expressed enough.

Allow yourself to take a moment to put yourself in his place. Take the time to fully realize his words and their meaning. Put yourself in a position where you can do absolutely nothing to protect and defend yourself nor your loved ones against someone who wants to hurt you. Whatever the monster wants to do will happen. You have no say nor any way to stop it. The monsters know this and will do exactly the worst thing you can imagine.

We can all pray we never witness this stage, as an individual or in a group/society. But we must learn to see how monsters work behind the scenes. They don't even need to verbally communicate their goals. They recognize movements that are working towards their ends. The decent people should see this too, but most of us are too naive and don't see the enemies within our own countries and cities. So we ignore the small signs around us. We ignore how step by step, our society is pathologized. Lies are spreading. Lies are being accepted as truth. Good men are being portrayed as evil. Evil men are seen as good. Have you noticed the trend of the last decades in entertainment? Humans are portrayed as all evil and have become the antagonist against the goodness and pureness of nature, animals, and creatures. It is no longer about the moral play between the decent and indecent humans. All humans are put into the pot of evil.

Do you think this is a coincidence? Who do you think benefits from portraying all humans as evil? Good people? No, because they will be put in the box of evil. The monsters want you completely defenseless. They will tear you down and make it, so you cannot stand up and speak against the lies.

Through Stages 1 to 3, they are doing what they can to operate within the rules, but it is ultimately all about Stage 4.

The place where they have utter control. Power against you as a person, group, or country and can kill, murder, torture, and leave as many lives in ruin as possible.

The burning fields of evil... happen again and again.

STAGE 5: NO POWER

The Fall of the Second Mask.

When evil falls, and it will, it cannot sustain its power because it is built on lies, deception, and brutality. Eventually, it will break down. Evil will attack evil, and from the burned forest, flowers will grow again. That is the good news. The bad news is that it can take decades and sometimes centuries for goodness and order to return.

When evil loses all of its power, you will see its deepest nature because it has two masks. One, to deceive us to not see its intentions to destroy us. Two, the mask that itself is unconscious of. The mask that hides its history and the reason for being who it is. This last mask will only come off when the person has no more options. Nowhere to hide or run, physically and psychologically. When that happens, they will regress into utter fear and show us hints of the origin of their dark soul. Stripped of all control, they become the little children that they truly are and were.

I don't believe there is a way out for them. I don't believe making them powerless and for the second mask to fall off for a moment is healing. I don't believe it gives them any insight. I believe it is almost a split personality that is seen that can only be accessed by force. But once you give them any way to escape again, their old hollow self comes back. It is death to them to go to their inner child. Why? We will look at this in the next chapter.

So monsters don't change, and evil doesn't stop even when it seems to have been stopped.

We must understand evil is always transforming itself and changing its shape and appearance. If it is lost, it will pull back and fade into the present culture in order to look benign or even positive and good.

Like the different stages, monsters hide in, the same happens with greater evil. What I mean by greater evil is many dark people work together for Stage 4, directly or indirectly. They need big movements that they can hide within, and they do it through associations and organizations. It is all about the groups. After a time when true evil has been defeated in a society, like the twentieth-century world wars, there will be a brief time of peace where evil seems to disappear. The reason is that the face of the defeated evil has been exposed. It can no longer hide within the defeated organizations. They need a new host to possess, to gain the trust of people and once again indoctrinate towards evil's goals. This takes time. Goodness must be tempted to let its guard down.

"That never happened…" or "That won't happen again."

And so, a new generation will grow up in a world void of past horrors, only with their parents as storytellers. Stories that will fade, until their voices finally are no longer. This is when the real dangers start again. The second or third generations who would have let down their guard. Perhaps they have even lost the belief in evil. After all, their parents never saw or felt it. So these next generations are likely to make the same mistake and not only ignore evil, but support it.

But how?

The face of evil will be very different than the old one from two or three generations before. They will not call themselves what the evil of the past did. Individual dark people, not high in IQ, might be attracted to the past. As an example, we know how evil Nazism was. But if you look at the few Nazis today, they have no power or ability to do much evil. That is not to say there cannot be some dangerous people among them. There are reasons why they are attracted to a group that murdered millions. But as a whole, they are now more laughable than threatening. Look at the rallies that they hold in the United States. They have to be protected from the main population by police. Not the other way around.

But we hear on the news media currently the constant drum of "Nazis! Nazis!" They are trying to deceive you and associate evil with groups like the old Nazis and even objects like guns. We then look for those evils and say, "Never again!" We will never let Nazism take over again. Never again will we let the KKK do what they did! But this is a misdirection. It does not prepare us for future evil nor coming present evil and sets us up to fail fighting against it.

Present evil will always be a new face, a new group. In the 1920s, no one had heard of the national socialist labor party in Germany (National sozialistische Deutsche Arbeiterpartei). It was a new political group with a new leader.

Evil will come from a direction of what is considered culturally good in each time period... And what has power or can bring power.

So don't look for evil through the lens of past groups unless they still yield enough power and opportunity to transform into its next shape.

Nazism does not matter any longer. The face of Nazism will never be used again for great evil. This means its name, symbol, and all of its association. Why? Because it will forever be linked to evil. For this very reason, new evil will never put this face on. It wants to represent innocence, victimhood, or as a protector of a victim. Not the oppressor of the past. So it will come with a new face, new symbolism, and a new cause. An obvious cause with a perfect slogan few could argue against. Evil's true face is never evil until it has absolute power, and then it will be too late. So we need to learn to look at actions and behavior. NOT names of the past or their symbols and slogans.

But now that we have gone through the idea of how monsters and greater evil hide within society in different stages of power, it is time to look more at how to open our eyes. Because there are hints and flags that go noticed but are ignored. We are so trained as decent people to not think bad about people that we try to justify bad behaviors, and if we notice odd behavior, we quickly forget.

But don't forget. You must see. Open your soul up to the fact that parts of the world are ugly. Your heart will never be the same. It will feel more pain and, at times, break in pieces from the world around you. But it will also love more. It will appreciate every little kindness you see.

The signs...

I will repeat myself. The monsters look like all of us. They are not easy to see if we do not use our mind, thoughts, heart, and gut together. Your body has cells that have captured millions of years of experience with danger and, therefore, evil. But your mind needs to learn. Your mind can easily be confused by evil. Your conscience can easily misguide the truth and, through guilt, apply right on wrong and bad on good. Our heart is no different. It sees what it wants to see. It's like a child. Beautiful and good, but so easily misled. Our gut is often the best one to ask, our best friend. The one who speaks the truth. It is sometimes referred to as our second brain lined with over one hundred million nerve cells with pathways that lead straight to our brain stem, communicating faster than an eyeblink. The earliest and most primal part of our brain.

So our gut knows evil well. But we need to know what to look for. The patterns we need to recognize are many, and they are complex.

Let's go through some of them.

Look for behaviors that show signs of their inner world. Is someones superego not in check? Do they not seem to have a self-critical ability? Look for signs of hyper-sensitivity where they are easily insulted and slighted by the smallest things. Look for their response. Do they quickly blame others for accidents and even their own mistakes? Are they quick to blame groups of the world for their troubles? When being served, do they ignore or look down upon people?

Do they not take responsibility for their faults? Do they push it off and resent the idea of personal responsibility? Do they vocally express anger and treat people, children, and animals with impatience or even cruelty? Do they talk with manipulative language that is filled with threats and hostility? Watch for anger. Especially the kind that doesn't seem to be related to anything. Look at their manners. Do they devalue one moment and the next, talking flattering words in an exaggerated and abundant way, only to again sulk, abuse, and humiliate later?

If you ask for personal boundaries, do they ignore you? Do they ignore your wishes, small or big, even with an air of arrogance and a smile? Do they give little but set very unrealistic expectations for you and others? Do you feel like an object or a useful fool for their gratification? Do they show very little trust? Suspicious of anything and everything? Do they always want and need to be in control compulsively, holding the keys, the money, the tickets, the passports, the bag? If one is away from them for a short period of time, does it seem to upset them? Make them angry? Do they expect you to ask them for permission to do things, such as visiting your family or meeting a friend?

Another sign to have your eyes open to is being rushed. Slow down your thinking and if you sense you are being rushed, make a mental note and slow your reactions down. Watch them. Are they eager to move on? Do they from one day to another "fall in love" with you? Do they pressure you to become their soulmate, quickly expecting exclusivity and instant intimacy, and once you agree, they rush you to cut off your friends and family? Do they ask you to leave your job? Your education? Do they put you in a position of vulnerability? Do they ask you to let go of your independence?

If they are a sexual partner, do they find sadistic sex exciting? Do they have fantasies of rape or pedophilia? Do they find it amusing to be extra rough during sex? Do they abuse you verbally? Curse at you? Call you insulting and emotionally hurting names? Are they physically violent, often in a laughing manner? Do they enjoy seeing you in fear and terrified?

Watch their body language.

Do they move with an air of superiority? Holding their head with the chin up high to the point of being over the top. Making it seem as if they think they are above others. Do they show amused indifference? A feeling of being mysterious. Do they socially interact with supremacy, as if they are so good and forgiving towards others with a virtue of perfection?

If you do all this and stay honest and open, you will begin to see. Not how we see with our eyes but in a peripheral way. A mindful way. The subtle signs with people around you will no longer go unnoticed: the small gut feeling, a quick thought, seeing a microexpression, an odd look, catching a small lie.

I will emphasize, some of these qualities can be found within all of us at times. It is part of our human flaws, but they are flags. Both for ourselves if we see them within us but especially if we see them in others. Too many flags and we should heed the warning.

You will be ready for the next step. The step where you will be able to unprogram yourself. Where you no longer will be ignorant.

It will be painful. but worth it because you will see a purpose.

CHAPTER 16

HEAR NO EVIL

The monkey is sitting, holding his hands against his ears. He will neither hear you nor listen.

What are our ears used for? They are our most primal pathway to listen and communicate with our fellow humans. Before writing and other forms of communication, it was all verbal. Our language made our cultural evolution possible, allowing us to communicate more complex thoughts. Share ideas and grow our knowledge and understanding of the world. One human cannot learn enough in his limited lifetime to even scratch the surface of our wonderfully mysterious world. But once we developed language, maybe a hundred thousand years ago, we could do just that. Grow knowledge. Seek the truth.

Seek right from wrong.

Take your hands and put them up against your ears. Press hard against your head. What do you hear? The ruffles of your skin and the blood pumping through your temples? A deep rumble that resembles the sounds of a distant earthquake? Imagine if you would never hear a sound again. No spoken word, no tune or song to move you. It is strange to think of losing our natural given sense of hearing. But many have their ears covered like the monkey. They cannot hear you. Not because they are deaf. On the contrary, their physical parts are all healthy. But because of two reasons. The first reason: They choose not to listen out of fear or out of ego and arrogance. The second reason, and the one to worry more about: They cannot listen because their ability to truly hear has been hijacked by toxic ideas that, like parasites, live in their minds and will not allow free thought to happen. To emphasize, I am not talking about the usual hardship of us humans to understand the world and the struggle to find the truth mixed with our wishes, beliefs, and egos to be correct. I am talking about parasitic ideas that are carefully thought out for ulterior motives and distributed by media and culture repeatedly, spoken as facts and absolute truths across media, filling people's ears with lies and false narratives. Once false ideas have entered ones ears and mind, the parasite idea can warp the thoughts and opinions of the person, paralyzing their ability to perceive truths and even common sense.

And this is what evil needs. It needs you to be unable to recognize danger. Even if it stares you right in your face, it needs to be able to operate in the open. Left alone to do its ugly deeds.

But how does this mind control work? How can it do that? How can evil people be out in the open and not seen? It can be done by making people think they are not seeing what they are seeing. Even if they learn what to watch out for, even if they watch with eyes fully open, those whose ears and minds are covered and filtered by "idea lies" will see nothing. To better understand this, we must revisit and think about how our thoughts work and how we use learned knowledge to make sense of the world. We talked earlier about the traps of words, and it is true.

Words are programming.

They are the foundation for our mind, our ideas, our beliefs, and our actions. They shape what we believe is good or bad and help us organize our world and how to function in it. They are how we learn and carry past wisdom, rules of our civilization. Now think about our world. Have you noticed words becoming more and more meaningless? Do you think it is by coincidence? Look around you and notice how language is changing. Notice the direction. Is it more beautiful words? New expressions of love, affection, and uplifting thoughts?

Think as a parent with a child. Would you, with pride, want to teach your children the words, their origin meaning, or the new meaning? How about "wicked" or "sick" now meaning "awesome." Do you think that is good? Making words that are used to represent bad things represent what is good, moving the language to more insidious expressions. What about promote cursing or the idea that words don't matter because "they are just words," then ridicule words of goodness as old-fashioned. This slowly removes the ability for people to express goodness and its viewpoint and their ability to defend themselves. Is it far-fetched? I know. It seems like it. But the forest doesn't die in one day. It dies one tree at a time. One person at a time. Dumbing down people until the balance tips. Then it will quickly escalate to a race to the bottom. Once the culture's language becomes a soup salad of nonsense, the people will be in a state of confusion. Unable to put logic together to defend themselves against any ideological attacks.

They are making the masses impotent intellectually.

Making them unteachable in the deeper subjects of life.

Making good ideas hard to teach to the new generation. Taking away words that express these concepts, which will die once the teachings can no longer be expressed.

words = ideas = knowledge = civilization

If you lose your words, you will lose your ideas, knowledge, and ultimately your civilization.

Think about those civilizations that protect goodness and individual liberty. These societies are natural enemies of darkness. Evil people have to operate hidden and, if caught, risk their lives and their freedom. They yearn for an open society where they can do anything they desire. But how do they transform a fairly peaceful world and its citizens? Consider the key features that hold a society together. Is it not shared values? Common ideas that bring people together? Now follow the rabbit down the hole and realize that a society can be destroyed by changing the meaning of words. Twist the words. Take truth and mix it with a lie. Confuse the language or, even better, take ideas and truths and flip them. Especially if you can cook up some emotional soup for why. No logic is needed, only a simple slogan that has a ring to it and sticks. Something easy to remember and with a common positive meaning. Then force its association to the flipped words and ideas while silencing anyone daring to speak against it.

Adolph Hitler wrote in his *mein kampf* about the idea of the "big lie." How Jews and Marxists would speak falsehoods and use the principle that there is always a certain force of credibility in the big lie. Because the broad masses of a nation are always more easily corrupted by their emotional nature than consciously. With the primitive simplicity of their minds, they more readily fall victims to the big lie than the small lie since they often tell small lies but would be ashamed to resort to large-scale falsehood. It would never come into their heads that someone would fabricate colossal untruths, that others could have the impudence to distort the truth so infamously. Even if the facts were brought to their minds, they could continue to think that there may be another explanation.

I heard of this famous idea since I was young and, superficially, thought I understood the idea. But I never really understood nor had any idea how true it was. On the contrary, in my mind, I thought I was wiser and more clever than those masses Hitler spoke of. But I was wrong. I didn't understand until I saw it myself. How my mind had been affected by big simple lies, and they were a part of my beliefs as if they were mine. I was deaf to any thoughts contrary to them for a long time.

These "idea lies" make people deaf to truths by putting traps in their heads, stopping thoughts that could lead them to the truth. Like a labyrinth, these parasitic ideas block an attempt to see clearly, leaving them confused unconsciously but consciously certain the lies are truth. It is mind control. Stopping people's freedom of thought until they eventually have no ideas of their own. Making the very thought of trying to question ideas a psychological crime, creating deep anxiety and fear. Done long enough to a person or a society, self-expression will end and ultimately free will, making you unable to defend yourself.

Leaving society unable to defend itself.

Which is the first step for evil to be able to take off its mask.

The second step? Devaluation...

Once you cannot defend yourself, evil will make you devalue yourself. Make your brain a mush of cowardice, self-doubt, and self-hate. Unable to see clearly, as if in a state of sleepiness. After that, evil will be able to fully unmask right in front of people. Most would obey blindly, unable to understand what is happening or unable to defend themselves. When bad things start, which are bound to happen, they will blame those they were told to blame.

Would you fall for it? Don't think so? Don't be so confident.

Ask yourself, Do I value myself? How hard do you think it would be for someone to manipulate you into devaluing yourself? Especially if you know you try to be a good person. A giver who cares about others. Given that knowledge of yourself, could they do it? Even a little bit? The hint is that it is all about turning a lie into believed "truth" by confusion. It stops your mind and common sense from seeing through the lie.

Let us try a thought.

Ask yourself again, Should I value my life?

I hope you answer yes.

Now ask yourself, Does evil want me to value my life? What happens when you don't? I believe you would agree you are less likely to defend yourself. Evil can do whatever it wants with you. Thus, you would indirectly serve evil's purpose. To destroy and to control... YOU.

But how can evil accomplish this?

It would seem too obvious if they were to tell you, "Do not value yourself. You are worthless. I'm the one you should follow. Submit to me. Do what I tell you to do. You have no power. You cannot take care of yourself. Let me take care of you so I can control you and use you as I want."

Would you follow this person? Highly unlikely. Even for the weakest and obedient person. Darkness needs to lure you in. Remember, evil NEVER shows its true intentions at first. Not until it has absolute power over you or is forced to show its hand.

So how does evil then make you NOT value your own life?

By using your self-doubt against yourself. Confusing you.

As an example, they could tell you only a very selfish person would ONLY CARE about themselves and then follow up with this question to you: "What would you choose? If you had to pick between either you dying or ten people dying? Would you save yourself and live and sacrifice the lives of ten people?"

Take a moment and analyze the question. The manipulation forces you to choose to either kill ten people or yourself. If you are good, the very choice to kill ten people is horrific. Perhaps you say, "I'd kill myself!" (because I'm good and could not kill anyone). At this moment, you have already devalued yourself a tiny bit. Both in terms of relationship with the person/group who asked you the question and your mindset. Because each time you pick a group's value higher than yourself, you are letting go of a tiny bit of power from yourself to the group. You are strengthening the group's power and weakening your power and value. With each question and manipulation, you are being drawn into submission no matter how small and insignificant. At some point, the scale of who's most important will tip from you to the group. Both from the group's perspective AND, more important, yours. When this happens, you will no longer have control of your own life. Your life will not have value. Your value will be what you can do for the group or person. Evil now has power over you, and it will appear that you have no RIGHT to choose for yourself. THAT would make you very selfish and BAD.

But what if you don't allow yourself to be manipulated? What if you choose to value your own life in the question at play? Choose your life as more important than ten other people. It might even make you feel a little guilty to say: "I'd rather live and have ten random people killed." But you take the decision and the risk to LOOK BAD and perhaps selfish. You might have avoided the manipulation so far. But let's see how far you can go. To your answer, the person/group gives you a new question. "What would you then pick, your own life or random ten thousand people? Would you rather die yourself and save ten thousand people? The ante is up. ten thousand people! That is a town of human lives. Lives with families. Probably a lot of good people, innocent lives.

How could you possibly not want to save them? It would be arrogant and very selfish, yes even evil, to put ten thousand people to death for one's own little life. Most might choose to save their lives and feel good about themselves. In this simple mind play, they just showed that they'd be a martyr. Ten thousand humans are certainly more important than one's own life.

Again, you have valued your own life as less than the group.

HEAR NO EVIL

Your purpose in life is to protect yourself and value your life. Be good to yourself. Take care of yourself. This strengthens good people because it takes power away from evil. Your own life is more important than any group or person. No matter how large. Your life is priceless. Evil values the group, never the person. There's no power in the person, but in the group, absolute power can be achieved. Evil will never want you to value yourself. That would mean you are not submitting to it but instead listening to yourself first. Evil, at the same time, cannot look for its value because it has none. It is void of value. A hollow hole full of rage, resentment, jealousy, and fear. So evil's mission is to destroy any goodness in people by making them weak. Use their self-sacrificing nature against themselves and make people devalue themselves. Either through culture, through group pressure, shame, guilt, or force. And by asking questions like the previous thought exercise.

So next time a similar question comes your way, value yourself highest and teach them your goodness won't be manipulated by group guilt. Each of those abstract lives are individuals and have the right to self-love and protect themselves, including you. Now think about it a bit further. Notice how your emotions reacted to it? Did you feel slightly uncomfortable with this simple thought experiment? I know I did in my thinking. And that's how they get you through wordplay and misleading analogies. They make you devalue your opinion and ability to protect yourself as an individual. All through simple words and making you confused through guilt. Unable to "hear" the truth and decipher what is right and wrong.

From now on, try every day to notice around you how words are used to manipulate, whether it is about changing meanings or to deceive, which leads to the idea of primers. Manipulative people often use words to "prime" the receiver before a lie.

Primers neutralize the lies.

Words are used to blind people to the truth. These words and what could be called primers come before the lie. If you can notice the primer, you can reverse their meaning and often expose the lie and agenda of the liar if you dare to see the truth. We talked about it with the traps in the prior chapters. But be careful. It is not easy. Primers are very powerful in that many people have not developed the skills needed to judge situations or do not have the guts to follow through thinking-wise. The good thing is that once you know the pattern, it will become more obvious, and you'll start seeing it everywhere in media, marketing, politics, strangers. Sadly, you will also see this with your friends and family.

How does a primer function?

It works with a few words being inserted prior to the lie, that prepare the mind to accept it. Putting the listener's mind at ease or uses guilt to make them mentally accept the next part, the lie. If your mind does not detect it and miss to put a flag of caution, it will be taken as accepted truth and become the Trojan Horse in your mind, leaving your ears covered and unable to know the truth.

Primers also work for nefarious groups and organizations. Look through history, and you will notice many primers with violent groups. They often name themselves something positive and true but then say you are evil if you disagree with their political position. Thus putting people in the intellectual, moral position of either bowing to the organization or being vilified. It is a false dilemma through manipulation. But for many who have not been trained in verbal kung fu, these simple mind tricks can imprison people and make them afraid to stand up for the truth. It is about deceit. As I write this, one example right now is the political group called 'Black Lives Matter.' We can all agree that the phrase ' Black Lives Matter' is true unless you are racist. And that is exactly what they want you to think. Now they have you, unless you see through their manipulation. They took this simple, true statement as a slogan and used it as the name for the organization. Thus setting up the primer for a large group of people to believe BLM's movement is true and good. If you find videos of supporters of BLM, you will see them repeating these words as if the organization is for Black lives. "Yes, I support Black Lives Matter!!". But when confronted with slightly more complex questions such as "What about Black cops, defunding police and those blacks killed by other blacks? Do they matter for BLM?". They will quickly deflect or not answer and get mad. You cannot reach them. No talking points or facts can change their understanding. They let 'Black Lives Matter' primer into their heads and connected it with their own personal, painful experiences. Once accepted, it takes a lot of inner work to see through and escape. The primer has caught the ego's tail... closing a person's ears and mind.

It is human nature. We are all very good at self-deception for endless reasons. Life is scary, and it takes courage to listen. It is a lot easier for us to cover our ears. When we listen, we are more likely to get hurt or find a painful truth. We don't like bad news. We want the world to be harmless. We want the world to be easy. So many walk through their lives in a state of denial of the world. It is the famous saying, "People hear what they want to hear." And this favors pathological people's attempt to control and manipulate us all through words, language. Re-educating us to believe four fingers are five. Leaving us unable to defend ourselves and giving evil people the opportunity to devalue us. And we will often do it for them. Once we have the toxic ideas in our minds, we will begin to self-doubt so much that we will become unable to see clearly and will now defend evil instead of ourselves.

This sets up for Stage 4 of evil unmasking itself, getting ready to take power away from us. Our perception of reality would likely be twisted so much, many will not see.

If we were to ask people during this phase in a safe setting, I would hope many would know what is going on, but be too scared to speak up.

But we must not allow this to happen. We must work on our courage to open our ears.

And prepare to speak.

CHAPTER 17

SPEAK NO EVIL

Once you can see and hear, the spell will be broken... mostly.

But the monkey with its mouth covered is the hardest step.

You will see the world for what it is—The real world. Not the fantasy world of make-believe. A bittersweet reality. Its ugliness is unavoidable to see each day. You will see trauma and abuse everywhere. But you will also see the light in a new and brighter way. Suddenly, the kindness you receive from a stranger has purpose and meaning. Love becomes stronger and more powerful because you know its value and how precious it truly is.

Though the world will be more clear, it will still be foggy and confusing. It takes a lot of energy to keep seeing and hearing, being disciplined in knowing your flawed ability to see the truth. But you are still miles ahead of the majority of the population who can neither see nor hear and do not understand the evil around them through their indoctrination. It is a mystery. Deep down, they know to fear it, but they have been brainwashed. The spells are real. Their brains block the train of thought if they get close to any realization of the truth. Just as they are about to grasp it, it is walled off and quickly fades away.

You are now ready to hear the last part... SPEAK NO EVIL.

And this one is about courage, and knowledge.

You need your courage to speak up, and you will need the knowledge to be able to speak correctly and defeat the lies and the twisted truths that people have been programmed with.

It is not a small task.

You need to not only be able to see their masks and how they lie to you with words but also understand how they operate and set up their games. We have gone through some of this, but let us look at it from another angle to better understand how they trick us. So we can gain the knowledge to defend and go on the offense.

The first part is the hardest. It is the one that we all struggle with.

Courage...

It doesn't matter how good we try to be. If we do not dare to speak and take action, goodness is meaningless. A great majority of us lack courage. It is not surprising. Courage is hard. There are many things to fear, and for good reasons. Life is dangerous, and speaking up against something wrong means you no longer can hide from the bullies who want the truth untold. A target will be put onto you, and you must be ready for the 'attention' of daring to rock the boat.

So why bother?

Let someone else do the job. There's always someone else who will stand up. Why be the one and risk losing one's lunch? Life is too short to become involved. Besides, it all is out of our hands. Mix with the crowd and let someone else take the beating. If they win, great. If they don't then it wasn't us. I think we all have those thoughts, especially in the heat of the moment. It takes a lot of bravery to take action. I know I have failed myself too many times. I wanted to be courageous, but I wasn't. The seconds when it mattered, I didn't do it. I had spent years, days, and hours thinking about how I would be brave. But when the moment came, I wasn't. My fears froze my actions. I would then spend hours afterward thinking about what I could have done, which frustrated me and strangely satisfied me when I thought about what I should have done. These human flaws are our greatest enemy. We all have them, more or less, and I know I battle them every day. The fire inside me was there, but it was not big enough to overcome my fears. The author Michael Hopf came up with the wise saying, "Hard times create strong men; strong men create good times, good times create weak men, and weak men create hard times." Some criticize Hopf's idea, but I believe they fail to see the truth or don't want you to see the truth in it. Look at yourself. When you had it comfortable in life, did you take the easy road or the hard road? In the same way, when you had no choice and your life was tough, did you grow? What are your proudest moments? Reflect on the easy life events or when you did something truly hard. You know the answer when you do the tough and right thing.

So again, why bother?

Because you know it is the right thing.

Now for those who are reading this? and saying, "well, come on. My society isn't this bad. I don't see evil around me. I am one person, and there's not much anyone can do." This answer is exactly what those who want chaos want to hear. They need people apathetic. It brings excitement to them when they see people blind to the subtle darkness everywhere. Taking the easy road. Hoping the bear won't come for them. Together with this attitude comes escapism. Spending lots of time being distracted from the real world, with a strong unwillingness to recognize the world as it is, and hating those who expose the real world. It is human nature. The more we try to escape from the truth, the less we want to face ourselves. And because of this, we need even more to build up our false selves. Should anyone question us or, perhaps worse, take action that we should have taken, the fear in us will express itself through anger and self-righteousness without any sense of shame. We become worse human beings. Author Jake Thoene said it well. "Apathy and evil. The two work hand in hand. They are the same. Evil wills it. Apathy allows it. Evil hates the innocent and the defenseless. Most of all, apathy doesn't care as long as it's not personally inconvenienced.". Author Theodore Dalrymple dealt with this in his book *Life At The Bottom*. He was a British physician working in a poor area of London. When he retired, he started writing about his experiences with the English lower class and, in his own words, "the cult of stupidity." He explained how one student, who ended up in his hospital from an overdose, was told, "You're stupid because you are clever." Take a moment to let that one sink in. They meant anyone who tries hard at school is dumb for wasting their time. He also emphasized there was a threat behind the "joke,"telling her to change her ways or get beaten up.

Those lost cannot allow anyone else to see. Through intimidation and violence, they will test your courage. And apathy and escapism will look very attractive when the other choice has little reward but plenty of sacrifices. Evil wants us to be tempted by the easy road. To be drawn by the siren's song of "none of this matters. You are only one person." Slowly letting you become part of it, serving evil even if you are not evil. And finally, should you try to speak up? You will be bullied for doing so.

It's not only "why bother?" it's also 'don't you dare!'

It is about silencing the few.

Even if we have little courage, remember that courage is like a muscle. We all have it, but some are stronger than others. For those who are weak, look for the brave ones and find out what made them courageous. Because no matter what. There will be a point in your life, unless you are especially lucky, that you will face troubles and darkness will come looking for you. Through small life moments or, God forbid, bigger events. Don't be the fool who thinks the bear won't come for you. It will come for you. Like the poem written by Martin Niemoeller: "They came first for the communists, and I didn't speak up because I wasn't a communist. They came for the Jews, and I didn't speak up because I wasn't a jew. Then they came for the trade unionists, and I didn't speak up because I wasn't a trade unionist. Then they came for me, and by that time, no one was left to speak up." Niemoeller was a submarine commander during World War 1 and an anti-communist who initially supported the early Nazi party until they turned against the church. Hitler had him arrested in 1937, and he was put in two concentration camps until 1945 and narrowly escaping execution. Had the war lasted longer, there is little doubt he would have been among the many thousands slaughtered.

So take some time to reflect. The bear is real. Especially if people keep silent, the bear might take ten years, maybe fifty years, to get to you. But it is patiently waiting until enough stay silent. State regimes murdered millions in the twentieth century. One of the ugliest centuries in human history. But because there has been a lot of good at the same time, we tend to forget. It only takes a few generations to cover up horrific events. Rudolph Rummel, a writer who coined the phase "democide" for mass genocides by governments, wrote of his overwhelming feelings when collecting the data for his studies and books: "Regime after regime, ruler after ruler, murdering people under their control or rule by shooting, burials alive, burning, hanging, knifing, starvation, flaying, beating, torture. Year after year, Not hundreds, thousands, not tens of thousands of these people. But millions and millions. Almost 170,000,000 of them, and this is only what appears a reasonable middle estimate. The awful toll may even reach above 300,000,000. The equivalent in the dead of a nuclear war stretched out over decades."

Were you aware of this? If not, ask yourself why? Sure, you knew about the World Wars, but were you taught about the rest? And the size of the horrors everywhere? I know I wasn't.

When we get beyond a few hundred people, the deaths become numbers too impossible to understand. The numbers are too big for us to comprehend. We are so far removed that understanding its evil can't be done. But we cannot allow that. I don't know if your heart has grown cold over the years or if you are in touch with to your feelings. But I want to encourage you to get in touch with the truth of these numbers. I need you to take time to visualize with me and see, feel, and imagine.

Think of someone you love deeply. The one who comes to mind first. It can be your son or daughter, wife, husband, mother, or father. Now imagine them right in front of you. You are on your knees, feet, and hands tied. They are on their knees, looking at you. A man in black is next to them holding a rifle against their head. Say their name, then say how much they mean to you. Tell them your deepest heartfelt feelings and then, tell them goodbye as you imagine them being shot and executed in front of you. The ground before them opens up as they fall into the grave. But not one grave. A mass grave. Now imagine the next person you love, saying goodbye and them being executed. One excruciating minute for each loved one murdered. Now eight foot graves are opening up as far as your eye can see. If you were to spend one minute by each grave and walk along with them, you would spend three hundred to six hundred years, many lifetimes of goodbyes. Walk ten to twenty times around the Earth from grave to grave to reach the number of innocent people murdered by governments, dictators, and rulers in the twentieth century. Remember, it's not fiction. It is all very real.

We cannot allow these murders to be silenced or forgotten.

We must fight! But how?

If the majority of people do not have the courage? Then what? We all know too many didn't say anything and instead looked away. It is a cliche, but it is true. How can we gain more courage in society? How can we learn from the brave? The answer is to fight as a group. A few courageous leaders can unite people to do better. Many "arrows" cannot be broken as easily as one single arrow. You likely have heard this saying from the Greek story of Aesop: "If you cooperate and stand united, no one will be able to break you. If, on the other hand, you quarrel with one another and act on your own, it will be easy for your enemies to break you."

And our enemy DOES want to break you and me.

So yes, uniting together and being a bundle of arrows is one answer to courage. It grows when you know you are not alone. In a large crowd, if one person stands up. The odds are a few more will stand, and given enough time, a majority could stand.

Swinging the balance towards the light.

But first, we need to heed a warning. Groups are also the way through which evil will gain power. There are many dangers in groups. We must always ask ourselves, What is the glue that makes the group stick together? Watch for cynicism and demonetization of another group of people. Especially if it is targeted. If there is any demonetization, seek out the truth yourself. There are good reasons to demonize someone who is evil. But evil is a master at projecting their intentions, and they use demonetization very effectively towards good people, groups, and anything that stands in its way. One good way to detect bad groups/people but also to use as a guide for doing the right thing when speaking up requires one to ask this question:

What is judged? Ideas or people?

What does a group or a person hate or criticize? Do they judge the message/idea, or do they judge and criticize the person? Where does the blame go? This will show the darkness or light. Darkness will go straight for cruel judgment of people. And the more power it has, the more vicious it will be unless the culture has caught up with its ways and is forced to be extremely deceptive.

So when speaking up...

ALWAYS judge the message. NEVER judge the messenger.

It is a prudent and honest way to see the world.

There can be a messenger with a bad message. The messenger might not even know. We all are so easily misled. Toxic ideas rarely come with salt but with sweet sugar and tempting hones-sounding ideas. They are like the sirens of the ocean, tempting the sailors. And in the end, it is always the message that should be looked at. So when a good friend, a teacher, a parent, or a stranger comes to you, tells you an idea. Judge the idea. Be critical and protective. Not towards the messenger but the message. It can be a good message or a bad message. Your judgment can be correct or incorrect. But it brings the odds in your favor. Same with the other way around. If a criminal, who might have many bad qualities, offers you an honest truth or a good advice then you could miss their gift if you judged the message by who they were. It brings up the old saying. "Never judge a book by its cover." It is good old advice. It doesn't mean the message cannot be bad when the messenger gives you a bad feeling, nor that you shouldn't believe your friends. It just means judge the idea on its merit.

It helps with speaking up and courage because it removes the personal aspect. Now, my anger is so much less when I am faced with very emotional and toxic ideas. I am better able to separate the people from the group and its ideas. Even if they are part of it and supporting evil. I feel I am also better at looking at groups and seeing if they are healthy or not.

What are their ideas? Their messages?

Are they vague? Do their messages, and slogans easily fit into anyone's issues and inner workings? Feelings? Look for very simple words. Look at how the group is being formed and by whom. What is their history? Both in words and in action. Do they divide? Do they lie? Is their message and what they "stand for" the same as their actions? How does the group treat its members? Look for any hidden abuse within it, especially from the top.

Evil seeks power over people, and groups are an easy way to influence its control.

A dark group desires one mind. Utter control. The needs of the group replace all the members needs. It might be difficult to imagine for a healthy person. But these ideas of bowing and obeying a "higher" purpose are tempting for those who come from difficult lives. Being lost and having a hard time figuring out life is painful. Those who want to escape their responsibilities see a hardcore group as a safe haven where they can be invisible yet heard and seen at the same time. They become one with the group. The group's strength becomes their strength. Looking in the mirror will no longer be scary because they will see the group and not themselves. This is why any of these groups need strong visual representation and easy slogans that can be regurgitated. Once joined, the individual ceases to exist. They can do no wrong. They cannot be responsible and thus, can let out their inner pathology, rage, and malice with the protection of the group. In fact, it will be encouraged without words. No need to say it. It is understood between the members, which is exactly what the leaders of these groups want. They want to use lost people as a great machine of destruction. Use their hate and anger towards the world. Creating empty vessels for their slogans. Someone who will scream any slogan, the more ambiguous the slogan, the better. So it can fill any hole that the member might have. All for the collective and their revolution or ideology. Leading the way to a free world of violence where evil can reign.

So watch out. Groups, like individuals, can often be deceiving. Gaining courage from the wrong one will ultimately lead to self-doubt and the destruction of courage. And it can happen to anyone, no matter their intelligence. Brainwashing is not to be underestimated. So if you join a group, ask yourself, What am I seeking in the group? And what is the group, especially the leaders, seeking in me? Is it "In unity" or "in bondage." Look for their symbolism, like a logo or written principles. These will often show a glimpse of who they truly are. But as always, watch out for the lies. It will most likely be a mix of truths unless the group already has a lot of power.

But you might be asking. "Will those who are lost joining nefarious groups not find themselves stronger, even if they are used by them? Won't they get stronger when they are part of the group and protected by the group" No, they will not be stronger. It's the opposite. Their inner weakness will grow bigger. Their inner hole, deeper. Evil, by its deepest nature is utter fear, expressed through the most horrific silent or not-so-silent rage. The individual members in a dark group can never be made strong. It will not be allowed. It will only be for the collective and a hierarchy of power at the top. From this, the hypothesis is that decent groups can be found through whether they are for a collective mind only or for individuals.

But why this conclusion?

The idea is rooted in the understanding that individualism can grow benevolent courage based on the self, while collectivism, by its nature, must crush any self-image. A dark group's main purpose is power over others, and there is NO power in individualism and individuals getting stronger.

At first thought, you might think that is wrong. Isn't individualism bad? Think about what you might have been told.

If you live in the Western culture, perhaps you have noticed the value of individualism disappearing. It is thought of more and more as selfish. Creating an egotistic and immoral world where people want everything for themselves and envy others. A world of wolves and profit. The idea is that IF an individual is ALLOWED to think about his own individual needs first and not the group, they would rarely want to give to others and naturally only take. If encouraged, people would eventually be full of greed and stop helping others and only take for themselves.

On the other hand, in some people's minds, the idea of collectivism is a loving community where everyone is taken care of, and there's little envy. A place of peace where the group is valued over the individual and no one thinks of themselves. A place of true altruism. Not a perfect utopia, but close enough. A place of social justice.

If one doesn't think too much about it, it is understandable how some are attracted to this idea. Indeed, we cannot live by ourselves. We need a community where we can help each other. We are social beings. So on the surface, it holds many truths, and this is likely why so many believe it. Especially those who were abandoned by those who should have loved them the most; parents, family, friends, and even society.

But it is a lie, in my opinion.

The word itself is a primer. Collectivism is not a collective. It is a herd for the wolves to use and for the most power-hungry to control. Study the history of political collectivism, and you will find an ugly past. The truth is that a group in itself is an abstract idea, which means the group doesn't exist without the individuals. The individuals are the ones who make up the group, and it is they, who give the strength to the group, only if… each individual is allowed to be themselves, for them to pursue their happiness and do what is right for them. This means, look out for themselves, take care of themselves first, take responsibility for their actions, and grow and challenge themselves first. If the group allows this, the group will be very strong because each arrow is strong on its own. But mighty strong together. On the contrary, dark groups function very differently. They work through fear and obedience. You are a body and an object to use. You can easily be replaced, and, if you dare to go against the group's constant chants and orders, you will be bullied, laughed at—or worse, beaten or killed, depending on what is at stake.

So think about it again and go deeper.

I firmly believe individualism is good.

It speaks to the truth of the world we are in. Whether you believe in GOD or not, it is clear we were given a mind and a heart for us to develop and find our way through life. We are our own little vessel, and we must learn how to take care of ourselves. Once we do, we can achieve many great things, including helping others. But think of yourself first. Not in a selfish way, but in a loving and caring way. This point is important. To care for yourself first is not selfish. It is the opposite. It is good and natural. Yes, we have a selfish side. It is one of many flaws we have as humans that we need to learn to tame. It is our ego. But at the same time, if we do not have it, it leads to no good. We become targets and victims. We cannot help others who deserve it since our energy will be taken by those who see our selflessness and weakness and use it against us. Consider the narcissists in our society who exemplify selfishness. They are the true selfish ones. Shaped by an utter lack of love and stability in life, where their ego and self were never able to see themselves in a positive light. Stuck in a little child's world that never went beyond themselves. In truth, they grew up in abuse and hatred to the point that their inner heart learned there was nothing to love.

So an important step to gain courage is to learn to care for ourselves more.

When we try to love ourselves, we learn who we are. The fear of looking inside will lessen and give us the chance to see ourselves in a more honest light. See our faults, our weaknesses, and our darker sides. And from these depths, courage will grow. From an honest look at the world and knowing who we are, for good and bad.

This will not happen overnight, and fear will never go away, but with patience, our courage will become stronger. It will be hard, and you will be tempted a lot and fail many times. But with consistency, the mountain will move. Never stop. Build that fire. Know you can only build the fire if you are honest with yourself. Find your purpose for why you are doing what you are doing. Find your moral compass and find it early. It is vital you look for it during easy times because once you are tested and life gets tough, there will be no time to relax or breathe.

So prepare, prepare and prepare.

Look for the fire in yourself and anchor your beliefs firmly in the ground to create a moral compass that will keep you towards the light. I have thought about this often while writing this book. I pray I will be prepared and do the right thing. But I do not know. It is easy to say and so much harder to do. True heroes are heroes for a reason. There are so few of them, but they do exist, and they give us all hope. You might be one of them. I hope so. I want to believe there's a hero in us all. Deep in my soul, I know it is true because we have all carried too much in this life. So much pain. I see it all over. I see the suffering. I see the dead eyes of coldness. I see the sadness. But I also see the love and the joy. We must all fight to become the hero of our lives.

I can certainly speak of the lack and struggle of courage. My weakness lies with people and wanting to please them. Some call this being an empath, and it is true I often worry more about other people's feelings than my own. I will avoid speaking up when I know it will hurt someone or be painful, which unfortunately only makes things worse.

So yes, I have too many times been a coward. But the fire in me wants me to get stronger. I struggle against myself.

In my struggles I have found ideas that helped me...

One thing is to not look up or down.

Meaning, when you are trying to accomplish something or fight for something, the mountain and the challenge will test your courage by the sheer size and perhaps even dangers. But if you focus on your next step only, putting one foot in front of the other. The next rock, the next stepping stone. The more doubt and fear will not enter your mind.

For bigger decisions, you need to think long-term and consider them carefully. Prepare physically and emotionally. Do the things you know you should do to be ready. It is all within your ability and control. For the rest, let it go. Do not waste your energy on things that have not happened.

And finally, the last idea to gain courage and the biggest answer I can advise, since it has helped me the most—is a religious answer:

Seek God. Speak to him. Get closer to him.

Whatever faith you might have, trust in God. Find him and let him take the burdens that are too much for you. Know you are not alone and know there's something much bigger beyond this physical world. Do not fear men. Fear God. Fear the moment you face God and what you did wrong. What actions did you not take? Did you speak up when you knew you should? Or did you keep quiet? I am not here to make you believe one way or another. That is up to you. But I do want to share with you that God gave me courage. I was personally lost and broken. But a soul friend of mine took the time and, with much love, softened my shell and brought me closer to God.

God and the belief in something bigger than you is one of the most powerful ways to gain courage.

We can, and we must gain courage and seek knowledge.

So through God and the belief in something higher than yourself, grow your courage, like you were always meant to do. Build your skills and grow as a person. Take responsibility and be your own master. Find your moral compass so you know why you are going where you are going and why you stand when you stand. Tend the fire in your heart for the truth and yearn to seek it. Take self-defense classes that build your physical strength. Eat healthy food and take care of yourself first. Learn to watch your ego and be patient yet firm with it. Look for those who do better and are examples for us all. Those rare people, often regular people, are the true heroes we all need. You might well become one of them. And if you don't, know that is okay also. You have your place and your ripples will also matter.

But ONCE you speak up, prepare for the bullying. That is, if you live in a free society. Otherwise, the consequences are more severe. But that means your voice is dangerous. In a totalitarian society, truth is dangerous.

The small monsters will come for you in force and try to silence you. They will laugh at you, try to make you feel dumb. Don't allow them to drag you down. Respond with respect but firmly in the truth. Stay humble. What they think does not matter. They are not your audience. Your voice is for those who listen and are willing to hear you and those who have no voice out of fear or threat. Your voice will give them strength. If it gives them the courage to speak up or helps them get through another day knowing they are not alone, it all has great value.

We can easily feel overwhelmed by it all and think, What can I do? I am just a little person. But it is important to realize evil depends on good people to stay quiet. There are rarely enough of the monsters. They cannot do this alone without the silence from us all. Your voice, no matter how small, has a real impact. It is a real threat to evil. So use it. Especially if you have been a victim. Use the anger, not for chaos but for motivation and courage.

They will attack you. Make you doubt your judgment and mind, saying "You are crazy." The whole trick is to make you doubt your intuition and ability to see the truth. It is a subtle but effective way to manipulate people who naturally try to do the right thing, targeting your healthy nature of questioning yourself.

If that doesn't work, they will intimidate you, smear you, lie about you. and demonize you.

And it works. We, as humans, listen and trust gossip too often. It is entertaining to hear about other's trouble and mistakes. But should we believe what is said? Should we repeat things we don't know about? We can only truly know our own experiences and knowledge. The rest is trusting the information. So be aware and careful with that. How many times do we repeat things we have heard without thinking? How many times do we judge people based on gossip? This goes back to fair judgment if it's a public person. Research and listen to their own words. If it is a close friend or family member, go and talk with them.

But this is not easy, which is why this is effective. Demonization brings fear in people who hear the rumor. They become afraid to ask and to know more. We are more likely to stay away from the person than speak with them. Same with public people. We often are more likely to believe the rumor and ridicule them without even knowing if they said it or not. Which, in return, hurts our ability to find the truth.

Which is EXACTLY the purpose. It keeps you away from other views and possibly any dangerous information to evil people or groups, the truth about them and the bigger truths about life.

Don't allow it. Never gossip. Never trust rumors. Research and stay humble in the truth of what you know and don't know. If you hear bad things about someone, then investigate. You might then hear with your own ears the ugly truth. But you might also find it was not true. A lie to confuse and mislead you.

Trust what you know, see, and hear from the real sources.

Lastly, when speaking up, understand that people do not see the world as you see it. We all come from different perspectives and experiences. We can only understand the world from our senses and how we were taught to view it, and from how we have learned to react and think. The world turns around each person, and until we have a way to enter another's mind, it will always be so.

If you know this, you know how to better work with people. Don't expect them to see your world or to even care. It does not make them bad nor evil. It is who we are. Most people don't even know their own world. How could they possibly see yours? How could they understand yours? So be patient. Be loving. Take nothing personally. If it is clear that some are not listening, then move on. Do not waste your time or energy. They are not ready to listen to others and might never be. Let them figure things out on their own. But do take the time with those who listen even if they highly disagree. Those are the ones you want to learn from and discuss and speak up to.

They will help you, and you will help them.

Are you ready?

The next step is to remove your hands of fear from your mouth and speak out, whatever it might be: child trafficking, domestic violence, government corruption, slavery. Or perhaps something that happened to you, big or small. Go where your heart guides you. Learn and speak the truth. Be ready to be wrong. Be your own worst critic but also your own strongest ally. Speak out. It will be awkward at first. You will feel uncomfortable. But know you are more than ready for the task as long as you stay with the truth.

Be humble and honest yet strong.

Seeing, hearing, and speaking. You are now ready for the fight.

SPEAK UP!

Warning! You will be wrong many times. So be extra careful. Stay self-critical and keep a check on your ego and your vices.

It is not about you; it is about all of us. Keeping evil in check.

I think the next chapters will help you see beyond the horrors and the bigger picture.

Perhaps a new perspective.

CHAPTER 18

IAN BRADY

It has been a long twisting road so far. The stories are disturbing and heartbreaking. No book can truly express the horrors of evil, and this is no exception.

But writing this book brought me to an unexpected alley. Not a dead end, but instead a way out. A truth I didn't expect to find. The desire was to put a spotlight on evil, and its influence on the world, which seems mostly asleep. But as I began to write and went deep into the darkest corners, I found answers that echoed louder and louder from different people. Ripples of truths. Answers from brilliant people who have largely been ignored or forgotten by our culture.

If you want to hold on to the taboos of our society, then I want to warn you. We cannot be honest if we are to be subtle and sensitive when dealing with evil.

The house of evil is raw, brutal. For a reminder of what lurks behind its walls, let's look again at evil.

This time, it is a house on 16 Wardle Brook Avenue, Manchester, England, which housed Ian Brady, a notorious serial killer from England who slaughtered five children plus his girlfriend, Myra Hingley. The words that come next are memoirs of Myra's brother-in-law, David Smith, who was a witness to the last murder.

David hears bone-chilling screams from the living room. Myra is yelling for his help. "Dave!" Ian is in the room, swinging a bloody ax over and over. "Fucking cunt. Dirty bastard. Fucking cunt!" An older kid is laying against the couch with blood gushing out from his head. "Mommy!" He falls to the floor and crawls under the table as Ian drags him out and swings his ax again and again. "Get the fucking dogs away from the blood, get the fucking things out of it.". The kid is lying on his face, dying. His head is completely destroyed. Ian kneels and strangles him, pulling an electric cord around his throat. David can hear rattles and gurgles as Ian pulls harder until there's silence.

"That's it, the messiest one yet," says Ian.

David goes on to recount that Ian is standing, breathing heavily, but casually looking at his hands drenches in blood. Ian passes the ax to David. "Feel the fucking weight of that. How did he take it?" David smiles at him. "Fuck me. I don't know." Inside, David is in shock. This can't be real. The brains of the kid are all over the floor, and he is standing, smiling at Ian. But it is very real. Ian looks at David with crazed eyes, his clothes full of blood, yet he is friendly and normal as if they were out in public. Myra's grandmother yells from upstairs about what is going on. Myra responds coolly, "It's all right, Gran, I dropped something on my foot. Just go back to sleep." Myra walks back into the living room and steps over the dead child as if he isn't there, and looks at Ian, who hurt his ankle. "Are you all right, love?" Ian answers "Yes, it's fine. I must have caught it, but I'm okay. Can you bring in the cleaning stuff?". Ian then looks at David, his eyes still demented. "There's a hole in the wall next to the fireplace. Put your finger in that. I felt the fucking thing bounce off his fucking head. That's when it swung back into the wall."

Ian, Myra, and David spend three long hours cleaning up the blood. The smell of the killing is strong in the air. It is a pungent smell of blood, brains, and defecation. Pieces of bone and black blood clots are picked up and dropped in a plastic bag. Ian straightens up and picks up his ax. He holds it in his right hand, then passes it to his left and back again, feeling its weight. He smiles at David and then puts it in its carrier bag. A great sense of relief rushes through David's body, but he holds back his emotions, staying calm and cold.

Ian grins, "That's it. We're finished. It's all done."

The victim was Edward Evans. Ian's fifth and last victim, and David Smith called the police the following morning.

Can you imagine the blood on the walls, the stench of the murder?

Let's step back for a moment and reflect.

Imagine this house on Wardle Brook Avenue. A common British house in a small town on the outskirts of Manchester. A place of beauty with its rolling hills and green trees. Yet within the walls of this particular house, something truly horrific happened. For a few hours, it became hell on Earth. But had you knocked on the door a week before, you might have been greeted with a friendly smile from Myra or perhaps a noticeable grin and rudeness from Ian.

You could never imagine the evil of these two.

And this is the problem we have. They were just another "nice" neighbors. Ian Brady, an aloof character, perhaps, but just another quiet guy. Certainly not evil. Yet he was. He was a true monster. What created the evilness in this man? Was he born evil? Did he choose to be evil?

Let us look at Ian's beginning.

What kind of family did he come from?

Details are hard to come by, but we know he was born on a Sunday, 1938. A pre-war World War II winter in Scotland. No father was named on his birth certificate. His mother, Margaret Stewart, was twenty-eight years old and single. She worked as a tea room waitress in a poor neighborhood. After only a few weeks, she put up a note offering one pound a week for anyone to look after Ian. The woman chosen was Mrs. Mary Sloan, a small housewife in her late thirties who was living in the slum area of Glasgow with her husband and three children. It is not clear when Ian was given to the Sloans, but we can guess it was a month to a few months from his birth. By all written accounts, the family was a nice and caring family. As one book states, "Ian spent the next sixteen years with his new family. The happiest time of his life."

Let us pause here. Almost all books refer to the Sloan family as a warm, nice, and caring family. Yet I believe we should ask how do they know? One source writes:

> *Margaret Stewart did her best to support the child... Mary and John took him into their warm and friendly home, where his mother, who now called herself Peggy, came to visit him every Sunday, bringing him clothes*

> *and presents. So it hardly seems that Ian Brady can be regarded as someone who was subjected to childhood abuse and brutality."*

Really? Staying open to the possibility, we must still ask ourselves how these authors can know this. Warm, friendly, nice, and caring aren't subtle words. It puts emphasis on a family who gave a lot of love and empathy. Yet Ian would later torture and murder children in cruel, sadistic ways.

Does it make sense to you?

The one problem we have is that we are not honest with each other. Calling a family warm and caring when we don't know, especially when it comes to murderers, doesn't help us see the truth. Maybe they were caring, but maybe they were not. Almost every book that talks about psychopaths puts loving words towards the parents without knowing the truth. It hurts our ability to find the truth. I only read one author, Emlyn Williams, who didn't put the Sloan family in an extremely favorable light. He wrote:

> *In a society where the fight for existence is unremitting, they were kind, as a family is to a pet... the kindness of indifference."*

Yet another author who worked directly with Brady thought Wiliams could not be more wrong. Who is right? Hard to know. For now, let's keep both options open.

Let's look at Ian's later childhood.

Ian would grow up knowing the Sloans as his parents. They were Da and Ma. On occasions, mostly on Sundays, his mother would visit. But she wanted to be named Peggy and not called mom. It is not clear to me if Ian knew she was his mother or not. Ian made the note in his book that he hated Sundays. He made a plot to murder a leading member of the Lord's day Observance Society in revenge for the miserable Sundays he had been forced to endure as a child. He hit puberty early at the age of 11 and told one author that he found joy in kissing so violently that both mouths bled. As a teenager, after threatening to kill his girlfriend, he was sent back by the court to live with his biological mother. Along with signs of his physical violence, his obsessions with books also showed a darker side. He taught himself German to read Hitler's 'Mein Kampf". We should reflect on this as he read it only a decade after the horrors of World War 2. He also enjoyed the works of Blake, Henry Miller, and even the obscure Marquis de Sade, whom we are familiar with from chapter ten. He would groom Myra and David with these books. Testing their appetite for cruelty, Myra passed with flying colors, but David thankfully failed so he could report the two to the police.

But we are back at our question.

What created the evil within Ian Brady?

Which road should we go down? The genetic road? Nurture and environment? Both? Do you see any signs of the answer? Brady seemed to have a decent foster family, even according to Ian Brady himself... His best years. Would he lie about this? Even if he was a pathological liar, we should ask ourselves why he would lie? Through the thick fog of not being able to go back in time and witness Ian Brady's behavior or what happened to him, we can still glimpse many signs of a disturbed, violent child.

We know he was a sadistic murderer, abandoned by his mother and raised by a foster family.

This reminds me of Beth Thomas's case from the short documentary *Child of Rage*. A six-year-old girl who had been adopted with her baby brother at the age of nineteen months old. The documentary showed a family and tapes from her therapy with Dr. Kevin Magid. In the therapy, she would explain how she wanted to hurt her little brother and her parents. At only six years old, her emotional state remained calm, yet what she said was chilling for any foster parent who might adopt a young child.

In the therapy session, when asked what her parents do at night, she calmly tells Dr. Magid that they lock the door so she can not hurt her brother or them. "Otherwise, I will try to stab them, stab them with a knife."

Dr. Magid asks, "Do you ever stick pins in people?" Beth looks briefly away and nods. In a short but firm tone, Dr. Magid asks, "Who?" Beth looks straight at Dr. Magid and replies. "My brother." Dr. Magid asks, "okay, do you do it a little bit?... or a lot?" Beth looks at him. "A lot," Dr. Magid continues, "okay, and what are you trying to do with your brother?" Beth pauses and looks down. "Kill him." Dr. Magid says, "Who else would you like to stick pins and needles into?" With no hesitation, Beth responds, "Mommy and Daddy." Dr. Madig questions further, "What would you like to have happened to them?" Beth answers "Die."

A sobering talk with a very innocent-looking six-year-old girl.

Tim and Julie, the parents, talked about how their dream quickly became a nightmare as they began to notice the troubling actions of Beth. They were told that Beth and John were normal and healthy, but the truth was very different. At seven months old, John was not able to raise his head or roll over as a baby. Beth seemed normal, but her sadistic side would take time to discover.

Looking at the parents, they come off as genuine. It is always hard to tell, but the mother, Julie, shows signs of utter fear and sadness in her micro-expressions. A sign that she is not in control. It is harder to tell from the father, but I don't pick up bad intent. If those impressions are true, then what is it? What can explain a girl wanting to torture her brother and kill her foster parents?

Maybe it is her genes? We hear about this all the time.

Let us go down this road more, the road of genetics and DNA.

CHAPTER 19

The MONSTER GENE

A GHOST OR REAL?

Maybe evil people are born. From genetics that makes them sadistic?

Is this the answer? To Ian Brady? Beth Thomas? To all the stories we have heard so far? Is evil simply bad luck in ones genes? Can certain genes explain what gives these people the desire to murder and destroy? If true, it is both a comforting and disturbing thought. Comforting for those who do evil because it would take away any responsibility of those who do bad. None of us can be at fault for our genes. It is disturbing for those who are decent because we would have no way to avoid it as a society or as a family. Could we trust the genetic tests? Would people be prosecuted for their genetics? A lot of ethical questions abound. Much of the media speaks of genetics as settled science, which is true for body attributes like our eyes and skin color. But is it also true for more complex issues, such as mental issues and human behavior that make people ENJOY hurting others? If you dig a little deeper in papers and science journals, you will find the science community at odds. The issue is that we do not have a much-settled understanding of mental disorders. Does evil fall into psychopathy or antisocial behavior? Even those terms are not well-defined. They overlap and both define patterns of behavior and "symptoms." Nothing wrong with terms. We need them for clear communication and getting closer to answers. It is important for science. For example, Robert Hare created the PCL (Psychopathy Checklist) and a pathway to help research malignant traits and diagnose people. But even with this work, there are disagreements and more new terms and views.

And here lies the problem.

If we cannot define the disorder, how can we define the genes?

Lionel Penrose, psychiatrist and medical geneticist, wrote in 1968:

> *The study of the genetics of schizophrenia is unsatisfactory from almost every point of view, with the first reason being that there is no certainty that the condition can be defined or even recognized."*

But you might say that was in 1968. We must have gotten further down the road, and you would be right. The human genome sequence was published in 2001. A much-celebrated accomplishment. It promised the holy grail for solving health issues, including discoveries in psychiatry and psychology. Stephen Faraone and his colleague, Ming Tsuang, wrote in 1999, "From the perspective of psychiatric genetics, The Human Genome Project is an immense factory, producing and refining the tools we will need to discover the genes that cause mental illness."

The only thing, it didn't happen.

In the book *Schizophrenia and Genetics* by Jay Joseph Psy. D., he goes into the details of the failings and the current crisis in the social and behavioral sciences, specifically towards schizophrenia.

There was a lot of hope that they would find various genes to be associated with it. But after decades of molecular genetic studies, all failed to produce a single gene that causes it. Timothy Crow, a schizophrenia researcher, wrote in 2008, "Success was inevitable one would drain the pond dry, and there would be the genes!" But he concluded, "The pond is empty."

Dr. Joseph continues with more examples of the problems. Though this is specific to the research of schizophrenia, it is still worth considering as it links to the understanding of the mind and sanity versus insanity. The major issue is with the science of the research itself. Stephen V. Faraone, who holds a Ph.D. in behavioral sciences, would describe the frustrating "non-replication curse" that had plagued psychiatric molecular genetic research for decades.

> It is no secret that our field has published thousands of candidate gene associations studies, but few replicated findings."

No secret? How many times have you heard of the struggles in genetic research? Dr. Joseph makes this clear observation "Non-replication is a secret because the general public has been told a very different story."

Sociologist, Aaron Panofsky, writes that molecular genetics "has been a major disappointment, if not an outright failure, in behavior genetics... This scientific failure has been a well-kept open secret."

As always, the public is told one thing and rarely the truth.

But genes! But science! are used as sprinkles in the daily word salad of the media. This is a tragedy for so many reasons. It kills the trust of the people, and it hurts science and stops us from finding the mysteries of life. If new generations of behavioral scientists are "encouraged" to stay in the lane and keep on the same road, even if the road has gone over the cliff, it will create corruption within science that will be hard to turn around.

We already see this.

So for those who have common sense and are not afraid to question the scientists, here are some new examples of behavioral, molecular genetic findings. Ask yourself why a human body built for survival and efficiency would use DNA/gene "space/memory" for these following associations... For example, a gene "association" to loneliness, a gene "associated" with predicting voter turnout, a gene that caused an increase of risk in joining a gang, a gene "associated" with credit card borrowing behavior.

On the surface, the absurdity is apparent.

What are your thoughts? Are we on the right road? Too early to tell? The road I see is very foggy. I know the view I am looking for. It is the one that will explain why Ian Brady's evil exists. Why all the evil that finds pleasure in torture exists. But I see no view. Only endless promises or vague "here we are" announcements with twelve-foot fog visibility of the valley. Part of the fog is the thick science. Perhaps, much of it is going over my head, and I fully admit I might be missing pieces. But it is clear to me there are big challenges with replicating the different gene hypotheses.

Maybe geneticists can't yet formulate their hypothesis in a clear and non-convoluted way. That doesn't mean they couldn't be right and are right in some aspects right now, but it does mean they do not yet see a clear picture of it or cannot explain this in any simple way. A LOT of abstract thought and giving names to abstract meanings is fine for setting up some organization of ideas, creating common words to help make headway for science to solve these big human biology questions. Still, it doesn't hold water for proofing anything yet.

And this highly wordy science can be used to manipulate the masses, much like it happened in the past with science. We always remember the good science and scientists but forget about all the bad ones.

It is like the math guy who lives in his own world of algorithms, trying to solve the universe. This might lead to some amazing new knowledge. But for most of it, it might also be a lot of loose ends. And for some... only loose ends.

So if something sounds convoluted, ask questions. Don't assume you are confused because you are dumb and not intelligent enough. Sure, that could be the case, but it could also be because the "genius" is lost in nonsense and has no idea what is up or down and has made a bunch of nonsense science salad. Too often, sounding smart is the goal. Endless words. It can be used as "intellectual" intimidation, making people think they are dumb and cannot follow because of a low IQ.

I think this might explain the gap between the public's perception of genes, and their success, compared to the reality of many decades of gene association studies with no replicated findings.

Biologist psychiatrist Robin Murray wrote that one of the mistakes he made in his long research career was to "follow the fashion of the herd" by thinking of "schizophrenia" as a discrete disorder. I expect to see the end of the concept of schizophrenia soon."

Powerful statement.

Is behavioral science doing the same with genetics overall?

Are they following the fashion of the herd blindly? Genes are popular, but do they have the answers for mental issues?

I believe we should give the benefit of the doubt and look at the true complexity of the tasks. All venues should be looked at. But with that in mind, the genetics/DNA field has far to go and much to prove before they can justify their current high acceptance in the psychology field. By the nature of genes being theories that hold zero responsibility to anything except to the abstract, it is an easy focus for those who want to push away from the already known abuse and violence. This is a clear truth. The violence is happening. But if genetic and chemical imbalances are what cause mental illness and psychopathy, then that is a gift to those who harm. It is also a gift to those victims who want to avoid the truth and hide the true violence in society.

DNA/chemical imbalances/genetic industry needs to continue with their work but need to be honest about their potential issue of knowingly or unknowingly helping the taboo, real violence, and keeping society ignorant. They must be held to a very high standard in reasoning and analysis.

The nurture/environment and neurologist studies do not have the same ethical issue as they do the opposite and put the spotlight on what is clearly happening: Abuse and violence in abhorrently large quantities.

And this matters!

Because if one cannot see clearly why something is… what it claims to be, the more likely it is to be false or misdirection. Sure the truth can be found within a fog, but sometimes the fog is smoke meant to cover true answers and direction.

CHAPTER 20

THE HIDDEN MOUNTAIN

As we are trying to discern what is true and what is not, we should keep asking ourselves whether we are on the right path or not.

If we are on the road of birth of Evil, what would we see on its path?

Would it not be victims?

A road littered with countless destroyed souls. The broken people among us, many of them unseen. Some with mental issues, hallucinations, hearing voices, a broken sense of reality and of themselves. Could these people not possibly have encountered evil? For a prolonged time? Possibly during the very important development time of a child?

Like the symptoms of schizophrenia.

Bertram Karon, Ph.D., in *"Take these broken wings,"* a film by Daniel Mackler, said:

> *I have never met a schizophrenic whose life wouldn't have driven me crazy if I had lived it. Not as the life is described in the hospital record by people who don't wanna hear what it was like. But the life as when I finally get to know what this person has experienced. There is no question I would be just as sick and in just the same way that this patient is... and in fact, I have never worked with a schizophrenic where I have not walked away from some sessions with a feeling my God, a human being has lived this way."* He goes on to say, *"If you are dealing with someone who's schizophrenic, you have to assume their life has been God awful. You also have to assume they are terrified."*

Terrified?

Let that sink in, and think about it. They ARE Terrified.

Not was, but ARE. Use your imagination. What would make someone terrified? Daily? Have you ever been truly scared? Not scared from entertainment but the fear of losing one's life type of scared. Cold sweat, fear that stops your ability to think. Your eyes lose focus. Your muscles shake... FEAR!

Does it match the road we are seeking? Does EVIL create FEAR?

Let's look at what the leading science says from The National Institute of Mental Health about schizophrenia:

"Many factors may cause schizophrenia, including: genetics. Schizophrenia sometimes runs in families. However, it is important to know that just because someone in a family has schizophrenia, it does not mean that other family members will have it as well."

Okay, so they start with popular 'genetics' and a very vague logic of "runs in the family" with a "not all members will have it." They continue: "Environment. Many environmental factors may be involved, such as living in poverty, stressful surroundings, and exposure to viruses or nutritional problems before birth." Poverty? Viruses? Prenatal nutritional problems? No doubt these can be associations, but do you think they are the causes? Stressful surroundings sound right, but the wording is clinical. They are too afraid to look at it honestly. Lastly, they put: "Disruptions in brain structures, brain function, and brain chemistry. These disruptions could be the result of genetic or environmental factors and, in turn, may cause schizophrenia."

It is a brain twister, for sure, at least for me. Nothing like a twisting sentence with a few key words people can repeat:

"Chemical imbalances!" or "genetic!"

If you think about chemical imbalance then ask yourself, what can I do to stop it? Nothing, right? That's the problem. End of story. Nothing more to see here. Move on. Convenient for evil, wouldn't you say?

And many believe it. Do you? If so, I don't blame you. We hear it over and over in popular culture and media. But take a step back. Think about where we have been, what you have read. Could all this be a chemical imbalance in the brain? A gene yet to be discovered?

What does your gut tell you?

Isn't there something seriously wrong with this world? If you think about it? Or maybe you don't see it? It is true it is well-hidden. I don't think Ian Brady's neighbor had any idea what kind of monsters lived next to them. Ask yourself, How many are near me?

None? One? A dozen? A few hundreds? Thousands?

Anna Salter, a psychologist, would express her concern when her eyes were forced to see something deeply troubling. After her Ph.D. in psychology, she went to a small town in New England with the hope of living a quiet country life. Help children with attention and behavior problems and sometimes consult for local schools. Maybe have a horse and keep a garden.

Things didn't go quite as planned.

What she found would shock her. The small town seemed to be the epicenter of abuse as she witnessed so much violence. Two out of three children she saw in the mental health center had been sexually or physically abused. The New England town had a tiny population of fifteen thousands. Yet it had a stunning number of incest cases, out-of-home sexual abuse, rape, physical abuse, neglect, and domestic violence. She would work the emergency line at night, and the violence was stark and very visceral. There was no running away from the truth. There was no denying what was going on. Unlike therapy sessions, this was in your face, gut-wrenching.

> " Over time, I developed the fantasy that my small town in New England was similar to the square mile in Mexico where all the monarch butterflies go; it must be, I thought, the center of violence in the known universe. It had to be. If the official estimate of violence were right. because there wasn't suppose to be that much violence anywhere, certainly not in small towns in the United States."

So was Anna Salter's little town unique?

She would continue:

> *In the years since, I've met many clinicians in different towns and cities all over the United States with the same fantasy that their own towns or cities were the center of violence in the universe. After a lecture on sexual abuse, a member of the audience will speak to me. "Do you think there's more sexual abuse in small towns?" She will say to me, puzzled, "We're seeing so much of it" A few minutes later, someone else will come up. "do you think there's more in cities," he would ask. "I just wonder because we get so many cases." This nation's dirty little secret, only now getting a small portion of attention because of the crisis of pedophilic priests in the catholic church, is the number of domestic violence, rape, and child molestation cases that are never reported to the police."*

At the time of her practice, during her awakening of the rampant abuse, the official estimate of child incest was that it affected one in a million! And during the many years of studying for her master's degree and doctor's degree at Tufts and Harvard in psychology, there was virtually nothing on child sexual abuse and physical abuse in any course she took! She had one lecture on the victims of child abuse. One lecture! And NO lectures about offenders. All the lectures she had during the years were on illnesses that are so rare that she never encountered even one in her twenty years of practice.

Take a moment to absorb those thoughts. If you have to, read the last paragraph again...

See the elephant in the room?

How can a major psychology and behavioral therapy field with their established institutions like Harvard be so wrong?

An oversight?

If only it was...

This is about the taboos we are not supposed to talk about or see. Just how Freud was ostracized for his book *Studies on Hysteria*. Academia with their master's degrees and doctoral degrees avoid in large parts the truth of just how widespread abuse and violence is in society. Only a few brave stand up and talk. Anna Salter was one of few who spoke. Another person who did the same is Daniel Mackler. He worked for ten years as a psychotherapist in New York but then decided to quit. He is now an author and filmmaker who wrote the books *Toward Truth* and *A Way Out of Madness*. In one of his many videos on psychology and life, he explains why he quit being a therapist.

> *I quit being a therapist because it was such a struggle for me to be a therapist in a system that was so messed up. The mental health system was not a healthy system, and that's the irony. It's a system that's supposed to help bring people who have mental health problems back toward mental health, yet the system itself is totally messed up and screwed up. The system presents itself as science, but it's not science. It's not even really social science. A lot of it is antisocial anti-science or maybe antisocial pseudoscience. For starters, therapists are supposed to diagnose everyone. I was a therapist in New York State, a licensed clinical social worker with my R letter, meaning I had six years of supervision*

> which allowed me to have the highest level of billing to insurance companies. Now social workers in New York have to diagnose everybody. They have to diagnose every client they see in therapy, and diagnosing people is incredibly stigmatizing. It can really actually cause people a lot of harm, and when you're in a field where you don't want to do any harm, why do you want to do something that's an intrinsic part of the field but actually so often harms people. Also, these diagnostic categories are quite arbitrary. Basically, you can stick most people in any number of these categories at any given time. So really what that does, that gives the therapists a lot of power to label someone with something that really doesn't have a lot of meaning."

It is, in many areas, sadly a BROKEN field of study.

It was one hundred years ago, and it still is today.

Alice Miller would become one of the leading voices in the late seventies speaking up about this. For many, she has been one of the most influential people talking about the unspoken truths. In her book *From Rage to Courage*, Alice Miller would write, "I no longer recommend psychoanalysts, because I feel that, unfortunately, they side with the adult and not with the child, as Freud did in his theories and his treatments. To recover from the tragic effects of child abuse, we need a well-informed witness who is not protecting the abusive parents." Alice Miller would get closer to the core in *The untouched key*:

> Several years ago I wanted to demonstrate that the works of writers, poets and painters tell the encoded story of childhood traumas no longer consciously remembered in adulthood. After having made this

> *discovery in my own paintings and in the writings of Franz Kafka, I was able to test it against other life histories. I wanted to share what I had found with biographers and psychoanalysts, but I soon learned that I was dealing with forbidden knowledge, by no means easy to share with "the experts"... And so I decided not to publish my study but to keep the knowledge I had gained by myself. Through these activities I gradually realized that my disappointment at the blindness of society and of the experts had something to do with my own blindness and that I really felt compelled to try to prove something to myself that a part of me refused to believe."*

And what was Alice Miller afraid to realize? That her own parents were not able to acknowledge the truth nor did they want to hear it.

> *For a long time, I couldn't stop hoping that my parents would someday be ready to share my questions with me, to stop evading them, react to them and not be afraid to join me in seeing where they led. This never happened when I was a child, and I thought I had long since gotten over my deprivation. But my astonishment at the reactions of people whom I had expected to be more knowledgeable revealed that I still had not given up the image of clever and courageous parents who could be convinced by the facts."*

This speaks to the greater truth.

Why this road to find the truth of evil is so hard.

There is a great amnesia in our world.

An amnesia in all of us. Some more than others. It is what keeps us from becoming stronger and healthier. It is the hidden world behind our psychological consciousness. The lost world of what happened.

An American psychologist, Arthur Janov would witness evidence of this amnesia from an event that would shock him and give him the insight to dig deeper. It was the crying scream of his patient as if he was being murdered.

The primal scream...

His patient, Danny, a young man in his twenties, during a group session had talked about a one-man stage show in London that fascinated him. In the show, the performer would wear a diaper and act like a baby drinking bottle of milk while screaming loudly, "Mommy! Daddy! Mommy! Daddy!" At the end of the act, he would vomit as the audience was requested to do the same in handed-out plastic bags.

Disturbing and disgusting, Yes. But in it hid a truth.

Picking up on his patients odd fascination, Janov followed through with his thought and asked him to do the same. "Try to call out loud, Mommy! Daddy!" Danny resisted. It would be childish. Janov kept on insisting for Danny to try, and finally, he gave in. As Danny started, he quickly became emotional. A deep, felt rush of emotions went through him as he started to say, "Mommy! Daddy!" Once he started, the emotions took over. Danny was squirming in pain on the floor. His breathing was fast and spastic as he continued screaming for his mommy and daddy. He appeared to be in a hypnotic state and was no longer in control. As his body would convulse, he finally let out a piercing, deathlike scream that rattled the walls of

Janov's office. The whole episode lasted a few minutes but left Danny feeling free, saying, "I made it! I don't know what, but I can feel it." Janov would spend time analyzing this incident and play the recording over and over. Still, even with his seventeen years as a psychologist and social worker, he could not explain what happened. The Freudian theories had no answers. After months, during a session with another patient, the idea returned to Janov when another patient, Gary, shared deep feelings about how his parents would always criticize him and mess him up. He had never felt they cared or loved him. Janov asked him to try to say out loud 'Mommy and Daddy.' Try to call for them. Gary felt it would be useless. He knew they didn't love him. Why bother? Janov insisted, and as Gary began without much confidence, his breathing became faster, and before he knew it, he lost emotional control. What happened next was similar to Danny. Spastic and near convulsions with a loud scream at the end. Both were shocked, and Janov now realized that what he thought was an accident must have more meaning.

Janov goes on to explain how he saw Gary being flooded with insights afterward. "This unsophisticated man became virtually another human being." Alert and insightful. His whole life began to fall into place right in front of Janov's eyes.

Though I suspect Janov is exaggerating in his book, I think there is no doubt he hit on a deep truth that we need to look at. He would call it the primal scream. The idea being that this scream is a product of the central nervous system, which brings into focus hundreds or even thousands of incidents that came out of hopelessness as a child.

It speaks of two things.

One, we have amnesia with a large part of our past.

Two, this past has mountains of unresolved emotions in it.

How to access it was found through Arthur Janov's curiosity and his openness to follow his hunch. He perhaps wasn't the first to do this, but he was someone who saw its importance and built a therapy around it, and briefly brought it into popular culture with John Lennon and others. This has great value even if one can argue whether he took it in the right direction afterward. My gut tells me he didn't. He took the surface idea and, unfortunately, promised a cure to those who were hurting. But that said, his primal scream insight was and still is true.

I say this because I found it myself.

I have always tried to work on myself psychologically as I work on my art, and when I learned about Janov through my best friend who was going to his institute, I read a few of his books. Like Alice Miller, I found much truth in Janov's writing, and I decided I wanted to try his theories myself. I knew I must have emotional pains towards my father. Since he was twenty-eight years old, he had multiple sclerosis, and I never remember seeing my father walk. The time I was born was the period where my father finally had to admit he would no longer be able to walk, and the wheelchair arrived. It was a very difficult period for both my dad, my mom, and my sister. He became extremely fearful of my mother leaving and became possessive for a period until my mother stood up and told him to stop.

I wanted to try to reach out to my dad, who had passed on, and tell him what I wanted to say as a child but never could.

I began to say "Dad" out loud and speak to him in heaven. I allowed myself to be vulnerable and open. Let any feelings that would arise... be. To neither fight them nor hold them back. I have, over the years, learned to let go even in my dreams. When everything inside you tells you to stop, you let yourself go. It is not about forcing yourself to stop. It is the opposite. It is going through the wall of stopping, if that makes sense.

As I began to talk to my dad, my tears began to flow. I felt a deep sense of sadness. Deep feelings surfaced on how I felt towards him; All the pain and suffering I saw him go through. It was pure love and wanting to save him. I remembered combing his hair. I remembered giving him the straw to drink, giving him food with the fork. I remembered tying his shoes and holding his legs down when he had spasms and pain. I continued speaking directly to him out loud, saying how much I loved him and how sad I was to see him hurt.

And then... I said something to him that broke me. It broke me completely. I didn't cry anymore. I was wailing on the floor. It was so strong it surprised me, but I didn't stop. Thinking as if I had wings, I opened them completely and fell into the abyss of my feelings towards my dad. It must have lasted a minute or two, and then a strange thing happened. I began laughing with the deepest joy, a wholehearted loud laugh.

I felt so good inside. I felt love for my dad, and I felt a sincere relief. After a few minutes, I began to calm down, and my mind was light. I was still giggling and just feeling high, but the analyzing "me" began to think back on just what had happened, and this is the strangest thing.

The thought that triggered it all was GONE. Completely gone. The sentence and words I had spoken out loud to my father I could no longer remember. I have, to this day, not remembered it again, but I know how true and powerful this small sentence was on how I felt towards my dad. It was both beautiful, deeply sad, and very powerful. But painful and too deep for my conscious self to be aware of it afterward.

The road that had opened in a second had fogged back in as quickly as it had shown itself to me.

So I can say with confidence that we have many mysteries and secrets in us, and they all hold powerful emotions and memories. One path to find them is to voice out loud the key primal word, spoken as the child you were, to the feelings you had back then.

Once you do and you let yourself be 1000 percent vulnerable, the labyrinth of your brain might open up and allow you to fall into those painful unvisited places that are buried deep beneath the mountain of walls and defenses.

Arthur Janov said it well:

> *I have come to regard that scream as the product of central and universal pains which reside in all neurotics. I call them primal pains because they are the original early hurts upon which later neurosis is built. I contend that these pains exist in every neurotic each minute of his later life. These pains often are not consciously felt because they are diffused throughout the entire system where they affect body organs, muscles, the blood,*

and lymph system, and finally, the distorted way we behave. Neurosis is a disease of feeling. At its core is the suppression of feeling and its transmutation into a wide range of neurotic behavior. The dazzling variety of neurotic symptoms from insomnia to sexual perversion have caused us to think of neurosis in categories. But different symptoms are not distinct disease entities."

And in this, I think we are on to something.

This could apply to evil as well.

CHAPTER 21

AMNESIA

The road we must go down, is, for many, a forgotten road. A road of amnesia that is hiding a broken world.

A deeply broken world...

It is much more broken than we think. With the Western world's clean streets, pristine houses, and great monuments, it is hard to realize this is true. Yes, the Third World countries are also broken. In some ways, more broken. But you will also find great beauty and love in the third world as any part of the West and sometimes more. It is not necessarily linked with a lack of wealth.

Amnesia is hiding truths we must understand.

It is now time for us to revisit Dr. Vincent Felitti and look at what he found. Another clue to the victims all around us, our amnesia and the great danger in speaking of it.

He was head of preventive medicine at Kaiser Permanente in San Diego and had created a risk abatement program that included a weight program. The problem he found was that he saw a high dropout rate, especially for those who had successfully lost weight. They would quickly gain the weight, and he could not figure out why. Desperate to help them and find the cause, he started interviewing people who chose to drop out. They were simple questions. What did you weigh when you were born? When were you in kindergarten? When did you become first sexually active? During one of these interviews, he misspoke and asked a woman, "How much did you weigh when you first became sexually active?" She said forty pounds and blurted out, "It was with my father." She began to cry and sob. The response shocked Felitti. It was the second incest case he had encountered in his twenty-four years of practice. Ten days later, doing more interviews, he saw another person with a similar story. In his mind, he concluded that it was unlikely to happen again. But over the next few days, he became disturbed as person after person shared stories of childhood sexual abuse. Felitti questioned his ears and eyes. This couldn't be true. Someone would have told him in medical school. One hundred eighty-six patients later, it turned out to be more than one out of two who had similar stories of severe abuse. Completely in shock, Felitti decided to have five other people interview another one hundred patients. Maybe he had somehow affected the results by the way he asked. But sadly, they turned up the same information. He brought up his finding to one of the people at CDC in Atlanta. They told him that no one would believe a study of only 286 patients.

Felitti could have left it at that and moved on. But he did not. Being a true doctor and courageous, Dr. Felitti took on the challenge together with Dr. Robert Anda at the CDC. Since he was in the department of preventive medicine, he had access to 258,000 adults. It was, in his own words, "fairly easy to ask 26,000 consecutive people whether they would be willing to help to understand more how what happens to people in childhood can affect their health as adults." I somehow doubt it was fairly easy. I believe few would have done what Dr. Felitti did. What he did was truly good and important. He created the Adverse Childhood Experiences Study (ACE). The largest study of its type. Trying to answer the question, How do you get from a newborn baby to a psychologically and physically broken man that we see and pass in the streets in our cities?

And what did Dr. Felitti find?

He found that adverse childhood experiences are remarkably common.

What is uncommon is the truth of this...

The truth remains well-concealed by shame, secrecy, and social taboo. Ask yourself, Have you ever heard of this study in the media? It has been more than two decades since it was released. But its significance cannot be underestimated. Adverse childhood experiences are the leading determinant of what happens to the health and social well-being of a nation's population. And Felitti didn't find adversity that was minor. As he puts it, it was on the heavy end of things, similar to what Alice Miller and Anna Salter found : mother's beating children with wires, wire coat hangers, or fathers punishing with fists, belts, or objects. And to what extent was this abuse? Sexual abuse happened to 29 percent of women and 16 percent of men. Recurrent emotional abuse occured in one out of nine people. Recurrent physical abuse recurs in one out of nine people. Households where one or more people was an alcoholic or a drug user, recurrent abuse occurred in one out of four people. People who grew up in a household where someone was mentally ill, chronically depressed, suicidal, or institutionalized were abused, one out of five times. People who grew up in a household where their mother was treated violently, experienced chronic abuse one out of eight times.

Do you see the unspoken truth?

What happens to us... MATTERS.

Stop looking away.

Abuse is everywhere, and it is out of control. It affects our health, physically and emotionally, into our adulthood. When you compare an ACE score of zero (no history of adversity) with a score of four or more, the likelihood of becoming an intravenous drug user some point later in life goes up 1200 percent. If you score six or more, it goes up to 4600 percent.

The question we can ask is, Where does evil fit in this?

What is the history of offenders and monsters? Do they share these experiences? Are they also high on the ACE score? Were they on the receiving end? To find this out is not easy and flawed at best. But we should look. One study that can give us a hint is the "Criminal Personality Research Project," which had Robert Ressler as principal-investigator. An FBI agent who played a significant role in shaping psychological profiling of violent offenders in the early 1970s. In the study, thirty-six of the most serious incarcerated murderers were interviewed, focusing on their history, motives, fantasies, and actions.

When Robert Ressler talked about their findings, he made an interesting statement first.

"Before going into the details of who these murderers are and how they became murderers, let me state unequivocally that there is no such thing as the person who at age thirty-five suddenly changes from being perfectly normal and erupts into totally evil, disruptive, murderous behavior. The behaviors that are precursors to murder have been present and developing in that person's life for a long, long time... since childhood."

Childhood...

The pattern we are trying to prove or disprove. Robert Ressler would continue and say that though it is a common myth that murderers come from poverty, the study found no such evidence. Their sample of killers came from all classes, with stable incomes. More than half lived initially with an intact family with both parents. They all were mostly intelligent children. Though seven of the thirty-six had an IQ score below ninety, most were in the normal range, and eleven had scores in the superior range of about one hundred twenty.

The homes had outward appearances to be normal though they were very dysfunctional. Half of them had mental illnesses in their immediate family. Half had parents who were involved in criminal activities. Almost 70 percent came from a family with alcohol and drug abuse. More than 70 percent had traumatic sexual experiences, from sleeping with the mother and being raped by a stepmother to being abused by the father.

But one of the most important points, all the murderers, every single one, had been emotionally and physically abused during their childhood. Their mothers were all cold, distant, unloving, and neglectful. One mother had put her infant son in a cardboard box in front of the TV and left for work, leaving him alone all day. The cardboard box became the playpen as he got older, but the TV remained the babysitter and his only simulation. Food was given, but without any love or care.

Let us ask ourselves, Do we know whether these incidents are true? No, not fully. To fully know a person's childhood, we must either be the parent, family member, or the child himself. Even then, it can be hard to truly know. Within families, things are often hidden and unspoken. One child becomes the black sheep, and the other the golden child.

But we see patterns...

Even with all the efforts by society to hide it—biographers talking about happy childhoods, Media interviewing neighbors amplifying "he was a nice guy" over and over—we know, in our gut, it doesn't make sense. It is covering up the mysteries, not exposing them.

So if the blood on the road is telling us these dark people went through some of the vilest abuse and neglect, would this be the answer to our question?

Are trauma and neglect the origin of evil?

CHAPTER 22

THE BIG DILEMMA

The short answer is, we have a problem—A big dilemma.

The dilemma is that many good and decent people also have gone through absolute hell from severe abuse.

Some of the best people have experienced the worst.

I kept asking myself why and struggled with the answer. It felt as if all the signs were leading to trauma and neglect for evil, yet I could not get past the fact that trauma and even being a victim of severe violence was not the realm of only bad people. Most of it was the opposite. The victims were decent and innocent people.

FBI Agent Robert Ressler made this same point as he also wrestled with the conclusions of their research. "It is true that most children who come from dysfunctional early childhoods don't go on to murder or to commit other violent antisocial acts."

To further Robert's point, I will bring up my own life because when I tried my best to put the pieces together of this mystery, I would come back to those I have met throughout my life. Some of the kindest people. My question always came back to if severe trauma can create monsters, how come there are as many, if not more, decent and empathic people who went through just as severe trauma, who did not turn dark?

I will share two such people for us to reflect on.

A good friend, the author of the book *Looking Through the Eyes of an Unseen Child* went through severe abuse as a young child and, in order to survive, split into multiple personalities, from being abandoned in the woods with her siblings to living in a homemade jail cell with her sister and experiencing severe physical and sexual abuse from her own father and stepfather. But the life force in her and the goodness in her always shined. Saved by a pastor, she turned her life around and became a protector of children like her. She would take in the most difficult children in her foster home and pick them up from the street to help them. She is one of the most inspiring people I know and a true example of Romans 8:28. God will take the bad we go through and use it for good.

Another beautiful soul, who has been a big part of my life, was the black sheep in her family. Throughout her childhood, a family "friend" terrorized and abused her with torture and worse. Her mother, being fooled by his charm, would invite this man into their home on a regular basis and ultimately favor his word over her own daughter's word about rape. I can only try to understand the deep pains inside her, and knowing her story intimately always broke my heart. Yet, she is the most incredibly strong woman. The man would end up almost killing her later, and if it wasn't for God protecting her, I don't think she would be alive today. But even with all that she had gone through, if you meet her, she is one of the most loving, cheerful, and genuine person.

I could go on. There are so many more I have met in my life that went through extraordinary painful events. A part of me thought decades ago that it was odd for me to meet so many, but today I know it was not unique to me, but more because I recognized their trauma and listened. As Dr. Anna Salter said, "it is everywhere." Once you see it, you see it everywhere, and it is a sad reality. Hard to ignore, which I wish I could sometimes. So I understand why most of our culture does not want to wake up. There's a comfort in being blind. One can live in a bubble and avoid the pain that is around us. Because it is a lot of pain... A lot.

All the roads are littered with victims. This painful reality is shining bright with its obvious truth. The gigantic elephant in the room is severe abuse and neglect in our world. Evil is very real and more prevalent in our personal lives than we might expect. Evil is all around us and has its hands in the trauma much more than we could ever imagine. But the question remains. If good people can go through abuse and remain good, how can severe trauma then cause evil? Is it a choice? Is it something else? Where does human nature end and choice begin? What is normal? What is our natural state as a human?

Are both good and evil normal?

As I was asking these questions, one road opened up with a hint. It was a road covered by trees and a dirt path into the deep jungles of Venezuela.

CHAPTER 23

TRIBES OF VENEZUELA

It is the story of Jean Liefloff, author of *The continuum concept.*

A woman who was both brave enough to venture into hidden parts of the world but also courageous enough to look at herself, her cultural beliefs, and allow some serious questions about our Western world... the question of what "normal" is.

Faith would have it that during her first trip to Europe, she ended up in Italy, where two explorers would give her a unique last-minute invitation. Join them on a diamond hunting expedition far into the Caroni River regions of Venezuela. She had twenty minutes before the train left the station. She knew the answer. It wasn't the diamonds nor the company that attracted her but the exciting thought of going back to the Stone Age and experiencing the jungle and living pure. As a native New Yorker living in Manhattan, the idea to live in the jungle felt to her as foreign as the moon. During the first trip, she kept writing in her journals and, without knowing it, began the groundwork of her ideas that would come together into some new insights about our human nature. What is our human nature?

Though she didn't have the words for it, she had a feeling that there was something original, something right about the jungle. It felt to her the place where things were pure. Things had not yet gone wrong.

When she flew over the jungle, a joy came over her. She saw the biggest jungle on Earth. The mystery of it all. The animals, the plants, the harshness. It was like one giant green ocean. She would live there for almost eight months at first and come to not only spend time with the two Tauripan Indians that they hired but with the whole clan. She got to live and spend time with families in their huts and see how they traveled and hunted. Except for a machete and steel ax that had replaced the stone tools, they were living as human beings lived during the Stone Age. They were small, less muscular, yet incredibly strong, and could carry heavier loads much greater distances than the Western team. Overwhelmed with new impressions, she absorbed it as much as possible, but it wasn't until her return to New York that she was able to put her lingering thoughts into perspective.

They were the happiest people she had ever met.

The children were all well-behaved and never fought. There were never any arguments or punishments. The children always obeyed happily and instantly. The jungle didn't give her any sense of rightness for herself, but she saw it all around her with the native tribes. As she again walked the busy New York city streets, it was as if she saw them for the first time. What had gone unnoticed before suddenly stood out to her. The way people walked with anxiety. How mothers would hold their screaming babies and put them in prams. Before, she had no perspective. It was the way things were. But now, her memories from the jungle made it all seem new and foreign. The concrete jungle was so different from the green jungle. As a world frozen in time all exposed, she saw the distortions of people around her and their personalities how the high state of well-being in the native tribes compared to the civilized.

But why? And how did she not see it before?

Jean would return and, on her second expedition, venture on a six-week march from the edges of Spanish-speaking Venezuela through the thick jungle to the Yeguana tribe. Here, she would feel again what she had felt from her first expedition. But the contrast was even more evident as these natives had never met any Westerners nor needed to cultivate a defensive blank face for strangers like the Tauripans. She would write in her journals to reflect on her own unlearning compared to what the Western world had taught her. What arose was the major idea of our human condition and how the West is raised with the thought that unhappiness is a legitimate part of life. An essential part. Without unhappiness, one cannot have happiness. So many assumptions she had were confronted by what she saw and experienced. A tribe that lived a life without anxiety, unhappiness, and especially violence. The "rules" of human behavior, as Jean knew, didn't seem to apply to them. As Jean put the pieces together of her experiences, she began to see more and more. It took her more than three years of living with them before fully putting the jigsaw together.

Where she had been blind before, she now noticed amazingly how easily the children behaved. They played together unsupervised. Tiny children from crawling age to walking age to twelve and fourteen. They never fought or argued. She noticed that she would think of them as little savages with their red paint, loin cloths, and feathers, and it made her not connect them to western children. But once she pulled down this mental wall of thinking, suddenly, things became much more clear. How many Western children are often crazed from mistreatment as infants and treated wrongly? We have, in many ways, unintentionally created an antisocial population where we now accept the idea that some children are born rotten and bad.

Jean noticed how some Western babies get colic. Ten percent to 40 percent of babies, according to the American Academy of Family Physicians. It is across all races and both in breastfed and formula-fed babies. If you read the literature, it is mentioned casually. Just a normal thing some babies do during their first weeks up to three months is many cry and spit up the milk. They accept it with no further thought. "The baby will get over it." But let's be honest. The baby is constantly throwing up. It is constantly crying. Remember when you last threw up? Was it pleasant? The babies are violently ill. Why would we believe humans evolved after hundreds of thousands of years and this be normal? No other animal does this.

Jean would compare the babies in the tribe, and unless they had a fever and were very ill, they would rarely throw up and certainly never routinely throw up. They also were not wriggling, struggling, arching, flexing, and squeaking like Western babies. Yet, it is normal in the West because it is rare to see a comfortable baby. So let's look at it with common sense. Many Western babies are so stressed from the minute they are born they cannot digest and keep the food down. Fear and the emotions connected from it appear in the stomach. And the baby's natural need to be cared for is up against the culture's will.

Jean would try to find flaws in her reasoning, and she did find one baby in the tribe that didn't fit the behavior of the others. The baby was sucking his thumb a lot and had stiff body movements, and screamed like a Western baby. Though when she checked the history of the baby, it still confirmed her theory. He had been taken away shortly after birth by the missionary and kept in a Caracas hospital for eight months until his illness was cured and he was returned to his family.

This leaves us with a question...

If this is true, is our natural state good? Not perfect, but good? And is our anxiety-ridden society a reflection on our beginnings and not our nature? It gives us the chance to see our Western world in a new light. An opportunity to reflect on it with judgment. Could our beginnings be so important that its passage of time becomes our foundation for our adult "eternal" now? Our constant anxiety? Our addictions? Our depressions? Our violence?

And our evil?

Many say no. Like Philip Zimbardo's idea that evil is in us all, Camille Paglia, Ph. D, made this quote: "Most people want us to believe that we are good. That we are involved in a continuous evolution toward moral superiority. But point in fact, Marquis de Sade's work demonstrates we are very much mired in primitivism and barbarism, and the history of humankind is one of development economic evolution. but not of spiritual perfection."

But perhaps Camille, whom I admire, did not consider that Marquis de Sades evil did not come from the jungle and nature's primitivism but from the 1700's French society, its cultural stresses that had diverted away from what is good. It is interesting if we look at Marquis de Sades early years. He was the only surviving child born into a wealthy French aristocratic family. His father abandoned him, and his mother left him for a convent. Instead, he was raised by servants, whom the biographer writes indulged his every whim.

Sounds familiar? Similar to Ian Brady.

So perhaps we are not stuck to our worst nature? Maybe we are not all evil inside. Because what Jean Liedloff found showed a very different world. People who were calm in daily life and full of happiness. A primitivism that was affectionate and full of love. Even the males with natural testosterone were calm, strong, and channeled their maleness through hunting and sexual intimacy. Not through manipulation or violence towards each other.

It shows anxiety is not normal... and that the extreme of evil isn't either.

CHAPTER 24

TRIBES OF ALOR

The pieces are coming together. The road is clearing. Do you see the path a little? Though it is hard for us to fully realize what Jean Liefloff experienced, she is helping us to look at ourselves. Our surroundings. What is right in front of our eyes. If you allow yourself to see your own world and neighborhood through the eyes of the continuum, you cannot unsee it. It is everywhere. Both the healthy, decent people who had a good beginning in life but also the people full of anxiety and pain, and lastly, the violent, manipulative sociopaths among us who likely didn't have a good beginning.

But we still have the big dilemma. Trauma and neglect aren't in the realm of evil people only. Some of the best people went through it.

So we could ask ourselves, What about tribes? Are all primitive tribes in the jungle the same? Easygoing, relaxed, and happy?

The question brings me back to New York City. Have you ever visited the Metropolitan Museum of Art? Art from all over the world from all periods of human history. When living in NYC, I would visit and sketch the statues. But a thought came to me on how all this art was a timestamp of the health of the culture. You could walk through this museum and get a broad sense of our world. From the present Western world to all the way in the past, with what values and beliefs each culture possessed. I remember the small Egyptian figures in the hieroglyphs, so many happy faces. The sensual Indian sculptures were voluptuous and bold. The stern but expressive Greek statues. And finally, art from tribes. More primitive yet beautiful sculptures. But it was the masks that made the biggest impression on me. Dark and somber masks from Africa and certain Pacific tribes. Some are quite frightening.

This brings up a question. Were the Tauripan and Yeguana tribes that Jean Liedloff met in Venezuela full of happiness because of the jungle's simple life? Or was it because of their culture towards their children?

For a possible answer to this, we will go back a few decades to 1937 and travel over the Pacific Ocean to the East Indies that is now Indonesia and the small island of Alor.

Here arrived an American anthropologist by the name of Cora Du Bois. She had studied the Native Americans and sought more answers to how the customs of tribes affected the people. In her book *The people of Alor*, she would describe her two-year stay.

What she found with the Atimelanger Tribe was very different from Jean Liedloff's Yeguana Tribe.

They were not calm and happy.

With a history of being headhunters twenty years before Cora's book, it gives us a macabre hint of their past. Though little is known about headhunting, it seemed to have been a normal way for revenge and to avoid further conflict between tribes. If an enemy had killed a man but not decapitated him, the home village of the victim would cut off his head and put it out for the enemy. Whether this was for rituals or not, it speaks of a culture that is very intimate with gruesome human body mutilation.

Cutting a head off is one of the most extreme forms of violence.

But even if their headhunting days were over, there were still plenty of other signs of an unhealthy and violent culture. All directed towards their fellow man.

Cora describes how she saw outbursts of rage but with an interesting note. Always towards human beings. She never saw an Atimelanger lose his temper at an inanimate object. With animals, they would shout loud and harsh but without a sense of real anger. But with humans, she saw rage.

And besides the rage, she saw signs of mental illness. Cora would tell the story of three people. The stories lack deeper context but can help us shape our questions. One was a woman named Matingmale, who got into a fight with a brother-in-law and afterward ran off killing chickens and pigs. With one pregnant pig, she reached in and pulled out the unborn fetal pig. While doing this, she was making obscene advances to the men in the village. The people tied her up, but she got away and continued her destructive rampage, even taking a small child and tossing them in the air. Another woman with the name of Lonmanima had been stealing food from her village all her life. She would often grab children and run off with them or attack people with clubs and stones. When given food, she would throw it away and return her disk broken or full of feces. The third story was about a man named Makonmale who would one day go crazy as if he was on the edge of suicide. He walked around the neighboring villages, shouting, swinging his sword, and shooting arrows at people. When the people threatened to kill him and sell his head, he dared them to proceed and escalated the tension by trying to catch young women and rape them.

Cora described her reaction to these stories.

> *Whether or not the individual's behavior is correctly reported, it is interesting that informants all stress as symptoms of insanity violence, both against people and property, obscenity, and scatologic behavior."*

It tells us something is going on in Alor that didn't seem to happen at all in Jean Liedloff's jungle of Venezuela.

What could it be? Was there any difference?

The answer is yes.

There happened to be a huge difference in one specific area.

Compared to the Yeguana, who raised their children in their arms throughout the day and night and never left them, the tribes of Alor had very different customs. The women would work in the fields each day and leave their babies and children all day in the village. New mothers would return to the fieldwork as early as ten days after the birth of their child. The babies would then be left in the village and cared for by older siblings or grandmothers who no longer could do the garden work. Though the babies would get food during the day and see their mothers in the evening, Cora witnessed how babies would reject good food. Infants would try unsuccessfully to nurse at the breast of any mother surrogate like the father or an immature sibling. Because of this, the infant nurturing needs for one consistent object, a strong attachment with its mother, was never formed. It is left confused without consistency. Cora described how babies would regularly scream and beg for food. Some were lucky to have an older sister who could better care for them, and Cora saw that breasts were available sometimes from other women in the village for other reasons. After the work in the fields, the mothers would return to the villages and feed their children. At nighttime, they would sleep alone with their babies until the children could sit up alone or crawl about. Then the father would join the mat with the mother and child at nighttime.

Cora would talk about how mothers would tease their own children. One mother would nurse someone else's child, and her own son, Padafan, would start to whimper and climb up on her lap. The mother didn't help him nor stop nursing until he had worked himself into a rage and begun hitting the infant. Only then did she surrender the strange child and pick up Padafan to let him, nurse. Cora noted that the adults are fully aware of infantile jealousy and got a mild amusement from it. Cora found the customs of prodding and tugging at toddlers. One favorite way was to tug the penises of small boys or to poke fingers or arrows into their bellies. The children would often become mildly irritable and aggressive, which was greeted with laughter and encouragement from others, saying, "Hit him!" "Kill him!".

See it? Tribe members were finding pleasure from seeing a toddler being irritable.

Could the poking and prodding be painful? A little? Should this be funny, even if done in a playful manner? One can view this as an innocent play, but it could also be similar to how an adult with abusive behavior uses humor and jokes to mask their intentions.

Frightening children was another game played. A five-year-old boy was watching a mechanical toy roll towards him on the verandah. He watched with great interest and was calm until a young man started yelling, saying it would bite the boy. Older children joined in the yelling, which sent the little boy into a spasm of fear that amused the group a lot. Constant threats combined with showing the knife and pretending to cut the children's ears or hands. The adults would do this in a playful way, but for the children, it was very scary. If children cried, they would be told, "Padahavelulua will come and hit you."

Cora would explain in more detail the striking forms of emotional expressions in the early childhood of Ateimelangers. Their temper tantrums. Rages were so consistent, so widespread, and of such long durations among young children that they were one of the first impressions for Cora about the tribe. If you find photos of the Alor Tribe, you will find a common facial expression, anger, which could not be more different than the smiles and clear eyes that met Jean Liedloff in the Venezuelan jungle.

So we have the answer to whether all primitive tribes in the jungle are the same.

They are not.

The jungle is sadly, after all, not the romantic source of human purity and goodness that Jean Liedloff thought about when flying over the jungle. Had her plane flown over the Island of Alor, she would have met a very different experience. Though both the people from Alor and Venezuela were primitive tribes, they couldn't have been more different emotionally.

One culture was full of anxiety and anger, and the other was full of calm and happiness.

Do you see the fog lifting?

CHAPTER 25

THE MISSING LINK

What do Alor and Venezuela teach us? Would it be safe to say that if those accounts that Cora and Jean told us are true, that the mother and child relationships and how their babies are raised and nurtured has a big effect on the culture and being content or unhappy. Could we also say that one tribe showed signs of goodness and the other tribe, without knowing it for sure, showed possible signs of malignancy?

To me, the road is clearing for us. We have a direction.

It's likely that how you are raised matters greatly.

With what we know now, I think it is time to look at the person who gave the final link. The one who solved the big dilemma of abuse happening to both those who turn into monsters of various levels but also to regular, flawed people who will struggle for the rest of their lives but never do what was done to them.

It is Dr. Bruce Perry, a renowned American psychiatrist, and neurologist who wrote the book *The Boy who was Raised as a Dog.* The book is a collection of case studies and paths to learn about child abuse and how to help them. These stories gave the insight I was searching for and was the last link to make everything make sense.

Let us start with the first story that gave Dr. Perry the title of his book. Bruce first met this boy, Justin, when he was six years old. He was at the Pediatric Intensive Care Unit, where the medical staff was about to give up on him. They had no idea how to stop him from throwing food and feces at them. With the call to Bruce, they hoped he could find a way to help the boy. When Bruce walked through the hospital and went to look for the nurse board, he heard a loud and strange shriek. There, behind him, was a thin little child. He was sitting in a loose diaper inside an iron-barred crib with a plywood panel tied to the top. The little boy was rocking back and forth, giving out whimpering sounds. He was covered in his own feces with food all over his face and a diaper soaked in urine. While Bruce studied Justin's records at the nurse station, Justin would continue to hum and moan and let out a loud, angry-sounding shriek every few minutes.

Justin's early life was traumatic. Born to a young fifteen-year-old girl, the girl decided to leave him with her mother after two months. Without knowing the details, all accounts of Justin's grandmother were that she took good care of him and loved him. But unfortunately, she had major health problems from obesity, and when Justin was only eleven months old, she was hospitalized and died a few weeks later. During her illness and after her death, Arthur, her boyfriend, took over, to care for Justin. But with his age being in the late sixties and having not ever cared for a baby, he called Child Protective Services to help seek a permanent home for Justin. CPS asked him if he could keep Justin until they would find an alternative placement. Arthur agreed. He assumed they would find Justin a new home as soon as possible and then get back to him.

But they never did.

What Arthur did next, we can question his sanity. Dr. Perry believes he didn't do it with bad intentions but from ignorance, and I believe Dr. Perry is likely correct. But it is still very tragic. Arthur was a dog breeder, and he decided to keep Justin in one of the dog cages with the dogs. Justin likely would have been screaming and throwing tantrums after losing his second mother, and Arthur probably did not know how to calm him down. So Justin's new home at the age of only eleven months became the dog cage. Arthur would feed him each day but never play with him, hold him, talk to him, or do anything a normal parent would do to nurture their baby.

This went on for five very long years.

Dr. Perry read through his chart and saw what Justin had been through. A doctor had looked at him when Arthur had brought him in for a medical checkup at the age of two. He had a severe delay in development and was unable to talk. Not even a few words when normal toddlers would have begun speaking in sentences. The doctors diagnosed him with severe brain damage of unknown origin. Scans showed that his brain looked similar to someone with advanced Alzheimer's disease. Dr. Perry points out that many doctors back then were not aware of the damage neglect can do to the brain. They assumed that something this physical must have been evidence of a genetic defect or exposure to toxins or disease. They never asked Arthur about Justin's living conditions nor followed up on Justin.

By the time Justin was five, he still couldn't walk or talk. To the doctors who didn't know about the deprivation the child was experiencing, it looked as if his brain just didn't work, and they assumed it had to be due to some unknown reason—an untreatable birth defect.

Not one doctor asked about Justin's living conditions... until Dr. Bruce Perry.

When Bruce asked Arthur about his conditions, he found out that Arthur, who probably had a mild form of mental retardation, had raised Justin the only way he knew. He never had children of his own and had been a loner most of his life. He gave Justin food, shelter, discipline, and sometimes compassion in his own ways. He wasn't cruel to Justin. He would take him and the dogs out of the cages daily for regular play and affection. But he didn't understand why Justin behaved like an animal, so if he didn't obey, he would put him back in the cage.

Standing in front of the cage with scared Justin, Dr. Perry knew he could not approach him fast. No quick movements and no eye contact.

"My name is Dr. Perry, Justin. You don't know what is happening here, do you? I will try to help you, Justin. See, I am just taking off my white coat. That's okay, right? Now let me come a bit closer. Far enough?"

Justin stopped moving around the crib. He was breathing heavily with a fast, wheezy grunt. Bruce thought he must have been starving and notice a muffin on a lunch tray. Taking the muffin and breaking it into small pieces, he put it slowly into his mouth and began chewing slowly, trying to show pleasure and satisfaction.

"Mmm, so good, Justin. Do you want some?"

Bruce reached out with his arm and held it with the food. He was now close enough for Justin to reach it. Waiting for Justin, he held his arm out, not moving. Justin wasn't moving but looking. Bruce kept his arm out and didn't move. Slowly, he moved for the food but got scared and pulled his arm back quickly. Bruce didn't move. Then before he knew it, Justin quickly grabbed the muffin.

"Good, Justin. That is your muffin. It's okay. It's good."

Bruce smiled at Justin, watching him eat the muffin, and slowly walked back to the nurse station. This was his first day, and already Bruce had gotten closer to Justin than all of the hospital staff and doctors. Determined to help Justin, Dr. Perry changed his situation and got him into a private room to decrease the chaos around him. Only a few regular staff were to see him with physical, occupational, and speech/language therapy. Bruce didn't know whether Justin could develop further. But he was not going to let go of Justin as many of his other doctors had. What happened next was truly amazing. Each day, Justin improved. He felt safer. He stopped throwing food and feces. He started to smile. There were clear signs he understood verbal commands, and in only three weeks, he took his first step. He had the most rapid recovery from severe neglect that Dr. Bruce Perry had ever seen, which changed his view on the potential for early neglect.

Six months later, Justin was transferred to a foster family that lived far from the hospital, and Bruce lost contact with him.

Until two years later when he received a letter from the foster family in the mail. Inside was a photo of Justin wearing a backpack and standing next to a school bus.

On the back of the note, in crayon, Justin himself had written.

"Thank you, Dr. Perry. Justin"

Reading this in Dr. Perry's book has moved me many times. I think I can relate to Justin in the hospital. I wasn't neglected as Justin was, but the child in me still connects to the story of doctors failing to do their job and no one understanding the scared child.

What insight can we learn from Justin?

Here is someone who was truly neglected for over five years. Yet, he bounced back in development. What Bruce Perry later realized was that Justin's fast response to the therapy was because he had been nurtured in his early months and during the first year. Even his birth mother had likely been good to him and his grandmother before she passed away. During these eleven months, their love and nurturing made his foundation strong enough to overcome the next four years. Four years of almost no development as a normal human being. Justin was just waiting for someone to take the time and patience to help him gain back the lost years. Though he will always have some developmental issues, he was able to gain back enough to save his life.

Early love was the difference for recovery.

And we will see more of its importance with the next story.

The story of Leon.

Bruce Perry would first meet him in a maximum security prison. Leon had been convicted of a capital offense and faced the death penalty at eighteen years old. His defense had hired Dr. Perry to testify. His crime? He had stabbed two young women to death with a table knife. Cherise was twelve, and her friend Lucy was thirteen. After killing them, he raped both bodies and kicked and stomped them. Though he had often been in trouble, nothing showed that he was capable of this violence. His parents were hard-working, married legal immigrants: no criminal histories, no history of abuse.

When Bruce saw him, he looked small and pitiful.

"It was an accident. I just wanted to scare them. Stupid bitches wouldn't shut up... I told them I wouldn't hurt them if they would just shut up." Bruce asked if their screams had enraged him. "Well, I didn't kick them. I just tripped. I had been drinking some. So, you know."

Bruce would describe the cold feeling he got from Leon. This was a predator whose only concern was what he could get from others. Bruce would continue and asked, "Now that you look back on all this, what would you have done differently?" Leon thought for a minute and then responded, "I don't know. Maybe throw away those boots? It was the boot prints and the blood on boots that got me." Leon's brother, Frank, had found Leon sitting in the living room, still wearing the blood-covered boots watching TV.

Chilling.

And what was Leon's history?

When Dr. Perry met Leon's family, he saw a mother, father, and brother who sounded full of confusion and guilt for what had happened. Neither of the parents looked Bruce Perry in the eye. But Frank stared at him defensively. Perry asked them how they met and their history. Alan and Maria grew up in a small rural community, and both lived in a large extended community and shared the same school and church. Everyone knew everyone. They got married when Alan was twenty and Maria was eighteen. They both worked and made a good living. When Maria got pregnant with Frank, it was a joyous event for both families, and Maria got plenty of help. She quit her job to stay home with their newborn child. Her parents lived next door, and Alan's family was only a block away. When interviewing Leon's parents, Dr. Perry would notice that Maria didn't say much, and over time it became clear to him that though she was kind and polite, she was mentally impaired and had a hard time following the conversation. Bruce decided to ask her a simple question. "Did you like school?". Alan stepped in and told Bruce she wasn't good at those things. She looked at Bruce sheepishly and nodded with a smile. Alan continued to talk about Frank's birth. Both families, grandmothers, aunties, and older cousins, had come over to spend time with the new baby and mother. When Maria felt overwhelmed caring for Frank, there was always someone who could help out.

But then Alan lost his job.

The factory closed, and they had to move one hundred miles away to another factory. Away from the community and into a small tiny apartment. Frank was now three years old, when Maria got pregnant with Leon. Alan would work long hours and get home late. Maria began going out early in the morning when Alan left and spent the whole day outside with Frank. Going to parks, museums , and out for groceries. We can imagine she felt alone and overwhelmed with the situation, and leaving the small apartment gave her space and something to focus on.

Which is when Leon was born.

Maria had never raised a baby alone, and Dr. Bruce Perry believes that the family likely understood her limited abilities and helped her give Frank a safe and loving environment. But with Leon, there was no help. She was all alone. "He was such a fussy baby, he cried," Maria told Bruce as she smiled. "We would wake up and feed him and then go for our walk. We go to the park, play for a while. Take the bus to the church and have lunch. Then go to the children's museum. Take the bus to the market to buy goods and dinner. And then go home."

Bruce asked, "So you were gone for most of the day?"

Maria responded, "Yes."

Bruce's heart sank when he began to realize that Leon had been left at home all day from the time he was only four weeks old. Leon would have cried and cried all day alone, seeking comfort and safety, but was met with silence from a cold apartment. And then, at some point, he would stop crying as his screams solved nothing.

Maria would say, "He stopped crying so much."

As he got older, he continued being very different than Frank. He never responded the same way, unlike Frank, who would always run up to his parents and hug them. Leon didn't like to touch or be touched, and he rarely showed emotions. He didn't care whether he let his parents down and always ignored their corrections. He began to use manipulation, like flirting or flattery, to get his way. If he didn't get what he wanted, he took it. As he got older, things escalated. He got in trouble. By fifth grade, he had become a regular in the juvenile justice system with many charges, from theft to vandalism.

Leon had become a sociopath. Cold and emotionless, drawn to the extremes and getting what he wanted. And now, at the age of eighteen, he was facing life in jail or the death penalty for his brutal murder of two young girls.

Do you see it? Do you see our destination on the horizon for evil's origin? To our biggest question? And the solution to our dilemma?

Could early neglect be the beginning of antisocial behavior?

Though both Leon and Justin had been neglected, they turned out very different.

The one who became malignant and sociopathic was neglected from birth. The other who recovered a great deal from his trauma, was benevolent and was neglected but not until he was eleven months old.

Think about it… The importance of the early months to the first year.

With this in mind, let's look at another story.

The story of Connor.

Connor came from a regular intact family with what looked like a nontraumatic childhood. Yet, he had gone through many psychiatric treatments, and was diagnosed with autism, childhood schizophrenia, ADHD, bipolar, OCD, depression, and anxiety. Dr. Perry would notice how he would rock back and forth and flex his hands, and hum to himself in a toneless drone for comfort.

He had no friends and was the target of bullies. Dr. Perry observed that he was odd but didn't show the classic signs of autism or schizophrenia. He wasn't completely isolated and would engage with other people. Another note Bruce made was that the boy was on so many medications it was difficult to even know where his illness ended, and the medicine started.

Looking at Connor's mother, Jane, Bruce saw a bright woman, yet anxious and at her wit's ends. She didn't live near any extended family members, nor had she ever had any experience with babysitting. A few years before Connor, she and her husband, Mark, had moved from New Jersey to New Mexico to set up a new business. Now that they were financially stable, they decided it was time for a baby. Jane soon got pregnant and had both good prenatal care, and the birth went well.

But one problem. The business was doing so well and was so busy that Jane decided to look for a babysitter only a few weeks after giving birth to Connor. Jane had heard horror stories about daycare, so they decided to get a nanny. Coincidentally, Jane's cousin had moved to the same area and was looking for work, so they decided to hire her. Jane felt guilty for having to leave Connor each day and go to the office. His screams and cries tore into her heart, and she was very stressed from his behavior. But then, he stopped crying. Everything seemed fine. One day when she, by accident, stuck him with a safety pin, he didn't even whimper. No crying.

She thought a happy baby was a non-crying baby.

But what Jane didn't know was that her cousin had taken another job. Instead of telling them, she would come in the morning, feed Connor, and go to work. Then at lunchtime, she would return to feed him again and then quickly return to work. Only just before Mark and Jane would return from work would she come back and pretend everything was fine. To be fair to Jane's cousin, she likely had no idea what kind of harm she was doing to Connor.

Slowly Jane began to feel something was wrong. She noticed that Connor was not developing as fast as some of her friends babies were. He wasn't sitting up or turning over. Concerned, she took him to a family physician who examined Connor but found nothing wrong. Dr. Perry puts it in a friendly way that physicians recognize physical diseases but do not know much about mental and emotional issues. He is right. Physicians have far to go with regards to broader knowledge. It is a problem. Instead, Jane was told that babies develop differently over time and that Connor would soon catch up.

So the neglect continued, and Connor got worse. The cousin would babysit every weekday until Jane and Mark came home.

One day, Jane got sick and had to go home early, which was a blessing in disguise. When she got home, she found a house in darkness. It was quiet, and there were no signs of the nanny. Thinking that maybe her cousin had gone for a walk with Connor, she went to Connor's room to check and smelled something awful. In the dark room, Connor was sitting alone with a dirty, full diaper. No toys, no music. Nothing to simulate or nurture poor Connor. Jane was shocked and horrified. Jane and Mark fired their cousin and, for the moment, was relieved that he had not been kidnapped or something worse had happened to him while he was all alone in the house.

But Jane didn't realize just how traumatic this event had been for Connor in his early months. He was eighteen months old when they found out. Eighteen months of being neglected and alone. Jane quit her job to stay home with Connor and tried to make up for what had happened.

But it was too late. He had gone through too much. Way too much.

As Connor grew up, the neglect showed its effect, and no one saw nor understood its impact. No one in the medical field or the school system had any clue. He was diagnosed with endless alphabetic named diseases and drugged to silence his inner screaming voice of help. None of it did anything to help Connor. He was just pushed through the system, and the system did its thing. No responsibilities, no rocking the boat, no questions asked. I have to admit I get bitter reading these stories. I am, in my mind, not as nice as Dr. Perry. What is stopping people from thinking outside their boxes? Throwing out their egos and asking themselves... why? But dogmas and small-mindedness keep us trapped in old knowledge, with the result being a fourteen-year-old boy rocking back and forth, letting out noises, humming. All alone without friends, extreme depression, scared to look people in the eyes, and who would have screaming and violent temper tantrums like a three-year-old at the age of fourteen.

This story is truly tragic because all parties involved had no bad intentions. Perhaps severe lack of common sense or selfishness from the nanny's point of view. But I have to admit that if you asked me fifteen years ago about young children and babies, how vulnerable they are, and how important the first year is, I would probably have told you I thought they were resilient and strong as long as they were not hungry and had food, maybe a toy. They would be okay. The reasoning would be that I cannot remember much of my early childhood. And I think if you ask a great majority, they cannot remember either before the age of three to five. The memories seem to be gone. So many think, including myself years ago, that the first years cannot be that important. But I could not be more wrong. Maybe this is how the nanny justified her actions to herself.

So here we are. Another story. This time, a severely mentally handicapped child who endured severe neglect. But though he could be violent as a child, frustrated and angry, he was not acting out of malignancy with any intention to hurt others and, more important, finding joy in hurting others.

He did not turn into a sociopath nor evil.

With the help of Dr. Perry and his team, Connor began to improve with physical therapy, and similar to Justin, he recovered in many ways. Though he is still socially awkward, he is now a computer programmer and doing well.

Connor, like Justin, did not turn into a monster.

But Leon did...

Which brings us to the story of Ryan.

Ryan was seventeen years old. A popular guy in school from a wealthy family. To celebrate admission to an Ivy League school, he had thrown a party. He invited a fifteen-year-old developmentally disabled girl, Amy, from the neighborhood for entertainment for his buddies. Some of them knew her, but she was not part of the "in crowd" as Ryan and his friends were. Amy's face had shined with happiness when she got the offer to go to the party. Little did she know how she would never forget this day. Not in good ways, but in horrible ways. Ryan's intentions were not noble but evil. That evening Amy was raped, used, and humiliated by Ryan and his friends.

"We did her a favor," Ryan told Dr. Bruce Perry.

"I don't know what the problem is, really," Ryan added in a polite, well-modulated voice. "She never would have gotten laid by anyone as good as us."

Bruce found his coldness and complete lack of empathy chilling. Ryan had laughed while his victim cried. He was the one who brought her to the party, who assaulted her, and who egged on the others. He thought it was one big joke until the police arrived and he got arrested.

Ryan's parents, Amanda and Michael, were horrified about what had happened, but their main concern was for Ryan to avoid any further consequences. Bruce observed them, and they appeared to have a good marriage. Michael was an investment banker, and Amanda would work on charities. They were very concerned about the whole situation and wanted it to go away. They would pay whatever it took to make this happen. They told Dr. Perry to diagnose their son with depression or anything, to make it all go away, so he could go to college.

But Bruce did not see anything that would hint Ryan was depressed.

Bruce began to ask about Ryan's history. His mother, Amanda, had never been much interested in babies as a child, but when she got closer to her thirties and got engaged to Michael, they both wanted a child. But neither she nor Michael had much experience. During her pregnancy, Amanda started to look for a nanny. She wanted her to be a nurse, someone efficient and who knew what they were doing. She wanted the best person for Ryan. As for herself, she would keep up her social life and her charity work. Her thoughts were that children needed mostly quality time, not quantity.

Dr. Perry asked her about what the nanny's impression was of Ryan.

Amanda responded, "Which one?"

Ryan did not have just one nanny, or two, or six, but eighteen nannies over his early childhood. At the early age of only eight weeks old, Amanda got jealous when she saw the nanny got more happy reactions from him than herself. He would smile when the nanny was holding him, but when Amanda held him, he seemed frightened. "It wasn't right." She was his "real" mom! So Ryan's mother fired the nanny and got a new nanny. Only nine months later, Amanda fired the second nanny. Ryan would often scream when being held by Amanda, and she felt that the nannies must have made Ryan turn against her. To better understand, Bruce asked more specific questions about Ryan and found that his parents almost knew nothing about their own son's schedule and upbringing. Their definition of quality time was an hour or less of snuggles and kisses and maybe a bedtime story. They didn't understand the vital needs of a baby and a young child.

But by the eighteenth nanny, he had calmed down, explained Amanda. He no longer screamed anymore if the nanny wasn't around.

Think about that.

THE MISSING LINK

A mother who left him from the minute he was born. A mother who found her social activities more important than her son. Yet she loved him enough to get the very best nanny? But was that for him? Or for her and her self-image as a mother to her friends? If she was jealous enough to fire the nannies, what underlying emotions could she have had for Ryan also? Anger? Resentment? I think so. When she says he was almost frightened by her, is she giving us a glimpse of the truth? If the anger and resentment were enough to fire the nanny when Ryan was only eight weeks old, then what kind of anger could she have expressed to Ryan himself? Emotionally and even perhaps physically?

Was it a coincidence that Ryan now was facing prison for raping a minor?

Ryan was not a murderer, but he had the coldness of one. He found joy in hurting and raping a young girl with no remorse. Our definition of evil. He was like Leon, another sociopath, but unlike Justin or Connor, who showed no cruel traits.

Are you seeing where the lights are leading us?

I believe there truly IS an explanation for the big dilemma we have.

It was when I was reading Bruce Perry's book for answers that it clicked.

Has it clicked for you?

CHAPTER 26

THE PUZZLE PIECES

Do you see it?

If not, let me go through the thinking and let you decide for yourself. I want to emphasize that it has been many years of reading in all kinds of disciplines for the search. I would not have found Dr. Bruce Perry nor likely understood his insights if it wasn't for all the others. Same with my friendships. For my best friends. From my own experiences. For the tragic lives, I had met and learned from as I read Bruce's four stories. All four are about neglect and trauma in early childhood. I saw a pattern between the two who were broken yet with their souls intact… and the two who had been broken and lost their souls, only for evil to grow within them.

Let's look at them again. We can start with Justin and Connor.

What overall pattern can we see?

Justin had a mother and a grandmother take care of him until he was eleven months old. We don't know the details of the care, but nothing hints at abuse. So if we assume that he was cared for with love, he received care and nurturing until the grandmother passed away. After this, he went through severe neglect by being with dogs, all day and all night. He had extremely little human contact except when he was released, and Arthur would let the dogs and him play outside. This went on unnoticed by society for four years, which is an eternity for a young child. From this abuse, he became a feral child with no ability to speak—scared, shy and angry.

Yet, once his true condition was understood, and he finally got treated like the child he was, developmentally stuck at one year old, with physical therapy and a lot of love and care, he began a miraculous return to the human being he was meant to be. How far he has recovered today is not clear, but he already had gone far as a young man in Bruce's book. He showed no signs of cruel behavior and seemed to have turned into a reasonably happy, and grateful child.

Now, let us look at Connor and see if there are any shared patterns.

Connor had a mother who was there for him during the morning and evenings, and on weekends. But during the weekdays, he ended up being left alone most of the day. The severe neglect went on for eighteen months before his mother finally went home and found him all alone in a dark house with dirty diapers. The neglect stopped, but it was too late to avoid the severe mental issues, compounded by poor health diagnoses and drugs that only covered up his pain.

Take a moment and compare. Any similarities?

Justin was nurtured and loved until he was eleven months old, when his life turned upside down. Connor received love during the evenings and throughout the weekends. Not enough to avoid psychological damage, but I believe enough to avoid his soul turning dark.

They both rebounded from their severe neglect without losing empathy. They were awkward but never became monsters.

Unlike Leon and Ryan.

Leon has a story that resembles Connor, where he was left alone for extended periods each day. But unlike Connor, who had a mother that nurtured him when she was with him, Leon had a mother who just left Leon alone all day on her own accord. The fact that Leon's mother was timid and had a low IQ does not excuse her lack of love. Being "simple" doesn't justify the inability to love. Reading how Bruce described Leon's mother, Maria, as "sad and fragile" reminds me of the fifty dollar guy that helped me move. The guy could fit Maria's description. He looked pitiful. Yet, it was a mask. Once he was with my friend and no longer with me, his real self showed how cunning he had been all along and how he intentionally destroyed my photos from jealousy and anger. Did Maria show Dr. Perry her real self? The self she had been with Baby Leon alone in the small apartment? With Frank, she had the attention and help from her close family. But this time with Leon, she was all alone and maybe emotionally overwhelmed. Maybe passive-aggressive? Maria neglected Leon all day, but I wonder what kind of abusive attention she gave him when she was home.

What about Ryan? Any common threads with Leon?

Ryan's mother handed him over to a nanny right from birth. When she didn't approve of his reaction of fear towards her, she fired the nanny and would repeat this 18 times over the next three years. Eighteen nannies were hired and fired. Ryan never got to bond with anyone. His moments of attachment were constantly disrupted. And for his birth mother, she was cold, jealous, and rejected him. Think about your emotions when you feel jealous. Is it not a mix of fear and anger?

Ryan did not become a murderer like Leon, but he was cold like him. Both were sociopathic and both enjoyed their horrific acts. One raped a young girl and the other murdered and raped two young girls.

Do you see a hint? It is not a clear answer to our question. It is complex. But it's there... the first year.

If their first year was not only neglect but also abuse with little to no affection, then the person is closer to becoming a monster of various degrees depending on the extent of the suffering.

If the neglect and abuse occur AFTER the first year, then one can become severely traumatized, progressing even to serious mental illness. But your soul and empathy will have taken root from its first year of attachment and affection.

The first year... of love, or hate.

Swinging the pendulum towards human or monster.

This could solve our big dilemma on how some can go through severe abuse and survive it with their heart and soul. They had love the first months of their lives. They had a mother who gave them the affection, human touch, and nurturing they needed. After that, they can go through the darkest events and still remain decent with a shine of goodness in their eyes. Even if the years afterward are so severe, they turn schizophrenic.

And those who had only abuse and neglect the first year would turn into monsters with evil desires for revenge even if they had riches and wealth, even if they got love later in the form of foster parents or help from the community.

I believe we have come to the hill with the answer. But we must look back and see if this pattern fits some of our stories of evil.

We can start with Ian Brady, the British serial killer. What happened to him as a baby? Does he fit into our pattern of trauma during the first year? I believe the answer is yes. To be fair, one of the bigger problems proving this hypothesis is getting trustworthy evidence of a child's first year. Yet, we can look at the overall situation. His mother abandoned Ian Brady the first weeks after his birth. This is a checkmark for us. He was then given to the foster parents, which we do not have any evidence of whether they were abusive or not. But they could have been.

Now let's look back at Beth Thomas, the six-year-old girl from the documentary *Child of Rage*.

This one shocked me when I first watched it. Beth's young age and her chilling coldness with violent yet calm language and how she wanted to hurt her little brother and parents. She put pins in her brother and squeezing little birds to death. I watched it over and over to try to understand. It was before the time I had realized the meaning of the first year. Yet, it had been there all along. The documentary even told the story mentioning the first year and foster parents. But my mind had, for some reason, skipped this part. Together with her brother, Beth had been adopted at the age of eighteen months and came from a very abusive household.

Here we see it again. The first year.

Beth would write, in the book *Dandelion on my pillow*, together with her foster family about her time as a toddler with her previous foster parents:

"They were again baffled by the amount of rage that poured from my little nineteen-month-old body."

"I was terrified of the water and the woman trying to wash me. Who did she think she was, my mom or something? I had a mama, and she was coming back. I knew it. And why was she taking my clothes off and putting me in this tub? What was she going to do? She could hurt me! I would just rather be dirty than do it her way because she'd probably try to put my head under the water or something. I didn't know her, and I didn't trust her. Strangers weren't to be trusted. Even people who supposedly loved me hurt me."

Beth would describe a recurring dream of hers as a young child.

"In terror, I would consistently see a man coming toward me as I lay in the dark. I'd back away until my body pressed against the wall, and then he would fall on me and hurt me with a part of himself. I'd scream and holler in my dream, trying to make him go away."

Without knowing Beth's true situation in detail, we have many hints. Her father, Ronald, was an abusive and deadbeat husband who barred Beth's mother from leaving home. There was never enough money. When she got pregnant with Beth, she tried to escape with all the children but got tempted into Ronald's control. The beatings were daily for both Beth's mother and siblings. Three months after Beth was born, her mother got pregnant again. But the births and the abuse were taking a toll on her, and she developed serious kidney problems. As her mother would go to the hospital, all the children were left with Ronald. His physical and sexual abuse escalated towards Beth's older sister and Beth herself. When her mother would return, little Beth would reject her.

"Each time she returned home, she would pull us children into her arms to hug and hold us, but I would turn and run from her. Eventually, I would warm up to her again and snuggle in her arms. A few days later, she would have to go back to the hospital, and the next time she came home, I would run from her again."

So much back and forth of the one person, what Beth needed most was her mother. With continued abuse and severe neglect, it all would finally end with Beth's mother dying fourteen months later, with Beth only being seventeen months old. Adopted a month later, we return to the story where Beth was torturing her brother and frightening her foster parents. In her book, Beth would describe her thoughts and actions:

"Twice, I grabbed my brother and pinched his nose, and held him under the water. His flailing arms and legs struck out as he struggled for air—the air I had taken control of and taken from him, the air that, if I starved him long enough, he would die without. I didn't let go until the arms of adults pried me off him and sent me out of the pool. 'He's fine,' I said. 'See! He's still breathing.' Bummer, I thought. Maybe next time. Stupid adults kept getting in my way."

See the water theme? Was Beth drowned? By her father or mother? Beth would explain how she went to hurt animals after getting caught more and more with her brother.

"The bruises on them wouldn't show, and they couldn't tell on me. When I'd get angry at anything occurring in my life, or my parents trying to control me, I'd take it out on the animals. The Golden Retriever became my prey. I felt so powerful when I could hurt such a big animal. If she were near me, I'd fall and land hard on her or 'trip' over her furry body, landing a solid kick to her stomach... I found a ball of needles one day and would stick them in her. Each time I'd approach her, she'd sit there looking pitiful and thump her tail on the floor. How pathetic! She doesn't even know to run from me! I felt I succeeded each time she cried. Another being I'd conquered, and I was only five... When no one answered her cries, they'd echo within me, and I thought, that's right. That's how I felt. I'd cry, and no one would come, and if they did, they'd scare me or hurt me."

Let's focus on the gift Beth gave us with her honesty and look at her last sentence. She would cry, and if someone came, they too, would hurt her. Could the hurt she cried from be abuse from her father? And the one that came to her cries, who scared and hurt her, be her mother?

Today Beth Thomas claims she has recovered.

THE PUZZLE PIECES

Was Beth Thomas a sociopath as a child? Did she recover through love and the trust and treatment by the Thomas family? Or is she still the same within but found a way to live life with her psychopathy? Only Beth Thomas can answer this. But I believe both are possible. I theorize that if she was healed, it would have been from a non-perfect mother who gave her comfort and love in the nightmarish early life before her mother died. If, on the other hand, Beth is a functioning sociopath today, it would hint that her mother wasn't that loving and that she may have been abused and neglected by her also. My humble guess is leaning towards a mix of some healing and still some pathology. But again, only Beth knows.

What are you seeing? Is it coming into focus for you?

CHAPTER 27

DO WE HAVE A MATCH?

Let us check two human stories that exemplify evil for us all. Two notorious serial killers: Ted Bundy and Jeffrey Dahmer.

You likely know the story of both, but let's recap.

Ted Bundy was a serial killer in the United States during the seventies. He kidnapped, raped, and murdered at least thirty young women, and twelve of them, he decapitated and kept the heads in his apartment to remember his killings.

Jeffrey Dahmer, diagnosed as borderline and schizophrenic, was another American serial killer from the late seventies to the early nineties. He murdered seventeen young men, most of them through strangulation. He would bore holes into many of his victims to inject acid or boiling water to turn them unresistant and submissive. When this did not work, necrophilia and cannibalism were next for his dead victims.

Chilling to think men like these exist. But monsters are real.

What is Ted Bundy's story? Was he born into a stable and loving family? We know the pattern we are looking for in this thesis... His first year.

According to Ted Bundy, he had a good childhood.

But did he? His mother, Louise Bundy, was twenty-two years old and alone when she gave birth. No father and no family. She had traveled some four hundred miles from Philadelphia to Vermont to the "Lund home for unwed mothers" where she gave birth to her son, Theodore Robert Bundy. Immediately after the birth, she left her little infant and returned home to her parents in Philadelphia. For three months, the infant Ted was without his mother. What conditions were at the Lund home is not known, and how they took care of him. But Bundy was abandoned until three months later when his grandparents and Louise picked him up. Their story to the families and community was that Louise's parents were adopting this boy. Even Ted was told his parents were Samuel and Eleanor and Louise was his sister. Louise never told Ted who his father was, and rumors are it was Louise's father, Sam. We do not know, but it could explain why she never did reveal who Ted's father was out of shame.

And what kind of place did Ted come home to at three months old?

Ted Bundy told Dr. Dorothy Otnow Lewis, a psychiatrist brought to his trial to avoid the death sentence, that his grandfather was "wonderful and loving and giving" and that all his memories were good. He adored him, and when Louise moved away to Tacomo when Ted was three years old, he missed his grandfather. But was this true? Interviews with family members described Sam as a man who terrorized his family with temper tantrums. He would shout, rant and rave. He was sadistic with animals and would kick the family dog. What kind of treatment would a man like this give a three-month-old baby, crying and screaming from neglect of the three-month abandonment? Did Ted have anyone to save him? To give love and affection? His grandmother was a timid, obedient wife with a deep emotional issue who would get shock treatments for depression and fear of open places. What about Ted's mother, Louise? Her sister, Julia, described Louise as being like their father, temperamental and secretive. Mysterious words, but not kind words.

A lot of holes and foggy details, but are you getting a picture?

Ted Bundy's first year was likely a nightmare, with neglect and abuse. Louise's sister, Julia, would go on and describe an event where she woke up after a nap and, in shock, found knives surround her in bed. Ted was standing by the bed, grinning. Ted Bundy's last words before being executed were to Dr. Lewis. He told her how, very early on, he was fascinated by murder.

Could Ted Bundy's story fit our pattern? I would say so.

Let's continue and look at Jeffrey Dahmer.

How were his childhood and first year? From the first look, we read in an article that he had a normal childhood but became withdrawn later by all accounts. Another article says he was described as an energetic and happy child up until the age of four. Other articles jump straight over his early childhood and go to him being seven years old.

Normal and happy by most accounts.

If this was all the info we had, it would not match our pattern. But in this case, Jeffrey's father wrote a book that gives us a chance for details. The book feels like a cry for understanding and gives us a closer look at Dahmer's household. His mother, Joyce, had extreme emotional problems leading up to Jeffrey's birth and had to leave her job from constant vomiting, nausea, and uncontrollable muscle spasms. Joyce got so irritable and angry at her husband, Lionel, for not complaining to the neighbors each day that they ended up moving to Lionel's parent's house only two months before Jeffrey's birth. The move did nothing to improve Joyce's condition. Instead, it got worse, and she began to develop episodes where her whole body started to tremble. Her jaw would jerk to the right and take on a frightening rigidity. During these seizures, her eyes would bulge like a frightened animal, and she would salivate and froth from her mouth. The doctors could find no medical reason for Joyce's condition, but they felt it could be rooted in her mental state.

I want to pause and mention that Joyce's symptoms sound very much like severe body trauma that is showing itself. Trauma is released because it cannot be held in any longer. Her pregnancy, with its stress, could have set it off, both psychologically and physically. We know from Lionel that his wife's father was domineering and explosive. She would often scream in her sleep and told Lionel that she had a recurring dream of being chased by a large black bear. Lionel was baffled by all this and couldn't understand it. But then, our society doesn't talk about this. To me, it's not a coincidence. Her vomiting could be stored memories of oral sexual abuse. Same with her nausea, her spasms, and frozen body. Sexual abuse. All unconscious memories being locked away for survival, now escaping through her body, bringing the past into the present.

Her condition worsened, and the tension in the house with Lionel's parents got very volatile. Joyce would spend most of the day alone and isolate herself. Lionel began to immerse himself completely in his work and would spend all day at the laboratory away from home, getting home late. Joyce's rage towards Lionel, his parents, and the pregnancy kept escalating.

And then Jeffrey was born.

Lionel describes Joyce as being happy during the birth but reading his words sounds more like wishful thinking. "Here's your son!" was her greeting to Lionel, holding Jeffrey for the first time. Maybe she was content. But the happiness only lasted days. Joyce didn't want to nurse, and the arguments returned. Joyce withdrew upstairs alone in her bed with Jeff in the bassinet, and Lionel would continue to go to work from early morning to late at night. Lionel's parents and Joyce and the atmosphere got so intense that they decided to move out when Jeffrey was four months old. Except for the parents now gone, the rest remained in the new house. Lionel would spend most of his time at work, even on weekends, and avoid Joyce as much as possible. But the rage from Joyce didn't go away. Things were both psychological and physical between the two. On one occasion, when Lionel fought back, Joyce seized a kitchen knife on him.

Let's pause for a moment.

Are you asking yourself what this has to do with Jeffrey? Family arguments and stress are common in families. Isn't it normal? And why would this tell us anything about Jeffrey? It is a fair question. The answer is that if you look at Joyce's behavior from Jeffrey's father's perspective, you will find warning flags that tell us Jeffrey would be in danger of physical and sexual abuse. Maybe you think, sexual abuse from a woman? A mother? We are now entering true taboo areas in our culture. Unlike male abuse that is commonly talked about for good reasons, abuse from mothers is silenced.

The book *Women who sexually abuse children* by Jacqui Saradjian presents this topic, and it seriously opens our eyes and minds. In it are fifty interviews from mothers who abused their children.

> *I hated him... he'd do anything to get at me... always crying, crying, crying... I'd tell him to 'shut up,' and he wouldn't... he does it to wind me up. Always wanting something. He'd look at me with that look, weak, pitiful, pathetic. He makes me want to hurt him."*

This is a mother talking about her son, whom she sexually abused soon after he was born until the abuse was discovered when the child was four and a half. The abuse she perpetrated was extremely sadistic. Jacqui would explain later that most mothers who initially targeted their infant children conceived these children in difficult circumstances. Almost all the women initially perceived the children they sexually abused to be "unwanted." Another important note was that with few exceptions, women who sexually abuse children do not target every child with whom they are in intimate contact.

Could Jeffrey's mother Joyce fit this narrative?

What could she have done with Jeffrey during the day when Lionel wasn't there? When was she alone upstairs, full of rage in the house of Lionel's parents or the new house all alone? Jeffrey began getting sick with ear and throat infections, and at the age of four, a small bulge appeared in his scrotum, which was diagnosed as a double hernia. Could that be signs of abuse? It is not clear evidence. But the story does give us a glimpse into Jeffrey's early childhood.

Now knowing this, could Jeffrey Dahmer's early childhood fit the pattern we are checking? The first year?

I believe it could.

It has been a long journey for us. You have been introduced to a wide perspective of the darkness that surrounds us.

Though we can never truly understand evil until it happens to us, the terrors are real, and they are happening now. All around the world, all the way to your country, state, town, and maybe even your street and area. Children are being trafficked and sexually abused. Women are psychologically tormented. Some are tortured in distant jails. People are working as slaves. Children are being abused by their mothers, beaten by their fathers. It goes on and on each day. Day and night, year by year, century by century. And in our journey, we have searched for answers that would explain this darkness and its source.

Do you see it? Do you see the picture I see?

Or do you doubt it? Do you still question if real evil exists?

CHAPTER 28

THE WALL OF DISCOVERY

I believe we have arrived at the beginning. The source, from where the bloody rivers began.

It is, in my view, the closest to an answer of evil's origin.

The time between the birth of an infant, through their first year, up to when he or she can leave their mother's arms and have their first taste of autonomy. Stepping into our mysterious world and explore with confidence.

If a little infant is abandoned during this time, left to die in an apartment, alley, hospital or in the hands of a rageful, fearful, and jealous mother, then bit by bit, trauma after trauma, the door to humanity closes, and the infant's heart becomes a rock to never feel again. It only becomes full of rage and resentment. Only full of the need to stop the pain of the past. The endless time of its first months.

Evil's origin lies here.

It would explain a lot. It would explain how some go through the most horrific abuse and adversity during their lives yet can be kind and have a heart of gold. No matter where they were born—in the jungle, in the slums of Mumbai, or on Fifth Avenue, If their mother took care of them during their vulnerable first year, These first moments in life, moments of love, would forever be there. Even if life later would take them through hell and back... their soul would still be intact. Perhaps full of pain, but not numb and destructive.

On the other hand, if an infant is born into an unwanted world with a rageful mother who sees the baby as an object... A pathetic and weak thing that cries to annoy and steal sleep. Their foundation will be an abyss of pain and rage, void of love.

Maybe the father is present but makes the situation worse with his temper and volatility. Maybe the father is extremely abusive, and the mother is weak and neglectful. The stories are many. Drug use, domestic violence, beating the baby, throwing the baby, raping the baby, or leaving it in its filth.

This infant, if nothing is done, could become a future monster.

Do you get it? It is all about the first year.

One important thing to understand is that it is not a black and white hypothesis. It is complex as human nature is. There are an infinite amount of combinations of nurturing and neglect and abuse. Where a person would fall on this early adversity spectrum will differ.

But if it is so complex, where do we draw the line with evil?

I believe we look back to the definition of evil. If "Pleasure to hurt others" exists as a drive in a person. Even if it is mild and well-hidden, it will qualify as evil. Because if these people ever get the chance to let out their inner monster in a safe way-in a world where the bad rule and the good are weak-they will be tempted to let their darkest side fester and metastasize into their darkest self.

What are you thinking about this right now?

Have I laid out the direction to the source? Have you thought, as I have, about our current culture? Do we not have a serious epidemic of early childhood abuse?

If this theory is true, we must find ways to prove it and educate our society to wake up.

But we have two big problems.

The first problem is how difficult it is to prove.

Do you remember your early childhood? What is your first memory? Mine is a vague, abstract memory of being in an ambulance, pushing my toy car down the hospital floor, and standing on my little feet on top of the radiator, waiting for my mother to visit. Anything earlier is beyond my reach. I cannot remember it. If I watch photos of myself as a baby, it's as if I am looking at a stranger's baby. I see no connection to myself or to the time and situation in the photo. I know I had good times and bad times, but I have no access to these memories. Now consider how we find details of someone else's first year. In most cases, the only way is to ask the mother or father. But if they are the offenders, how likely is the info trustworthy? Even if they are open to sharing their wrong actions it is not likely all the truth will come forth.

I have sought stories and found details, but it is unknowable how accurate they are. It is only by patterns and seeing story after story match that the unobservable is beginning to shine through.

If this problem wasn't big enough. we have a second problem.

Those who do not want this to be proven. Those who want it to stay hidden and taboo.

I get it. It is not easy being a parent. Children have their own personalities and make their own choices. Life is hard, and we all are flawed, both as children, adults, and parents. None of us do a perfect job. Many parents try their best but hurt their children from the cycle of violence or ignorance from never dealing with their own inner childhood trauma. So the cycle of trauma continues. If we cannot face it ourselves, how can we react to someone talking about it and challenging us to look at it? And even questioning parents, saying evil lies with the first years.

It is a real problem.

I encountered this myself when I made a comment on FaceBook. It was an article about a seventeen-year-old boy who murdered his mother by first strangling her unconscious and then stabbing her 117 times. thirty-eight times in the forehead, sixty-four times in the neck, and sixteen times in the arm. The son had been admitted to a mental health hospital, attempted suicide, and recently changed his name and gender.

His 999 call after the murder was casual and ice cold. Reading the article, it was clear the murder was very intimate and extremely rageful. When you strangle someone, it is up close between the victim and the murderer. A very visceral and ugly death. Same with a knife. And then to stab the person, your own mother, 117 times... It reveals a mountain of rage.

From these observations, I made the short comment:

"Severe abuse/neglect from mother and maybe father."

I don't know whether the abuse came from the mother or father, or both. But I have zero doubt that the rage came from a real place, and the mother had a place in its beginning.

Then came the response. I was called all kinds of names: sexist, misogynist, cockwomble. "Why is it always the mother's fault?" "I was abused. I never murdered anyone." "You have NO idea, and it's highly inappropriate to speculate." "Mansplaining to the extreme." "That's a lot of words for 'The bitch deserved it' Your words are disgusting." "That's right, blame the victim, not the psycho."

And then I got this reply. The only positive one out of sixty comments.

"Thank you for saying this. My mother abused me, and I wish more people would realize that there are some very evil mothers out there. It is hard to tell people as most can't or won't believe it."

The last one made it worth it because it speaks to a sad truth.

Talking about abuse from mothers is an even bigger taboo than abuse from men. We cannot allow this. We must hear these stories. It is for the best. I do understand the fear and the anger from all the other comments. It is personal and painful. It makes me wonder how many of you, while reading this book, threw it aside in anger?

I do get the fear and take no offense in the offense. It is truly a painful subject matter, which is why we must look deeper.

What research do we have about the infant's first year?

What do we know?

CHAPTER 29

THE FIRST YEAR

Let us first consider that human beings are among the species where babies cannot move on their own after being born. The infant's survival at birth is based 100 percent on devoted parental care... for a long time. It is dependent on food, protection, and survival. During the first weeks, the infant's ability to process information is extremely limited. For example, the baby cannot process extra information if it is in distress even when both internal stimulus of hunger and external stimulus of a nipple and breast. Any tension must be stopped by a discharge of movement or something vocal before any other stimulus like hunger can be processed.

Tensions override hunger. It is THAT important.

Dr. Rene Spitz, a twentieth-century researcher in child development, did extensive observations with both disturbed and normal children and what he found is the pattern we are looking for. If infants are deprived during their FIRST YEAR, it leads to severe emotional disturbances, and the babies gave the impression that they had been deprived by the most vital elements of survival.

Let us read that again.

"The most vital element of survival."

If the mother rejected the baby overtly with a rejection of motherhood, the cases were difficult to follow, but the child frequently died, either accidentally or through infanticide. If the mother passively rejected the baby, it could, in extreme cases, lead to comatose and severe illness. Margaret Ribble, an American psychoanalyst who specialized in young children, would describe these rejections. One sixteen-year-old girl who had become pregnant by temptation did not desire the baby. The birth itself was uneventful, but the first attempt to nurse after twenty-four hours was unsuccessful. The mother had milk, but during nursing, the mother behaved as if her infant was alien to her and not a living being. Her behavior was rigid and tense. Another case was a mother who stopped nursing because the child would vomit. The baby would vomit whether it was breastfeeding or taking formula, and the mother refused to continue. Three weeks later, the mother got sick with influenza and had to be hospitalized. When she was separated from the child, the baby instantly stopped vomiting. Six weeks later, when the mother returned, the child started to vomit again within forty-eight hours.

Dr. Spitz saw how the loss of a caring mother for a period of time would cause depression in the infant. Observing infants, they would see how the baby would change behavior and start laying immobile in their crib. Not lifting their shoulders and barely their head. Weeping would often be soundless, with tears running down its face. If spoken to in a soft voice, it would only make the baby weep more, intermingled with moans, and whole-body shakes. Take a mental note of how the body releases trauma through shaking and tremors, getting the tension out. If the separation was less than three months, the infant would quickly recover, but if it was over five months, the baby would not recover. It became irreversible damage to the baby in the 1st year.

BUT this was only if the mother and infant's relationship was good.

For bad relationships, Dr. Spitz did not see a single case of depression. In these cases, any substitute mother was better.

Think about that. As traumatic as losing a mother is, to the point where the baby cannot recover if it lasts over five months, it does not compare to a bad mother or an abusive situation. The emotional effect on the baby is that much more impactful and negative.

This screams to us how vital the emotional life of a baby is...

Just like how Dr. Spitz saw emotions and tension affected infants, the American physician, Alexander Lowen, also echoed these findings. He studied the body and showed how trauma and tension in our bodies are related, and how the loss of the mother develops into a threat. All infants need unconditional love. Their survival depends on a loving connection with their mother. Infants in nurseries who are fed and cleaned but not held or played with develop depression and die. In thirteenth century Europe, King Frederick II, a Roman Emperor, wanted to experiment on babies to see what language is native to humans. What language did Adam and Eve speak? So he ordered an experiment where he forbade foster mothers to speak to their babies. They could feed and bathe them, but no human interaction was allowed. What language did he discover? None... as all the infants died.

This story tells us how important human connections are. Giving the baby love is life-giving and stimulates the infants, especially breathing. An unborn infant has this contact in the womb, and if a newborn doesn't get it, it goes into shock. Alexander Lowen talked about how many of us do not appreciate how dependent every child is on a loving connection. Any break in this connection results in a shock to the infant's organism, paralyzing the functions. Have you ever felt an electric shock to your back and through your spine? This is a glimpse into the infant's world. Every shock is a threat to its living process. A sudden loud noise can cause a baby to go into shock momentarily, known as the startle reflex, which is present almost from birth. Its body stiffens, and it will stop breathing. As the shock passes, the baby begins to cry as it restores its breathing and the tension goes away.

For the first part of an infant's life, as we said prior, the infant can neither reason nor react with its mind yet. Knowing this, we can speculate that the baby does not know the difference between itself and the mother or the world. They are born conceptually blind. What a face is, is new. Everything is new and has to be learned. It likely does not know how to sense time. An hour could feel short or infinitely long. It is a ball of feelings. The baby is aware of its well-being or pain. It senses its body and emotions, but it cannot think about what is next. There's no perception of what a minute is, what a day is. The baby is as vulnerable as it ever will be until the end, when facing death. In this way, the infant is very closely connected to the raw, unconscious fear of death. It is real, and it is feared on a deep biological level.

But when the natural state is good, and the baby is in its mother's arms... all is good. When a mother's arms are around the baby, the baby hears the mother's heartbeat, feels her warm skin and senses her distinct scent. It is the expected place. The continuum, as Jean Liefloff puts it.

Liedloff explains it beautifully:

> *The feeling appropriate to an infant in arms is his feeling of rightness or essential goodness. The only positive identity he can know. Being the animal he is, is based on the premise that he is right, good, and welcome; without that conviction, a human being of any age is crippled by a lack of confidence, of a full sense of self, or spontaneity, of grace. All babies are good but can only know it themselves by reflection. By the way they are treated. There is no other viable way for a human being to feel about himself; all other feelings are unusable as a foundation for well-being."*

Emotions are your body's language. Instead of words, it uses sensations that go from your face, down your neck to your back, to your chest, your heart, and finally to your gut. They are all in the area of survival for your body. And it seems that an infant's emotional universe is fully developed by birth. The mind is only beginning to take form, and the primal emotional centers are ready for the new world. Ready to be loved.

In the book *Birth Without Violence* by Frédérick Leboyer, a French obstetrician made these observations.

> *People say and believe that a newborn baby feels nothing. He feels everything. Everything utterly, without choice or filter, or discrimination. Birth is a tidal wave of sensation, surpassing anything we can imagine. A sensory experience so vast we can barely conceive of it. Admittedly, these sensations are not yet organized into integrated, coherent perceptions, making them stronger, more violent, unbearable, and maddening. The hands that touch the child reveal everything to it: nervousness or calm, clumsiness or confidence, tenderness or violence. The child knows if the hands are loving. Or if they are careless. Or worse, if they are rejecting. Inattentive and loving hands, a child abandons itself, opens itself up. In rigid and hostile hands, a child retreats into itself, blocks out the world.*

If true, the infant's emotions are like a sea of impressions, amplified a thousand times, and its attachment to its mother is so vital that without it, it cannot exist.

And this is exactly what we see. A mother's love is the oxygen for the baby's inner emotional world.

Biology echoes this truth with a hormone that is often called the hormone of motherly love... oxytocin. It is released in large amounts during birth and helps facilitate the birth, making it go faster. But it has a big role afterward as well, both for the mother and the baby. It calms and connects the baby to its mother or caregiver. But it takes time. It is not instant, and it needs to be continuous. It is almost like there is a pattern of trust being built between mother and baby via the oxytocin, bringing them both closer. If the mother loves the baby, the oxytocin is released, bringing calm throughout its body and relaxing stress system, telling the infant that all is well. The world is safe. But it only works with the trusted mother or a few caregivers. The baby needs time to bond. Attachment is everything. If this doesn't happen, the oxytocin isn't released, with the result that the baby does not form the same associations between a human and pleasure.

What happens when there were little to no connections made?

When the stress system isn't calmed? When there is NO love?

CHAPTER 30

THE SOURCE

Of the River of Blood

To think about this, we must realize the reality that we, as humans, have needs. We are born needing, and we live our entire life needing and struggling with unmet needs. But there is a big difference between adult needs and the needs of the infant. The infant's world of needs is our foundation for all needs. We are dealing with the deepest primal needs. When those are not met, the infant hurts, and this pain is all it knows until it is resolved. And the pain is on another scale. The baby knows subconsciously that if it is left alone, it is left to die. It cannot do anything but feel the empty void of pain. It can cry, it can scream, it can kick and thrash its legs and arms. But if no one comes to hold the baby, to feed it, then the fear and tension continue to build, making the baby more and more frightened for death. This is a life or death matter for the infant. There is no reasoning. No understanding that the mother is in the other room. There is no understanding she is coming back.

For the baby, there is only the state of being. Comfort or discomfort. Relaxation versus tension. Peace versus Pain.

Thus everything in the baby's core knows the importance of a protector. Without which the baby would die. It must have this deep connection and keep it, to feel loved and safe. Anything that might hint this state is going away is terrifying, even for a moment.

A video of an experiment called the "still face" by Dr. Edward Tronick shows how a baby reacts when the mother stops reacting to the baby. The mother is told to sit down and play lovingly with her baby. She gives her baby attention and lots of smiles. The baby smiles with love and joy. But then the mother is told to stop responding to the baby. The baby tries to get her attention, smiling and pointing. But the mother doesn't respond, only offers a blank stare. The baby tries to reach for her mom, and when the mother still doesn't respond, the baby quickly gets very uncomfortable. Its body becomes full of tension. The baby squirms in its seat and lets out a loud squeak. With some relief from the tension, the baby tries to look at the mother again but is met with a dead stare. The stress is too much. The baby tries to look away from the mother, away from her face and her eyes. Then again, the baby goes back and tries reaching out with its little hands. When the mother doesn't respond and continues the stare, the baby starts crying.

This all happens within a few minutes. When the mother finally responds to the baby, the baby's world returns to normal, and the crying stops and is replaced with a smile.

Mom has returned. The state of the world is again okay.

A nanny from Norway, Lise-Lotte Austad, did this experiment with a small change. She added a cell phone. It is interesting how the emotional face of someone looking at their phone is eerily similar to the blank stare from the original experiment. Her baby's reaction was very similar, which also ended up with the baby crying within a few minutes.

Do you see it?

There is a threat of no mother, no connection with mother, a strange detached mother, and the alarm bells go off for the infant. It is in danger. Stress!

But once back safe in the arms of the mother, peace resumes.

The more the stress system is in alarm, the worse it gets for the infant's survival, both psychological and physical. We see this in observations of animals also. Dr. Levine Seymour, a psychologist and neurologist, found that only a few moments of handling young baby rats by humans were enough to change the rat's stress response system for life. And as with human infants, baby rats without nurturing, which for them would be grooming and licking, would die. Renowned researcher on stress and maternal care, Michael Meaney, continued this search for understanding. He set up an experiment where he watched hours of videotapes of mother rats to see a difference between them. He found that some licked and groomed their pups much more. To see if this greater amount of nursing had an effect, he separated the rats into two groups; those with twice as much grooming for group one and the rest for group two. Then he put them through various stress tests. He found that the more nurturing mothers had a big impact on how the pups behaved when they grew up. They were much calmer in stressful tests, from putting them into open fields to mazes and hidden platforms in the water. Also, the hormones that affect pulse and circulation were much lower in the more licked rats. The experiments showed a clear contrast between the less affectionate versus the affectionate mothering. Interestingly, those female rats that came from more nurturing mothers had much more oxytocin activity in their brain's pleasure regions. Meaney also found that the rats raised by the more affectionate mothers had an enhanced GABA-A receptor, which acts like brakes for the stress response system, stopping it from overacting.

In so many words, those loved rats had a much more calm stress response system. One can ask then, maybe it is not the affection that produces these results but the genetics. Could it not be inherited genes? To see if it was the genes instead of the love, Meaney switched the babies. He took the babies from the high-licking mothers to the low-licking mothers and vice versa. What were his results?

There was no measurable genetic effect. None.

Love was the answer. The babies born from the low licking mothers and given to the high licking mothers showed a calm stress system. The babies taken from the high licking mothers and given to the low licking mothers behaved just like the babies born and raised by low licking mothers, with a much more active stress system.

It was all about the mothering.

But what happens to those rats that have not only less affectionate mothers but also abusive mothers? A paper by neuro-endocrinologist Bruce S. McEwen and his colleagues gives us a hint. From their research when they put the rat mothers in stressful environments and pushed the mothers to become abusive, they found that their pups not only had higher levels of stress hormones, but it became chronic. Not only that, when these pups were put back with their mothers after a stress test, they would not calm down. Instead, their stress levels would continue or even spike higher.

Their mothers had become a source of pain-a feared threat.

So what happens with continuous fear and stress? When the abuse and neglect continue, the infant is left with no choice. It cannot leave. It cannot run away. It cannot defend itself. There is only one direction for the energy. After weeks and many months of crying and screaming, there is only one place to go. Go inside and close up. Thus the tension becomes greater and greater until the pain becomes too much and a split is needed. Disassociation.

It is one of the most primitive reactions when there is no option to escape. The infant must disassociate from the extreme stress. During this state, the brain prepares the body for injury. Blood is pulled away from the limbs, and the heart rate slows down to reduce bleeding from any wounds. The body's natural opioids are released throughout to kill the pain and produce calm, taking the infant away from what is happening. No fear, no pain is felt. The infant is transported far away to a place where no pain and no fear exist.

But does the pain and fear still hit the body without the conscious mind knowing it?

Theodore X. Barber, an American psychologist, did experiments that give us an idea. He found that when he put subjects under hypnosis and gave them pain stimuli, though they would report no pain, the physical measures showed their body reacted. In other experiments, he would look at their brain waves, and though the subjects reported feeling nothing, the brain waves showed pain. This indicates that though we might be disconnected from feeling pain, the body and brain likely are constantly reacting and sensing it all. The pain is still stored, but it is not felt at the moment. It is put behind a wall. A dam that holds away all the suffering. The injuries to the physical as well as the psychological. This is the pain behind the primal scream that Dr. Arthur Janov discovered. Stored in the body, yet not felt. For many, a gigantic mountain of pain.

You might not remember. But your body does.

I know this from my own stress response system. Though I don't remember being deadly sick at two years old, I see my body's response. When I lived in apartments that had mold, a simple shower gave extreme discomfort. My eczema would overreact and tell my immune system something was wrong. Taking a shower was utter terror. Not only from the itching but from the stress response my whole body would enter. I could smell what seemed to be my dying cells as my immune system went full force against my skin. Just standing there in the shower, my pulse would hit between 150-165 bpm, shaking and itching. The situation of the shower could never justify the high pulse, but the stored trauma of the past when I was close to dying from an infection could.

You might think that pulse cannot be true with standing still and having such a high pulse. I thought the same until I tried it. This idea of measuring the pulse when trauma is triggered came from Dr. Bruce Perry. He discovered it by accident when he began running marathons and wore a heart rate monitor. One day, visiting a family and their foster child, the boy asked him what the monitor on his arm was. Bruce took it off and gave it to him. His heart rate was 100. Not an abnormal rest pulse for a boy his age. While talking with the boy, Bruce realized he had forgotten some paperwork and asked the boy if he wanted to go to the car for the papers. Immediately, the boy's pulse shot up to 148. Bruce noticed this but didn't think further until he asked the boy again if he wanted to join him. The boy froze, and the pulse went even higher. This puzzled Bruce, but he didn't want to make the boy uncomfortable, so he let the boy be and went down to his car himself. Later, when Bruce went back to his office to check the boy's chart, he found that his mother's boyfriend had sexually abused the boy in a garage. Bruce put the two together. The man would likely have said, "Let's go to the garage," which meant he was about to get abused. So when Bruce said, "Want to come to the car with me," the boy was triggered. Traumas are so deep and big that words or other senses like scents, tastes, sights, and sounds become sensitized. As much as it affected this young boy, it must affect infants. But only more. Much more. Enough for some of them to die.

Do we see the signs that match the importance of the first year? Are we seeing how important nurturing is in the first year And if the infant goes through severe neglect and abuse, could this cause severe changes to their brain, body, and being?

Are we seeing the river of blood? The source?

Are infants much more sensitive than we might think?

Infants are not born resilient. They are extremely vulnerable. Not only can events in our lives be damaging, they can change the very core of our being if it is early enough. Our brain develops from the womb, birth, all the way past twenty years old. But for the first three years alone, our current research tells us it is around 85 percent of the brain's growth. That leaves only 15 percent left after three years old.

This should shock you if you really think about it.

Three years = 85 percent of your brain's growth and learning.

It is our foundation.

But does that mean it's the source we are looking for?

Would it not be true that many of us have been through trauma as infants and toddlers also and did not turn bad.

This is back to the main problem that is often raised with nurturing. The first year and early enough cannot be the only answer. So what else could lead a small child down the wrong river? Not towards the river of life and joy, but the river of destruction and evil.

One last clue can be seen in drug use, and its effects on the body. A drug can give very different reactions depending on how it is used.

If taken frequently and in small doses, the drug loses strength over time. The drug user becomes tolerant and thus needs more and more to feel the same high. On the contrary, it has been tested that if you give an animal the exact same amount of drug but in large and infrequent doses, the drug actually "gains" in strength. In two weeks, a dose that caused a mild reaction on day one can cause a profound and prolonged overreaction on day fourteen. Sensitization to a drug, in some cases, can lead to seizures and even death.

Same drug, same amount, but one pattern leads to tolerance. The other leads to extreme sensitivity.

What if we apply this to trauma?

I noticed how this matches those I know. Infrequent but big traumatic events do seem to create severe sensitivity. It is anecdotal, but for example, a dear friend reacts with utter fear from just hearing the name of the person who abused her. The fear is visceral and powerful. She also has similar reactions to the smell of coffee and seeing milk. What happened to her? Was it daily abuse? No, It was not a daily event, but on and off sporadically during her pre-teenage years and into her young adulthood. Her trauma and response fit the sensitivity hypothesis as post-trauma from soldiers in war.

The question now goes to tolerance.

This one is more complicated but might lead us to our big question. What happens when an infant is being neglected and abused? But not a few times. Not where the mother is absent for a few days or a week. Not where the mother might get angry and frustrated at life and take it out on the baby only to embrace it moments later. On the contrary. This is a situation where hate and abuse are overwhelmingly bad at a very early age. Weeks of crying does nothing except make it worse. The entire world of the baby is neglect and abuse. There is no escape. Could it be possible that when the baby begins to dissociate that this is the first step to tolerance of the abuse? The baby becomes numb. Nothing can affect it. Even its heart rate might go down as it knows there is no fighting the abuse. It is interesting to note that low resting heart rate has been shown to be a common trait among aggressive and violent youth and psychopaths.

Adrian Raine, a British psychologist, found in his study with 1795 children at the age of three years old that a low resting heart rate predicted antisocial behavior later on at the age of eleven.

There is nowhere to go. A mind not yet developed. A body that cannot yet move on its own. Could this combination be the source of the river? Could tolerance and dissociation from the constant stress and fear of abuse be the last part we are looking for? Combined with the early age of an infant?

A time during which the baby needs the most—love, care, stability—Could persistent maltreatment and cruelty in the first years be the second birth... the birth of a monster?

The source of the river of blood?

I call it the river of blood because we must NEVER forget what evil is. Let us not forget the many stories we have read. Gulsoma, who had to endure beatings with electric wires, sleeping outside the house, freezing. Her back covered in scars from being treated as a human tabletop with food being cut on her back. Ms. Soon ok Lee who survived the camps of North Korea. How guards would force water into her until she nearly drowned. Water running out of her body from her mouth, nose, anus, and vagina and then jumping on her with a board on top of her stomach. It is hard to imagine this level of cruelty and thousands of events happening right now as you read this. But it is extremely real.

While still considering all the complexity of human personalities and the wide spectrum of abuse and neglect, I believe we have arrived at the source... It all makes sense.

This is the hypothesis for EVIL'S ORIGIN...

The Origin of Evil

"Regular and often NEGLECT and SEVERE ABUSE, with little to no affection or love DURING the first months of the infant's life."

That is it.

This could be the reason for the biggest sickness the world has ever known. A sickness that has thrown the longest shadows over human potential and destroyed so many innocent people's lives.

A river with blood so thick the edges are hardened, and the flow is so slow one could stand still and barely see it move. A river that has run from ancient time to present time and eerily seems to be widening. But the waters of the future are yet untouched. If we can understand it, test this hypothesis, understand if this is true, then determine what drives it. Then we can lessen its toxic control and take back more of the beautiful river of life.

I pray to God we do.

Because as I am writing this book, I see the world turn darker by the day. I sense that we could witness true horrors in a not-so-distant future if we do not wake up.

So let's try to understand its core. Understand what happened.

For this, we must imagine going to the darkest place. The likely Origin itself and try as much as we can to understand its beginnings.

CHAPTER 31

THE SECOND BIRTH

The Birth of a Monster.

Day zero.

You have been floating for nine months in the womb. Grown from a tiny single-cell up to the baby you are now. The womb has been warm but not peaceful. Sensations have shot through your system, from the rush of your mother's stress hormones to loud noises from a strange world beyond the reddish glow. But the constant rhythmic sounds of a heartbeat brought comfort. You are not you yet. You are senses and mostly asleep as you grow. The deep, muffled voice of your mother has become familiar, whether it's quiet, loud or screaming.

And then it happens, your birth.

The wonderful beginnings of your life. Full of potential. Coming out from a wet environment into a cold world with harsh bright lights. Every cell in your lungs feels the painful sensations of breathing air. Your inner soul screams for the next natural step. Reunion with your mother outside for the first time. The natural and beautiful moment where the everlasting bond happens on top of your mother's chest. You and her. But something is wrong. You are harshly handled and sense no sign of your mother. The separation is unbearable. You scream. You emote what you cannot process or understand. All you know is the world is not in harmony. Where is your connection? Your protector? The one you were one with for nine months?

An eternity passes, and you wake up in a crib.

It's day seven. It's been a week. You've grown. You've been given food. And you have finally been united with your mother. But something is off. There is something deeply disturbing. You cannot understand it. All you can feel is that the world is not right. When your mother is present, you are handled roughly. But not the sensations of experienced busy hands. No, they feel dangerous. They push your fingers in. They squeeze you hard. It hurts. You scream and scream when you are hungry, and nothing happens. It feels like years and years until you get a bottle pushed into your mouth. But now the milk is choking you. Your whole essence is frightened. Where is the sense of peace, security? Is everything bad? You are your mom, your sensations. It is all a ball of fear. You ARE only your senses with no escape.

Day fourteen. You begin to recognize the face of your mother: her eyes, her nose, and lips. You see other faces as well, but it is mostly a blur. You are still only a bundle of images, sounds, and sensations. But with an enormous need yet unfulfilled. Where is the love? Protection? You don't know what it is, but you feel the world isn't

THE SECOND BIRTH

in harmony. It is the opposite. It is dangerous. Painful. Lonely. You scream and feel a hard hit on your cheeks, the skin burning. You see a face. Eyes of steel with the familiar voice from your womb. Your mother. The two become one. The old, warm place has been replaced with a cold and shivering frightening world.

A world of wrong, day in, day out. Waiting for the feeling of love.

Day thirty, it has been an eternity. There is no time. Only forever. The pain is forever. The natural need for love does not exist. There is no understanding of the loss of hope or what could be. Only what is, and that fills your every sense of being with dread. Every cell. Tensions fill your legs and arms as your gut turns inside out, vomiting. When will you see the angry face? Will it laugh this time? Every feeling of need inside you is screaming for protection and love. The fear is turning into a soup of infantile anger. You sense the boiling heart. You must protect me. The world is not right. This is not right. Pick me up. Hold me. Kiss and touch me with love. I am important to you. I cannot do anything for myself. I am not even myself yet. You are me. I am you. This is my world, and it hurts. Every second of pain lasts a thousand years.

You cry and cry. You feel more sadness than the universe can hold. But it is all in vain. Nothing changes.

The second month starts with a loud bang. Your body goes into shock. Screams surround you. Then silence. You are picked up with forceful hands and put underwater. Your natural instinct kicks in as your heart rate lowers. You open your eyes. It's not the familiar warmth of the womb you once knew a time long ago. This is cold, and a new choking sensation fills your body... air. You need air. But like with every other need, nothing is happening. You kick and try to scream. Your lungs are again filled with water, but this time the sensation is all danger. Utter terror. Death. You sense it. You know it. Blackness surrounds your being as yourself disappear.

Voices, smells, vomiting. Sounds of laughter.

You are back. Other eyes stare at you. You smell a strong scent. Alcohol. Yelling and chaotic noises blur to nothing as you disappear again.

Fourth month... Time is suffering. It is all too much. Inside, a bottomless well of rage is building. This is not a just world you entered. Every sense of being in you knows this is not what you were meant for. This is not right. Everything is wrong. But you have no escape, no control over each minute. The screaming cannot stop it. The kicking and moving cannot either. The world surrounding you is full of danger. Sometimes there is nothing. No sounds, no touch, no food. Only slow seconds of forever. Then other times, it is chaos. Pain is so terrible, you must leave your body. A shadow is over you. Objects put inside you, skin burned. Dropped and beaten. You still don't understand the separation of yourself against the world. It is all the same. Sensations of horror, and there is nothing you can do except to escape. You want it to stop. With all your rage, you want it to stop. To END. But you have no power. You are utterly helpless. The world is you, and the world is out of control, hurting you. So you disappear. You go numb like a rock. Inside you are on fire, but outside you have become cold as ice.

THE SECOND BIRTH

Six months have passed. You are alive, and your body and brain have grown in leaps and bounds. You know what to expect from each day. A constant routine of endless silence and hunger, then the dreaded punishment of the world. You know what will happen. Sometimes it is worse. Sometimes it is less. But it is always a matter of time before it happens again, and you are powerless.

One year has arrived, offering you no true affection or love. You look just like any other toddler. You are praised for your cuteness. You are dressed and shown off by your mother to a new interesting world: more faces, more sounds, and more experiences. You are put next to another baby. Without understanding, your instant sensation inside burns to hit the other baby. Hit hard. Make them feel what you feel. And as you swing your little fist as hard as you can, hitting them, the response shocks and surprises you. They start crying. You can barely remember crying. But then another feeling inside grows, a sense of power over the other. It feels... GOOD. You want to hit again. You want power, control. You want the world to know your pain. You want the world to feel your pain. You want to flip the world, become the terror and the other, the weakling and the pathetic thing you were once, that had no escape and no choice but to take it.

And thus, we finally have the second birth... of the monster.

You are only one year old, but a path has opened for you. A path that will chase power, control, and destruction over everything and EVERYONE else.

You choose. What happens next in life will either amplify this darkness or hold it down. But healing from it is unlikely. The earlier and the longer the abuse, the darker the monster.

Are they human? Yes. Do they have a choice? I would say yes. But have the deepest parts inside of them been turned ice cold and hard?

Yes...

WITH a desire for utter revenge against the world.

CHAPTER 32

THE NEED OF EVIL

Monsters look human.

Many are hard to detect until they take gruesome action, whether being a serial killer or abusing their own children. They come in all sizes of personalities, and they carry a giant well of pain, in all depths. Shallow or world destruction deep. But if this hypothesis is correct, they have one thing in common. At the most vulnerable vital time of their lives, they had little to no love and protection, and they now feed off the pain of others, finding great pleasure in it.

Their needs are very different from the great majority.

Do you see it now? Has the fog lifted? Can you better understand the turmoil of our human species? How some cultures stayed healthy, and others became more and more sick and evil? Why we fight wars. Why we use other humans as slaves. Why we humiliate others. Why we laugh at the pain of others. Why we slaughter innocent humans. Why the very thought of genocide starts.

EVIL'S ORIGIN

I once saw a world full of people with different opinions on how to make a better world. I thought, for the most part, the end goal was the same. All good things in life. Peace, liberty, love. A purpose.

How wrong I was.

What I didn't understand was that there are people who desire the opposite, war, chaos, hate, and destruction. This desire to control is not only of their partners or their employees but against their countrymen and all on Earth. For them, they learned that human beings are a torturous threat. Every fiber in their being burns to be in control. The opposite of what they experienced as infants. They desire to have so much power that the pain inside no longer needs to express itself. For some, it's a smaller burn. Yelling at one's wife, controlling one's husband, maybe enjoying the power of being a government officer. Maybe a security guard. For others, it is a bigger burn inside... the need to control a larger group. Maybe become a politician of an authoritarian party. Maybe a warlord in a poor country or the elite for a global one world government. Enjoying absolute power over everyone.

As I write this, I see evil spreading everywhere. It is 2023, and I am shocked at how fast the spread of control has happened all over the world since 2020. But what scares me more is the apathy. I have seen this with a large majority of the people. Especially in the West, which has lived mostly in peace for sixty to seventy years. I fear too many don't understand just how dangerous this is. They don't understand genocides are not accidents. They don't understand that tortures in North Korean camps aren't about Korea but evidence of what can happen ANYWHERE that allows evil to grow.

This is indeed deeply serious.

Yet people walk around ignorant. They don't investigate themselves. They don't question things. They don't read. They spend zero time on serious matters and all their time on frivolous matters. When cities burn around the country, they ignore it. When churches and small businesses are locked down and decent citizens arrested, they ignore it. They see no similarities with the European Jews. They will even defend the propaganda they see. They accept it without second thoughts and attack anyone questioning it. I admit I am writing with frustration and anger.

Don't they understand we must fight evil?

I've come to the conclusion many don't.

And these are mostly good people.

Which is one of the main reasons why I started this book. People's inaction and apathy made me ask myself again. Are we really that different from evil?

Are we any different from monsters?

Do those who are not evil deserve to be called good?

Are we decent? Are humans good?

CHAPTER 33

DOES GOODNESS EXIST?

This is a question we must answer.

Are humans good? Is it innate?

I believe the answer is complex. It is yes and no.

Goodness grows out of love and care. The opposite of what we found with evil. The connection between the mother and the born baby. The baby is pure and innocent. Full of potential. Beautiful in its miracle of life. If given the maternal love it needs, it will learn about a life that is safe, protective, and giving... and from this, this little person has been given the greatest chance of being good.

Yet, it is an untaken journey.

Because our human nature isn't simple. Zimbardo could make people believe the statement "good people turn evil" is true, because unexamined, there seems to be a truth to it. We have the potential for being good but also equally for being bad.

Not evil... but bad.

The difference lies in the end goal. Evil desires utter power and control. It needs and lives on suffering. It hides behind the false mask until it has gained enough power to unleash the inner rage. Which ultimately, if not stopped, ends in true horrors that can last for hours to centuries, from domestic abuse, child abuse, human trafficking, slavery... up to totalitarian mass control and genocide of millions.

Goodness seems to be like a trajectory. Like a rocket heading for the stars. If its launch is destroyed during take-off, it will crash and burn. If the infant is abused and neglected enough, the seed of goodness is crushed. But given enough love and care, the rocket will take off and, for the rest of its journey, have this first moment, the first year, as a good trajectory.

But now enters the world and human nature with its almost infinite amount of obstacles... and choices.

Being human is hard.

Every step that happens next will either foster and teach goodness or knock off the trajectory. Are we given continuous support and love as children? Or does life take a dark turn and we lose our parents, or an abusive stepfather comes into the picture.

Life brings pain and temptation, and as we grow older, our own choices become more and more important. Choices that are based on what we have seen from our mother and father, then family, strangers, and eventually our culture. We watch them and pick up right and wrong, learning what we can do and what we shouldn't do. Do we live among thieves or farmers? Do we see productive people or wasteful people? Do we witness justice or injustice?

Life becomes a path of choices. The theory of judge, decide and watch. Our inner mind and personality will either lead our lives or be led by others and the world. We can decide not to judge and think we will be released from the responsibility of decision. We can watch and hope for the best. I know I have done this myself a lot. I am not proud of it. It is a child-like choice where the parent takes the lead. It is normal and healthy for a child. But as we mature, it becomes dangerous. Who are we led by? Bad company? Are we being used? Not taking decisions can lead one down dark paths. This is where I want to bring in the seven deadly sins that originated by Evagrius Ponticus, a Christian mystic from the third century AD.

Lust, gluttony, greed, sloth, envy, wrath, and pride.

For some, the idea of sins is old. Religious fanatics trying to control others by guilt. What did some old monks in Egypt, 1700 years ago, know about people's lives today? I thought this when I was younger coming out of school. In my mind, the concept of sin was dumb. It is simply a part of human nature. Moral judgment has no place in our modern world. But because of my youth and inexperience, these seven words and their wisdom went over my head. What I didn't understand is that human nature hasn't changed. We are the same as five thousand years ago. Our inner world, a sea of emotions. Sometimes calm and warm. Other times a storm of anger, jealousy, and rage. The original intentions of Evagrius Ponticus and the desert fathers, I believe, were to teach and warn us. To educate us in our ability or lack of ability to make good choices. For our own good and even more so for others.

These ideas surround the very question about goodness and who we are. They teach us how to be better and how to avoid the traps within ourselves. At least try to. To wrestle with them and overcome.

We all have been bad at times. Making bad decisions is easy.

Let's take time to think about these seven sins and reflect on them.

Lust. *An uncontrolled and overpowering desire and craving, often sexually.* How many lives have been ruined by lust? I know I have made some terrible decisions and paid for those with both shame and long-term pain. Think about **Gluttony**. *A lack of self-control, giving in to an excessive desire for pleasure.* Eating too much, drinking too much, watching TV or social media all day. Is this being good? To yourself or others? Now think about **Greed**. *Excessive, extreme desire for more power and wealth.* Have you ever had the chance to take? Not only take, but take more than you knew inside was fair. Maybe from a stranger or even a friend? Even lie to get what you wanted. What did it fill you up with? And what about **Sloth**? *Being lazy, indifferent, and passive.* No courage. Both regards to daily life but also your own purpose and soul. Does this bring goodness? or lead us into a dark cycle of hopelessness? Possibly giving us temptations to do bad? To avoid doing the work. And **Envy**. *the feeling of jealousy that someone has more than the other.* What goodness can an envious person achieve? It cools the heart and fosters anger. A feeling that burns bridges and becomes obsessive. Which can easily lead to our next sin, **Wrath**. *the raging storm within.* Mountains of pain all focused on a group or person. Blinding all reason. No person in hatred or rage can bring goodness in the moment. And finally, **Pride.** *Arrogance.* The mirror on the wall. Our twisted perception of ourselves. We all have an ego. The ego is natural and healthy. It is partly what gives us drive and confidence. But like a child wanting to be right all the time, it needs to be checked often. So watch if it goes from wanting to needing to be right. This can freeze our hearts and isolates us from others and the truth about ourselves.

Do you see it? Do you see the shadow of our human nature?

All of us have committed these sins. We have many temptations. We are dangerous. We are violent creatures. It is in us. To protect our loved ones, to fight for the survival of the tribe. Even the most civilized of us have the potential for great violence. Some of these actions can be good. But sometimes, we don't see things. Often we are wrong in our judgments, and we make terrible mistakes, all driven by emotions and primal instincts. Life is not easy. Dark fantasies can tempt us to take actions we will forever regret. Our emotions can become the master of our actions. No evil is needed to assist the disasters. Our flawed human nature and poor actions do it all. But that said, we are given a choice. We are given the opportunity to be good, and if we choose to grow and learn from our mistakes, we can be good.

With this, I come to the best answer I can give.

Goodness is not perfection. Humans are not holy.

But goodness exists...

Goodness is a potential... and at first, if we are blessed, it's a gift given to us through love, by our parents, our friends, and society. But later, this gift is put into our own hands for us to foster or... for it to wither.

Goodness is made. It is taught, tested, challenged, and ultimately a value that can grow deep roots. So yes, humans can be good. So very good. If given the love and taught the lessons, you will see it in their eyes. This cannot be taken away. Early love is their foundation. They cannot turn evil. This is why, when I see a homeless person with distant goodness in his eyes, I know that he was given love from his mother. I know he got the gift of love from the beginning. But then a harsh life entered with trauma and pain. This man, who got the right start, became lost. I've seen and spoken to those men and women. Good people, but broken by life. Your heart breaks for them. The same in the criminal world. With tattoos all over, they grew up in a bad neighborhood surrounded by gangs and crime. Perhaps with a loving mother who had three jobs. They had few other options than to toughen up to not become a target. As flawed people, they may have done bad things, but not evil. Somewhere in their actions, you would see the light, even if it's small or barely there. The word evil should never be used for these people who do bad things and make mistakes.

That said, it's complicated. Very complicated.

I want to theorize that good versus evil is, from a practical perspective, a yes and no answer. But looking deeper, that does not mean there's no spectrum on each side and that the middle, the battleground of when a monster is born, is hard to know and define. It could also be a spectrum. How and when it happens. What broke the camel's back? What made the person go from an abused, hurt child to the numb person who enjoys hurting others? Who will do anything for power and control over others? I theorize it is during the first year. Yet, it is so far a hypothesis. We have a lot of hard work ahead of us to understand this. To prove it or disprove it.

But time is precious. I sincerely sense darkness is growing.

It's easy for those of us who are blessed with love and a good life to be ignorant about this world. But you have a responsibility. You didn't create the peaceful world you enjoy. It was a gift to you, given to you by those who sacrificed everything, including their lives, fighting evil.

Apathy towards evil has no excuse.

Educate yourself about the reality of the world.

But what can we do?

Is it not much bigger than us?

CHAPTER 34

PREPARE

Learn of the seven virtues...

We MUST fight evil...

To do so, we must first acknowledge it exists.

I hope you see it now. I hope the fog is gone and you see it clearly by now. Evil is very real, and it doesn't want you to think it is.

Now, if we have acknowledged it, what can we do? A subject matter that could fill up books, but we can look at a few ways.

First, we must understand its deepest intentions. Evils drive.

If the hypothesis of evil's origin is true, we have a place to go for more understanding. If you put yourself in the situation of the infant and try to understand its screaming desires, then we might have a formula to guess what the drive is. And if we add human nature and its dark attributes to it, a way for us to see what is boiling within. Think of the second birth. Think about being a baby. Not able to move on your own. Not able to escape. Neither physical nor psychological. If you are severely neglected, hurt, even tortured and raped over and over, what would be the biggest desire? Would it not be to STOP the abuse and the person doing it? By control, by power.

Absolute POWER... Absolute CONTROL.

As the heart, body, and mind grows cold, the baby never develops a human connection. Instead of love, rage is formed. Instead of trust, infantile envy and hate are formed. Any vulnerability, sadness, and fear have been destroyed and replaced with an empty void that desires revenge. An abyss so deep there is no going back to the original starting point of life as a decent human.

Only a shell of a person, a robot of selfish motives.

Now take those deep desires of hate and rage and look at our world. Consider every sociopathic person. From the worst serial killers to corrupt politicians, down to an unskilled worker who has a job that gives a sense of power. What would be their ultimate wish? Their deepest desire. The desire they had the first minutes, days, and weeks before the flame of humanness went out? Would it not be to control you and me? Control the world? Have power over all of us. Make us suffer as they suffered. To no longer be the one who took it but the one who gives it.

I suspect this is where evil's pleasure in hurting others comes from. A high of finally being the one inflicting pain. The one who dictates what happens next. A God-like position of punisher and judge maker. But not from a truth or justice point but from the twisted fantasy of the sadist and new monster. Depending on where they are on the spectrum of darkness. Depending on how deep the trauma is, their drive is for absolute power to hurt others in small ways within a family circle, all the way to global genocides.

Do you see it? Does the past make more sense now?

This is where evil men are different from bad men. They desire the suffering of others. This is why one should never bow to their demands. They will never be satisfied until you are licking their boots and shot in front of them. And even then, it is not enough. It is never enough because none of it can solve the original trauma. Their own trauma.

So this is my warning. Most people do not understand the threat that is around them. Especially those of us who grew up in peaceful times in the West. Throughout your own country and in your towns and cities are people waiting to take off their masks. To express their deepest desires. To pose power and control over others and cause suffering. In small or big ways. This is worth repeating because we often think about power in big ways and not the smaller ones. The power over a child. The power over the old and sick. A professor, a parent, a bureaucrat.

Power and control OVER OTHERS is the sign to watch out for.

If we understand this, we can understand that we must avoid being put in situations where we are controlled and under someone else's power. If we have ways to do this, we have ways to fight evil.

But how can we avoid this?

The key is knowing.

Once you understand that evil wants to control and have power over you, you know you must keep and gain control and power over your own life. Not others, but yours and those you love who cannot defend themselves, who need protection. So this leads to the question. How can you keep power and control over your life? This question is not easy as it's complex and difficult to answer. Life isn't simple. Having control is almost the opposite of life. And having power is a limited wish for most, especially those who do not desire it. One can be lucky to live in a country run by either benevolent rulers or have a constitution that protects the rights of the individual and limits power like the USA (if we can keep it). But one can also be living under a tyranny of various degrees. Those who do, know that once dark people get power and control, it is not the end but the beginning... To make others suffer, hurt, and beg.

We must work hard to understand this and change direction throughout different cultures. Some cultures serve evil more than others. We must see this and make the changes to slow it down. A Native American tale talked about how a tribe would deal with those who were sociopathic. If a member had a long list of dark behavior, the elders would gather and make a judgment. If they decided that the person could not be trusted, they would take them into the wilderness, far from the village, and kill them. Once they were considered to have a dark spirit, it was too dangerous for the tribe to keep them.

There is a harsh truth to this. Cancer cannot coexist with a healthy body. It wants to destroy the organism. It is one or the other.

PREPARE

This is true for society as well. But as the native American tribe could heal and avoid greater damage from their tough choice, I do not believe this can be done in a just way for a larger society. We, as humans, are too flawed. Once, we are no longer a small tribe with elders who are good and wise, and once society grows larger, the risk of it being used against those who want to do good, goes up by a lot. Just consider how difficult it is to know who a person truly is, just with one person. Let alone a society of people. To do justice would be impossible. Besides, it would play into the hands of evil as it would find great pleasure in taking decent people and portray them as evil and then remove them from society.

Instead, we must do what is harder. Look within ourselves and come from the direction of love and understanding first. Yet, at the same time, learn to know the true nature of evil and not be soft and easily manipulated. Be strong. Be firm.

This means we must prepare. We must educate ourselves.

Get to know yourself. Know your strengths and your weaknesses. Be honest with yourself and ask the closest people you love about the truth of how they see you. Look at what you are afraid to see. It's okay. It is for the better. Observe yourself. Watch how you can go down the wrong paths as you battle yourself. Do not be overconfident in your own abilities to know. Work hard to grow.

One warning.

For those who have a hard judging inner voice, I want you to be easy on yourself. There's a healthy judgment of yourself, and there is an unhealthy one. I want you to become stronger, not weaker, and if you have gone through traumatic events and had an abusive childhood, this could be a difficult path to walk. Be gentle with yourself. Know you are not the harsh voice. Once you realize this, do not fall into its negative game. But seek ways to heal. The more you heal, the more you are less likely to be controlled. I know this is easy to say and very hard to do. But fight it because this voice will make you an easy target among evil people. Don't allow it to run your life. You can become stronger, and you can become more aware, making it harder for others to control and use you.

But how do you fight your weaknesses and improve your discipline?

I believe our first step is to accept the goal to grow and know our weaknesses is a choice. Understand we are often our own worst enemy. Prudentius, the Roman and Christian poet from the fifth century Spain, wrote this:

> *I see the better thing and approve of it... I choose the worse."*

How true this is. I see it with myself. I know better, yet a lot of times I ignore my better judgment. Prudentius would write the poem "Battle for Our Souls" where our vices was confronted and defeated by virtues.

The virtues were:

Faith, Chastity, Patience, Humility, Hope, Sobriety, Good work and peace

PREPARE

Think about those qualities. Do you have them? Do you try to practice them?

Through time and different cultures, we have had virtues to look up to. For the Japanese Samurai, they had the Bushido Code, "The way of the warrior."

Their virtues were:

Mercy, Honesty, Loyalty, Honor, Valor, Respect, Justice.

Think about these. Are they good? Do they challenge us?

It is important to learn about the wisdom from the past. Don't forget we stand on the shoulders of many giants and our ancestors who created the majority of the culture we enjoy today. The same with us. We are building the structure that future generations will stand on.

Will it be better, or will it be worse than ours?

I worry...

For the last century or so, there has been a great push away from Western and Christian values and replacing them with values that glorify victimhood as envy, hate, pride, and relative "truths."

In many ways, it glorifies the seven sins. If you asked people today as I write this, are you feeling safe and good about the future, I think a majority would hesitate and give a negative answer. Especially after 2020 and seeing how the whole world was forced in one direction by a seemingly unknown force.

2021 has shaken and awakened me. Evil is on the rise.

We must fight and change direction. Let us step up and make sure we do not fail future generations.

I believe working on ourselves is the first step forward.

So lets look a little closer at the virtues. Here is the more modern version of the capital virtues.

Chastity, temperance, charity, diligence, patience, kindness, humility

Each virtue can be viewed as a solution to a sin.

Let us think about this...

Chastity could be the answer to lust. Chastity means being virtuous and modest. Absent from sex. Many people likely view this idea as old-fashioned. But I think we are missing the point and have forgotten there are reasons behind considering the sins and why virtues can lead us to a better life. Lust is like a fire. It has its place between a man and woman but can easily burn down your house and you in it. Chastity is having the discipline to play carefully and know the dangers involved. Sex is powerful. It is wonderful. But it can lead us into trouble and make a good person lost in a sea of powerful emotions. I am not saying sex is bad. It is great. It is part of love. But watch out. Find ways to be strong and disciplined.

Next is temperance. Self-restraint. The virtue that can help us with gluttony. We all have things we are addicted to. Endless social media, desires to eat or drink. But with self-discipline, we can learn to say no. To not drink that extra beer when we know it will bring us trouble. Learning temperance, self-restraint will help us. Like a muscle, the more we push ourselves, the more we learn we can keep a balance and get stronger against our weaknesses.

And then we have charity. Give to others. Be helpful. Understand that greed can never fill up your soul but can easily lead you into destruction. Remember Tolkien's Lord of The Rings series? How the ring destroyed Gollum? Its theme is both greed and power. To rule (and control) everyone. So what would be the opposite value? Would it not be to let others be free. To help others. To be charitable with what you have, instead of lying your way to more materials. So be careful. Balance the urge of greed with honest charity.

After this, we come to diligence. The opposite of sloth. The act of being devoted to a good job. Working hard with the utmost effort. No matter the size of the task, big or minuscule. It brings joy and helps others. It stops a bad cycle of waste of time and your own value. You are here for a reason. It is not to be wasted away. It is for you to discover what you can accomplish. And you can accomplish great things if you are diligent.

This brings us to patience. It requires a lot of patience to keep going. It is easier to be lazy and look at others with envy. Wanting what others have. Wanting to take from others. But did you put in the work? Patience can quiet the mind. It can bring focus to your flaws and give you hope that in time you will get there. Don't be envious. Have patience. Focus on running your own path. Things are not meant to be easy. Endure!

And from patience, we come to kindness, which is the antidote to anger. Anger lives within us all to protect us. But it can blind us and lead us in bad directions. We need both patience and kindness to fight it. Think about how often we are kind and how often we can choose to be kind, to help others. These questions and actions will help ease the fire within.

And then, we have the last virtue. Humility, The answer to pride. The more you learn about the world, the more you realize how little you know. The more you learn about yourself, the more you realize your flaws and not trust your judgments and actions. Be careful with yourself. Be humble because the truth is, we should never become too self-absorbed. It leaves us vulnerable to fake flattery and manipulation, which will ultimately feed and perpetuate evil.

That is it. These are the seven capital virtues.

Virtues that are sadly almost forgotten in our current society. We must bring back the thoughts of virtues. I sincerely believe they can make us stronger and better humans and help us prepare to fight evil in all its forms. Whether it's a bad domestic relationship or a totalitarian movement.

Because we cannot fight evil if we are weak and vulnerable to manipulation.

One thing, for the last virtue with humility, I am aware of the contradiction. Judge others fairly to not fall victim of ignorance but at the same time saying, "Don't trust your judgments because you will fail to see the truth many times."

I believe it is all true, and it shows how hard it is to be human and how hard it will be to turn our world around. To have it turn away from its own destructive desires and to slow evil's spread. We can be our worst enemy. But it is in the effort we can grow and learn to balance it more and more. To both be hard and soft. To work hard and to rest. To prepare so we can be strong, brave, and gentle.

Because if we don't, evil has an agenda, and it has been working overtime to gain power and control over us all.

EVIL people want people weak, dependent, and needy.

They want us to fall into the seven sins. The more, the better. It gives them the POWER to temp us, to control us. And when good men are weak, evil men can take over.

So prepare yourself. Be better. Be stronger. Be disciplined. Protect those who cannot protect themselves. You will then be better prepared to have the courage to fight the darkness around us.

Because it will take real courage to face the depths of evil.

It is much darker and deeper than many of us realize.

CHAPTER 35

KNOW ITS DEPTHS

EVIL IS BOTTOMLESS

We have come far in this journey by exploring history, stories, and looking into the source of evil's origin. But I noticed something about myself. I easily flip back to the perspective I know, a decent world. I have never faced true evil, so it's hard for me to keep it in focus. This is why we must, for the last time, venture into the darkness. For us to end with its cold reality.

Evil is not cool. It is not entertainment.

It is brutal. It is unforgiving. It is terrifying.

Do you KNOW IT by now? It cannot be imagined. It can only be felt.

Have you been to Belgium? Maybe Poland? To one of those historic and beautiful towns of Europe? The documentary *Eyes of the Devil* by Patryk Vega takes us into the world of sex trafficking in Europe. It shows us the truth of what is going on inside quaint family houses.

Patryk Vega is sitting relaxed on a couch. He is talking to a blurred-out and voice distorted sex trafficker whose job it is to find young pregnant women. Women who will offer their child for money. A baby who will be born without a birth certificate. Out of sight, unknown to society.

Eyes of the Devil:

Vega: "So it's kinda like human breeding?"...

Trafficker: "Yes, exactly."

Trafficker: "Those intercourses take place before a child is taken away for organs."

Vega: "Does the client have to pay more for that?"

Trafficker: "Of course, I believe the price amounts to... It must be around half a million euros. And he's aware the child becomes useless after that."

Vega: "Do those four-year-olds live together? with seven or eight-year-olds, or do they go somewhere else?"

Trafficker: "Seven- or eight-years-olds are good for regular sex and those little kids are separated."

Vega: "From what age can you have intercourse with a child without risking tearing them apart?"

Trafficker: "They can have regular sex from the age of six or eight and earlier. That is when recycling begins... He likes it when he shoves his dick in... blood spilling. He massacres the child."

Vega: "Does he murder the child or leave it to die?"

Trafficker: "Whatever turns him on, but then the child is a wreck anyway."

Vega: "How long can a child survive in such conditions?"

Trafficker: "If there's a client for the VIP satisfaction, then they won't survive."

Take a moment...

Let this last brief view into evil linger. Imagine being the child. The little baby... breed for evil.

Is it real to you? Ask yourself, Am I aware this is happening today? Did I know? If you didn't, ask yourself why not? How many journalists are there around the world? Some four hundred thousand in Europe, thirty seven thousand in the US. How many journalist stories have you read in the last decade? We consume news every day. Yet did you hear about this? Likely not. Ask yourself why? How many of the journalists deliver CONTROLLED news?

Could it be they don't want you to know?

I'm not saying all of the close to half a million journalists in Europe know this. Most probably don't. What I am saying is there is almost no one doing the job of a journalist finding the truth. Exposing the truth. Except for people like Patryk Vega, who's not even a journalist but a writer and director. What I am saying is, someone doesn't want this to be talked about. And they might be very powerful, in control of much of the media machine... VIP people.

Do you realize this?

Same with other fields. Psychologist Dr. Anna Salter wrote about how she first thought violent offenders would be put away, at least when the abuse is reported. Later she realized this was often not the case. During one case with a rape of a five-year-old girl, the offender was the same as another case of a girl of similar age just a few years before. She learned that the offenders were often believed more than preschoolers, and if they were convicted, judges would give them little time, and then they would be released without any treatment. Most rapes she heard about were never reported at all.

The point is. It's everywhere around us, and most do nothing.

Evil's actions are both in doing horrible things... But also in COVERING IT UP.

This goes for both VIP global elites and the regular family monster. It is being covered up. People stay silent. Doctors look at scans of brains instead of the girl in front of them. Judges ignore the cries of the child and release the family offenders. Government social shelters are given to psychopaths to run. The crimes are swept underneath the bed so we all can pretend it doesn't happen until the fire starts in the bedroom and spreads to the house, and eventually takes down the town in fires of pain and suffering.

SILENCE KILLS...

Are you going to look the other way like most do? Or will you take action? I am asking again and again because I see it being ignored. OVER AND OVER.

It is a serious question.

No one can answer it but you.

START WITH UNCOVERING THE TRUTH... Around you, your family, city, and country. You can do it. It's local. It is not a town in Iraq.

If you were a victim of evil, of a monster, then I ask you to bravely tell the story. Let others know, who are too afraid to speak. Let them know they are not alone.

If you were not a victim of evil, find victims and help them. Support groups like The Underground Railroad, O.U.R., who track down trafficking rings and catch the monsters. Or if you have the skills to start groups, organize one. Find your strength and seek ways to use them. There is so much to do.

We are behind. Evil is way ahead of us.

And unlike most of us, evil has a plan...

CHAPTER 36

FIGHT EVIL

THE PLAN

Evil has a plan.

The plan is to control you and then make you suffer.

It is this simple. But so easily ignored. Because it is both right in the open but also well hidden, it is not necessarily organized. It is simply a common goal. Big or small. Whether it is on a small individual level with domestic abuse, child abuse, or a global scale, like totalitarianism, the varieties are endless. But the path is not. The first goal is to gain power: power and trust. As the goal is to make you suffer, they cannot use any truth. True trust can never be achieved, so the best "trust" is through programming. So they must draw you in with various gifts or promises or with fear and protection. They need to frame their lies in a way that will take root in your belief system, so later, when suffering begins, it will be part of your ego, hard to escape. There will be endless targets to blame instead. All strategically set up, of course.

Ask yourself, What do these frames of ideas have in common?

It becomes a game of changing cultures. Of transforming a free society into a more "open" society for those who wish to control others and have power over them. To enslave and enjoy the show of human beings become numbers that can be used for anything.

How is this done? By words...

We have talked about this in previous chapters. Our culture is built up of knowledge and values. All are shaped through words and language. If a culture helps goodness and protects others, it will have words and customs that values this. This is a threat to anyone who wants control and power OVER others. They must remove these words and meanings. Doing so makes people blind to the true realities of life. North Korean escapee and survivor Yeonmi Park talks about this in an interview with Glenn Beck. North Koreans are so isolated from the outside world that there is no concept of even romantic love between a woman or a man. Only the love of the dear leader and the communist party. Take the time to think about this. The basic concept of human love does not exist in the minds of North Koreans. No thoughts on it. The communist party steals this truth from them.

This gives us a great insight into how vital culture and words are. Without any external influence, art, philosophy, religion, no one can gather their own wisdom.

The chains are both of mind and body.

I have been fortunate to grow up in a peaceful culture, but unbeknown to me as a young person, everything that I watched and saw was playing a mind game of chess against the populace. Especially young people. It was a battlefield of ideas. No blood spilled, but plenty of destruction of the very foundation that made it possible for me to live in peace. Crack by crack. Idea by idea. Values were ridiculed while new values were glorified. Virtues were laughed at, while vices were encouraged as good and natural.

I now see my own birth country turn over their limited freedom to a potential ending of it. Time will tell. As I am writing this book, I see the fall in slow-motion of the world. Hoping enough people will speak up and stop it. Who will not obey. But so much silence among people. I suspect it was always so in the past as well. It is just hard to see unfolding. I do not know what will happen. But you, the reader, will know when enough time has passed.

Learn verbal kung fu. When you seek and speak the truth, you will be attacked. This can be painful if you are not used to it. You will be called names and, if your point is strong, vilified as evil. They want to shut you up. This control never ends and only gets worse. To fully understand this, in North Korea, during executions, the person's teeth are broken, and a rock is put into their mouth, so they do not stutter a word against the regime. So if you think that they will stop silencing people once they have 100 percent power, you are underestimating evil's need for control. It never ends.

So speak up early before they literally have the power to break your teeth.

When speaking, resist arguments or following their narrative. Do not fight with their framing. With this, I mean, they set up the angle. No matter what you say, you will be on the defense. Some arguments are better not played. Speak the truth and move on. Any energy spent on a lie is spent in the mud. Question your perspective.

Catch your misguided thoughts. Be as honest as you can. Vulnerable yet firm. Avoid demonizing people/groups as much as possible. This way, you stay true to yourself AND it makes it easier to see when others do it. You can then watch out for this, and should someone keep talking bad about others, you can move on and stop wasting energy on someone who has a big potential to be poisonous.

We must remember their goal is to release their poison in the world. They cannot do this with a society that is strong on individual rights. They need a non-thinking mob, a baby, uneducated cult members who they can control to push power over the few who dare to speak up.

So I ask again, Are you the person who will turn in your neighbor? Who will close your eyes and ears? Who will celebrate the lies? Believe the lies? Will you cross the sidewalk if a stranger is unjustly taken in by the police ahead of you?

Who are you?

Will you join evil's plan? It will be "easy" at first.

Or will you stand?

It's time for our plan. To fight back.

FIGHT EVIL

#1 Know evil exists. Do not be in denial or naive.

#2 Know evil's past. Know what it is capable of.

#3 Prepare with discipline.
Psychologically and physically.

#4 Watch your weaknesses and flaws.

#5 Train your courage. Start small.
Add daily tasks of courage.

#6 Be good to yourself first.

#7 Then be good to those who need it and deserve it.

#8 Speak up. What you know,
What you see. Be humble.

#9 Become a warrior of truth. Take-
down lies. Takedown snakes.

#10 Expose evil's plans.

#11 Live a good life. Build a strong,
health-loving community.

#12 Love and protect the children.

#13 Help those who struggle and who could
potentially cause harm to their babies.

#14 Forgive but never give in to evil. Fight it early.

#15 If evil gains violent power. Fight
it brutality and relentlessly.

Do everything with strength and do it with love.

CHAPTER 37

IT CAN BE DONE...

A BRIGHTER TOMORROW

We are a traumatized world... full of broken people.

Let's have a very serious last moment. There is something I want you to think about. It is one of the biggest obstacles I see with what is in front of us.

I see the trauma everywhere. EVERYWHERE!

It breaks my heart to know how widespread it is. But what is much worse is a society that is running away from dealing with the source, child abuse. We can do better. We must do better. We MUST talk about this without taboos. We must have the hard talks for future generations. Because if we don't, society will get more sick with each generation, and evil will grow to a level where hell on Earth will be normal. A sick, demented, evil world where the monsters are free.

We CANNOT allow this.

We are at a fork in the road. Evil has taken a hold of what used to be free societies. Writing this, I don't even know what will be reality in five to ten years. In many countries, hell is already here. North Korea, China, Afghanistan. Too many places. In the West, the move towards totalitarianism is starting. I pray it does not get there, but it could. In the USA, we are more divided than ever. Things are equally bad or worse in Canada, Europe, and Australia. I want to sound the alarm. Many people don't understand there are small monsters all around us, waiting for the opportunity to have power over others. By now, their cruelty should not surprise you, but I suspect they still do. They do for me. I think of the research I did, where I saw videos that made me physically sick. I saw a skinny girl in her teens jump with her one foot on top of a small puppy, squeezing it to death. It was not a quick death. Her laughs as she forced her foot down and around, over and over, made something very clear. She, as a mother, would bring into the world broken people, if not monsters like herself. I have no compassion for her or her evil act, but I pity her soul and have sorrow for the innocent baby she once was. These monsters create broken people and create fallen societies. I saw images of baby corpses left to rot in puddles by the street curbs. It was shocking, frightening, and heartbreaking.

We have no time.

We must slow down this cycle of broken people. We need an explosion of awakening. There is so much ignorance on trauma.

The good thing, there is a north... We have an answer:

IT CAN BE DONE...

THE SOLUTION

"It is the baby's first year. It is motherly love. It is protection, care, and a calm, welcoming world."

It is a beautiful truth. It is so simple.

Yet many of us have forgotten it.

NO LONGER!

We MUST change direction and realize just how vital the first year and years are for our children. Yes, each child has their own personality and, if you ask me, their own soul. But they still desperately need love and security to set a healthy emotional foundation for their lives. If they do, they are well underway in life. Ready to make their own good and bad choices. But not choices coming from pure rage and sadistic needs for power over others.

With our knowledge and God's help, we can heal our nation and world. We cannot fix the already broken, but we can help them and, through generations, move towards a more empathic and decent culture.

That is if we have the fortitude and discipline to not look away and to educate ourselves of these taboo matters. Openly talk about them and then take action. Calm our righteousness and get to work on solutions. Children need their mothers by their side. Births should not take place in cold, clinical rooms and, when born, taken away from the mother. Parents should raise their children. Not leave them behind and have others raise them. Work practices need to change. Mothers can work but at home with their children. It is best for the child and them. The joy of being a mother is the biggest gift and the highest honor a human can have. Fathers can do their part by being the rock, the hard-working man who provides, outside or at home also. Yes, the old way of parenting at home is better. The evidence is clear. It is time to turn around. Our societies have grown colder by each decade. No more. We can no longer claim ignorance.

This insight is a cry for those willing to listen. Cultural ideas always start with a few brave souls who are not afraid to look outside the tribe's taboos. That later becomes the commonly shared values. If the book's hypothesis is correct, we can make a strong and decent society again. Not a perfect one. But a good one. One where mothers can care for their children. A place where the father gives protection for the mother so she, in turn, can care for the child. I do not want to sound too rosy. I realize we are still dealing with humans and their flaws. Many will not listen. Many will disagree. But there is a path for us. We must educate ourselves on how we can better protect our infants and provide a more safe environment. How we can educate the next generations, young parents, young mothers. How we can find ways to help those mothers who are having difficulties. How we can foster the vital knowledge that we all need to do the right thing.

We must get more of our empathy back. We must avoid creating more monsters. Together, we can do it. But do not wait for your neighbor. It starts with you. Ask yourself, What can I do?

PREPARE YOURSELF. BE HUMBLE. BE STRONG. TAKE ACTION.

I see a future where the light shines brighter. Where the great majority of children grow up happy and content, whether it is big or small cities, people are as happy as in the jungle of Venezuela that Jean Liedloff found in the 1970s. A place of love. A place of strength and support from each other. A good community.

Will there be evil people? Yes, there will be. But they will be much fewer, and they will not be in charge. They can still live within the decent society rules and use their trauma to do good. But any violence and abuse will be met firmly with action. The victims will always be number one.

But we have far to go. We are almost over the cliff. The world could turn dark for centuries.

Are you ready to fight the good fight? Let's do it!

For the unborn children!

For a decent society with empathy and love!

Acknowledgements

Could not have done it without you.

There are so many I want to thank. Writing this book with its topic has been a journey that at times overwhelmed me. I likened it to walking from one end of the Amazon river to the other. Years, days, many thousands of hours, one day at a time, trying my best to write in clear language and find my way to the truth as much as I could.

Thank you to my dear dad, Lauritz Laursen, who showed me how to be a man. To be strong in the face of suffering and never forget to laugh. Thanks to my sweet mom, Ninna Laursen. You taught me love. You gave me the most precious gift I will ever receive. You gave me the second birth, of love, which gave me my foundation for love and kindness. Deep thanks to Alexandra for your beliefs in me and your never ending support. No one supported me more than you. I could share my deepest fears with you. You guided me and gave me light when I was lost. You gave me insight to see things from a different perspective, from a true victim yet survivor and truth warrior. You truly honor your name, protector of humankind, and are an angel! Thank you Amber as well! Thank you Clarita! You were there in the early beginnings when the book idea was born. Your love and patience gave the artist in me, the space to grow. My obsessions were met with kindness and help. I am lucky to have met you and for us to have been together. I will always be grateful to you and your mother! Thank you, Lenni, for your love, patience, and giving me the right environment to focus and speed up my writing. As the world began to burn faster and faster, I knew, time was up and there was no longer time to waste. It was writing every day, at night, nonstop. I could not have written as much as I did without your help. You gave me the quiet place and you always understood. I will forever be grateful to you! Thank you, Chris! Our friendship was no accident. It was meant to be. I doubt this book would have been written if it wasn't for our friendship. Many of the ideas here came from our deep conversations. Many of the teachings I have learned came from you and your own unique and brave journey. You are a beautiful soul! A true warrior. You are like a brother to me. I hope your story comes to light and I will have the ability to help. Thank you, Daniel, for the great journey we had together. Teaching me so much, forgiving me for my faults, and being a good friend after all we went through. You mean a lot to me, and I could not be the artist I am today if it wasn't for you. I hope to work together again someday. Thank you Peter, for our friendship that never grows old. We will remain eight years old forever with our friendship. We have been a apart but always close as best friends. Thank you Lars, for being a true great friend. Air Brothers! I have always looked up to you and learned so much from you. All the laughs we have had! I am blessed to know you. Thank you Jette! Thank you Danilo, for our partnership and sharing the road we've been on. Your skills that I did not have, you helped me with. Through storms and through sunny days, we have

ACKNOWLEDGEMENTS

helped each other stay productive and work on so many great things. Always a joy. Thanks Rod, Matt, Andrew, always great to work with good and talented people like you. To all the great artists over the years I have worked with. Who have been there, believed in me, took me in to be part of their projects. Patrick Gilmore, Martin Alper, David Perry, Brian Horton, Tarrnie Williams.

Thank you, Diana and Dave, for what you've done to help this world, doing good. Helping children. You are an inspiration for us all. We must help the children who have survived the worst. Thank you to all my family. To my dearest Nan, who always was there for me as I went on the journey to the US. My second mother and protector. How lucky I am. To my dear sister Sussie, Bjarne, Kenneth and Nanna. To the rest of my extended family, Marianne, Bodil, Fleming, Jonas, Susanne, Hans, Sofie, Morten, Christian. For being a good family and patient with me as an artist always doing too many things.

I want to thank all the great artists and people I have worked with, whom I learned from, who helped me over the years: David Lovins, Robert McActee, Shaila Vaidaya, Tim Colceri, Lisa Roumain, Jesper Kyd, Chuck Dulin, Henrik Munch, Karsten Lang Pedersen, Jon Gregerson, Matt Hall, Rion Vernon, Ron Volz, Kenneth Bedsted, Rob Wright, Stephen Townsend, Mikko Tahtinen, Dave Prout, Joel Payne, Darran Douglad, Rolf Mohr, Rebecca Hanck Liu, John Haley, Monica Haley, Lori Pietruszka Sussman, Rene Vidum, Scott Kramarich, Lisa Stacilauskas, Bill Baldwin, Jens Albertsen, David Guldbrandsen, Karsten Hvidberg, Jens Schmidt, Martin Jensen, Solveig Wierenfeldt, Drew Love Taylor, Lillian Lassen, Araceli Theard, Evelyn Gonzalez, Marilyn Tampoya, Gilma Ruiz, Leonard

Cremer, Arielle Caron, Macy Galla, Melanie Herman and no doubt many more. You know who you are.

Thank you to my book team! Steven Fox, my attorney and Mary Jo Courchesne, licensing and Miriam Pinedo, printing.

Thank you Jenna Love Schrader. For taking a close look at the book's edit and making sure it all made sense. It was a joy going through the book and seeing the fixes and how you catched my mistakes. Thank you so much!

Thank you Suzie Hyun, for helping me pronounce the Korean names for the audio book.

Thank you to those who have passed on to a better place, but who all had a big influence on me as a new American and helped in so many ways. Maximo Munzi, Richard Fraade, Martin Alper, Sydney Balbes. God bless you and RIP.

Thank you, to all those who help traumatized children. To bring light to those who have seen too much. Thank you, Dr. Bruce Perry. Not only have your books been a key part in my journey in writing this book, but what you have done for neurology and science, seeking the truth. Not afraid of going outside the box of "doctor." Being a human foremost. Thank you Operation Underground Railroad, for the good you do, saving children from slavery.

Life is a journey and the people you meet along the way shape you in all kinds of ways. I would not be the person today if it wasn't for all these people and even strangers I met once but left me with an impression.

Thank you all!

References

Benedict de Spinoza, (2017): *Of Human Bondage or of the Strength of the Affects, Ethics.* Penguin Classics, p. 424. ASIN B00DO8NRDC. (Original work 1677)

Kevin Sites, (2009): *In the Hot Zone, One man, One Year, Twenty Wars.* HarperCollins, ISBN:9780061745096

Ms. Soon Ok, (2002): US CONGRESS testimony. www.judiciary.senate.gov/imo/media/doc/lee_testimony_06_21_02.pdf

Alice Miller, (1985): *For Your Own Good.* Farrar, Straus and Giroux (first published 1980.) Am Anfang war Erziehung. ISBN0374518599

Caitlin Matthews, John Matthews (2004): *Walkers Between the Worlds: The Western Mysteries from Shaman to Magus.* New York City. Simon & Schuster. p. 173. ASIN B00770DJ3G.

Philip G. Zimbardo (2007): *The Lucifer Effect: Understanding How Good People Turn Evil.* Random House (NY). ISBN 1400064112

Marquis de Sade (1791): *Justine.* J. V. Girouard (France.) Original title Les Infortunes de la Vertu

Richard Freiherr von Krafft-Ebing, Joseph LoPiccolo (2011): *Psychopathia Sexualis: The Classic Study of Deviant*

Sex. Arcade; Reprint edition (August 1, 2011) (Original Book 1886.)

Raymond T. McNally, Radu Florescu (1989): *Dracula, Prince of many faces*. Little, Brown and Company; Revised ed. edition (October 31, 1990) ISBN-10:0316286567

Friedrich Paulsen (1899): *A System of Ethics*. Creative Media Partners, LLC, 2019 ISBN 0526396695

Jung Chang, Jon Halliday (2006): *Mao, The unknown story*. Anchor (November 14, 2006). ISBN-10:0679746323

Reza Kahlili (2013): *A Time to Betray: The Astonishing Double Life of a CIA Agent Inside the Revolutionary Guards of Iran*. Threshold Editions; Reprint edition ISBN : 1439189684

Viktor E. Frankl (1946): *Man's Search for Meaning*. Beacon Press; 1st edition (June 1, 2006) ISBN-10:9780807014271

Blaine Harden (2012): *Escape from Camp 14: One Man's Remarkable Odyssey from North Korea to Freedom in the West*. Penguin Books, ISBN-10:0143122916

Jeffrey Moussaieff Masson (2012): *The Assault on Truth*. Untreed Reads Publishing, ASIN :B007JPNLXC

Sam Vaknin (2015): *Malignant Self-love: Narcissism Revisited*. Narcissus Publications, ASIN:B00HDJF7HC

Anna Salter (2004): *Predators: Pedophiles, Rapists, And Other Sex Offenders*. Basic Books; Reprint edition (March 31, 2004). ISBN-10:0465071732

David Smith, Carol Ann Lee (2012): *Evil Relations: The Man Who Bore Witness Against the Moors Murderers*.Mainstream Publishing; Illustrated edition (April 1, 2012.) ISBN-10:1780575394

REFERENCES

Emlyn Williams (1969): *Beyond Belief : Moors Murders.* Pan MacMillan; New Ed edition (February 1, 1969) ISBN-10:0330020889

Dr. Kevin Magid, Beth Thomas (1990): *Child of Rage.* HBO.

Jay Joseph (2017): *Schizophrenia and Genetics: The End of an Illusion.* BookBaby; 1st edition (September 4, 2017). ASIN :B075DDG6F9

Daniel Mackler: *Take These Broken Wing* (DVD). Studio Daniel Mackler. ASIN:B00C2YOYQI

Alice Miller (2012): *The Untouched Key.* Anchor; Reprint edition (May 9, 2012). ASIN:B009N989PM

Alice Miller (2009): *From Rage to Courage.* W. W. Norton & Company. ASIN:B002PQ7B6S

Arthur Janov (1981): *The Primal Scream.* TarcherPerigee (January 1, 1981.) ISBN-10:0399505377

Dr. Vincent Felliti, Dr. Robert Anda (2010): The Child First and Always. Presentation. www.acestudy.org.

Robert Ressler, Tom Shachtman (2015): *Whoever Fights Monsters: My Twenty Years Tracking Serial Killers for the FBI.* St. Martin's Press (May 19, 2015) ASIN:B00VQ1HK28

Jean Liedloff (1986): *The Continuum Concept: In Search Of Happiness Lost.* Da Capo Press; Reprint edition (January 22, 1986). ISBN-10 : 0201050714

Cora DU BOIS (1944): *The People of Alor; a Social-Psychological Study of an East Indian Island.* University of Minnesota Press; 1st edition (January 1, 1944). ASIN: B000IA5MLO

Dr. Bruce D Perry, Maia Szalavitz (2017): *The Boy Who Was Raised as a Dog: And Other Stories from a Child Psychiatrist's*

Notebook, What Traumatized Children Can Teach Us About Loss, Love, and Healing. Basic Books; 3rd edition (August 29, 2017). ISBN-10:0465094457

Beth Thomas (2010): *Dandelion on My Pillow, Butcher Knife Beneath: The true story of an amazing family that lived with and loved kids who killed*. Families By Design Inc; First Thus Used edition (April 15, 2010). ISBN-10:0970352522.

Rebecca Morris (2014): *Ted and Ann: The Mystery of A Missing Child and Her Neighbor Ted Bundy*. Notorious USA (April 18, 2014). ASIN : B00JSKAILE

Lionel Dahmer (1994): *A Father's Story*. William Morrow and Company, Inc.; 1st edition (March 1, 1994). ISBN-10 : 068812156X.

Jacqui Saradjian (1996): *Women Who Sexually Abuse Children: From Research to Clinical Practice* (Wiley Series in Child Care & Protection) 1st Edition. Wiley; 1st edition (December 1, 1996). ISBN-10 : 0471960721

Rene A. Spitz (1966): *First Year of Life*: A Psychoanalytic Study of Normal and Deviant Development of Object Relations. Intl Universities Pr Inc; 1st edition (June 1, 1966). ISBN-10:0823619605

Alexander Lowen (1995): *Joy: The Surrender to the Body and to Life* (Compass). Penguin Books; 1st edition (December 1, 1995) ASIN:B004HW88OC

Frederick Leboyer (1975): *Birth Without Violence*. Knopf (february 12, 1975). ASIN:B010TTMXL0

Dr. Edward Tronick (2007): HELPING BABIES FROM THE BENCH: USING THE SCIENCE OF EARLY CHILDHOOD IN COURT. Lovett Productions, ZERO TO THREE.

REFERENCES

Lise-Lotte Austad (2018): Youtube Still face Experiment. https://www.youtube.com/watch?v=bOR7jId8wYk&t=2s

Dr. Bruce D. Perry, Maia Szalavitz (2010): *Born for Love: Why Empathy Is Essential--and Endangered*. William Morrow Paperbacks; Reprint edition (April 5, 2011). ISBN-10:9780061656798.

Patryk Vega (2021): THE EYES OF THE DEVIL OCZY DIABLA. Documentary, Drama. Poland. https://www.youtube.com/watch?v=G1y38N4LQiU

PSALM 23

The Lord is my shepherd; I shall not want.

He makes me lie down in green pastures;
He leads me beside still waters.

He restores my soul;
He leads me in paths of righteousness
for His name's sake.

Even though I walk
through the valley of the shadow of death,

I will fear no evil;
for You are with me;
Your rod and Your staff,
they comfort me.

About the Author...

Christian Laursen is an American Artist & philosopher. From Award Winning Video Game Artist with Disney, DreamWorks, EA and Sony Pictures to assembling a power house studio in the game industry with world leading talent to filmmaking as screenwriter and film director, to creative director for virtual reality tech. And now, an author for "connector of dots" of one of the oldest mysteries, "EVIL"... What was always a burning question throughout his art, became a quest for an answer, After two decades of research in psychology, history, and anthropology, the book took him on an unexpected road, to a possible answer for evil's origin.